# Man Sent From God

*There was a man sent from God, whose name was John.*

*The same came for a witness, to bear witness of the Light, that all men through him might believe.*

*He was not that Light, but was sent to bear witness of that Light.*

—John 1:6-8

# Man Sent From God

## A Biography of Dr. John R. Rice

### By
### Evangelist Robert L. Sumner

SWORD OF THE LORD PUBLISHERS
Murfreesboro, Tennessee

ISBN 0-87398-550-8


Library of Congress Catalog Card Number 59-12933

Printed in the United States of America

**Dr. and Mrs. Rice with their six daughters: Jessie, Mary Lloys, Libby, Grace, Joy and Joanna.**

# INTRODUCTION

I have learned from the Bible that the only way to really judge men is to judge them by the things to which they respond. A man who loves music is at heart a musician. It is a compliment to Evangelist Robert L. Sumner that he even wanted to write a story of the life of my good friend, Dr. John R. Rice. I regard Dr. Rice as one of the greatest spiritual assets this nation has. He stands for something. America is suffering from a bankruptcy of character in the pulpits, in educational institutions, and in all the various fields.

Once in a while a man like John R. Rice comes along and has convictions strong enough to dominate him. He stands for something. Dr. Rice is an individualist with a heart in his bosom big enough to take in the whole world. A man does not have to beg for respect. He may have to plead for sympathy and pray for friends, but this old world still tips its hat when honest, upright, fighting, uncompromising men of God walk down the street. Dr. Rice is God's man doing God's work in God's way at this time when multiplied thousands of people are selling the Lord Jesus Christ down the river simply because they haven't enough character to stand up and be counted on the side of God.

Dr. Bob Jones, Sr.,
*Founder Bob Jones University,*
*Greenville, South Carolina*

Union revival campaign in beautiful Kleinhan's Music Hall, Buffalo, N. Y. 3,094 people present April 23, 1944; 114 churches cooperating; 76 public professions of faith in this service; 997 during campaign. View from balcony shows less than half of audience.

# AUTHOR'S PREFACE

It has been a distinct joy to write this biography of the man who has done more than any person living to bring back the days of great mass evangelism to America. My own heart has been stirred and blessed as I uncovered the details of his life, challenging me anew and afresh to lay my all, without compromise, completely on the altar of service for Jesus Christ. If my readers feel just a small portion of the challenge in their souls that I have felt, the many months of research and writing which I have expended will be amply rewarded.

My principal purpose in writing this book has not been to honor Dr. Rice, although I am glad to do so and he does deserve tremendous honor for his faithfulness to the fundamentals of the Faith over the years. Actually, my main concern has been to help young preachers and ministerial students—plus other young Christians who have what some would call the unfortunate experience of living in this day of compromise—by placing in their hands a challenging example of a man who would not yield. I have recently been appalled again and again at the number of ministers selling out for the thirty pieces of silver—*or less!* Men whom I thought had strong Bible convictions and would not bow to denominational hierarchy or the pressures of worldly interests have succumbed even before the fight waxed warm. My prayer to God is that this book might encourage other men to stand fast and stand true. Perhaps the incidents recorded herein of the various crises when it looked as if Dr. Rice must either compromise or lose everything (yet when he stood true God vindicated him and rewarded him with greater service than ever before) will help others to do the same.

There is no man living whom I admire more than John R. Rice. I admired him from a distance when a young minister, and I admire him much more now that I know him intimately. Perhaps my admiration has colored this biography. *Undoubtedly it has!* Someone has said, I believe Dr. R. A. Torrey for one, that if men had written the Bible, they would have glossed over the bad points of its characters. I make no apology whatsoever for having glossed over the weak points of John Rice. He is not perfect. *No man is!* Yet the amount of perfection in this humble servant of Christ is so much greater than what is found in the average Christian, I think his experiences and example will challenge others to higher living. Like the beloved apostle, he could say, *"Be ye followers of me, even as I also am of Christ"* (I Cor. 11:1).

Perhaps I should say that I was not asked to write this biography. Neither is it exactly true that I obtained permission to do so. I simply told Dr. Rice I felt led to write it and that was that. At my request, Dr. Rice read the first sixteen chapters, following the completion of the first draft, to check the details for accuracy. He did not see the last chapter, "Personality Portrait," prior to publication since it pertains to matters he did not need to check and which another could evaluate better than he.

It might be in order to confess that I am *not* Dr. Rice's son-in-law. It is profoundly perplexing how false rumors begin and how swiftly they circulate to distant places. Where this strange story got started I do not know, but in all parts of the country folks have said to me, "You married one of Dr. Rice's daughters, did you not?" *I did not!* The closest kinship I can claim to him is brother—*in Christ!* However, I doubt that if Dr. Rice were my father-in-law, I would think any more of this man who has been my warm friend, counselor and inspiration.

Several statements in this book will not be pleasantly received in some quarters. When honestly reporting the facts of my subject's life, it was necessary to name some of the controversies in which he has been engaged and to call some personalities by

name. I have honestly tried not to hurt anyone—living or dead—
by what I have written, but neither have I side-stepped the issues
nor toned down the truth.

There are many acknowledgements of help received which
should be made in this Preface. However, since it is impossible to
name each one who has so kindly assisted me, I trust it will suffice to simply mention Dr. Rice's personal secretary for many
years—Miss Viola Walden. Her help has been invaluable. Her
sweet personality, her humble spirit, her enthusiastic willingness
to cooperate even with tiresome details have been a distinct
delight and blessing to me. Incidentally, Miss Walden has been a
tremendous help and asset to Dr. Rice during the long years she
has faithfully served him. I honestly doubt that even Dr. Rice
realizes how much she means to him and the work of *The Sword
of the Lord*. Many, many details—some of lesser degree and
some of considerable importance—she has taken from his
shoulders. She will surely share in much of his reward at the
Judgment Seat of Christ.

I would also like to say that I deeply appreciate the
graciousness of Dr. Bob Jones, Sr., founder and chairman of the
board of Bob Jones University and one of the greatest evangelists
of all time, for consenting to write the Introduction to this book
about his close, long-time companion and friend, Dr. Rice.

Let me close this Preface with a statement made by another
associate of Dr. Rice, who has also been with him nearly a half of
a century, Miss Fairy Shappard. She wrote in a letter to the
author:

"Because of his humility, his way of life, his deliberate choice
of going with Christ and the minority, many people do not
recognize his greatness. Some, however, have said that he is one
of the great men of our day. I believe with all my heart that
history will prove him to be not only one of the great men of this
generation, but also one of the great men of all generations.
*Heaven alone will reveal all his influence for Christ.*"

Miss Shappard has expressed my sentiments exactly!

# PREFACE TO THE REVISED, ENLARGED EDITION

God, in His matchless mercy, permitted *Man Sent From God* to receive a wonderful reception by the Christian reading public. Eight consecutive printings contributed to its continuous circulation following its original release in 1959. Among many other kindly words, the late Senator John L. McClellan of Arkansas placed into the *Congressional Record* a review written by Dr. George S. Reuter, Jr., Research Director of the American Federation of Teachers, describing it as ". . .one of the best biographies of the century about one of the greatest men who has ever lived."

After Dr. Rice's death, following his eighty-fifth birthday by less than three weeks, friends and associates strongly urged me to revise, enlarge and update the stirring story of his life. This I have done, adding two full chapters while revising and strengthening the others.

*Man Sent From God* did much good in its original format. Lives were changed, preachers got a new vision of what could be done for God, others developed new convictions, and many serving the living Lord discovered how it pays to stand for right even when everyone else is taking a contrary position. It is my earnest prayer that this new edition will accomplish even more good and circulate even more widely.

Dr. John R. Rice was one of the spiritual giants of the 20th century—or any century—and more people are coming to this conclusion now that he is no longer present on the earthly scene. While *Man Sent from God* is his only biography to date, we expect many more will eventually be published. His widow, Mrs. Lloys Rice, hopes to release a pictorial biography and perhaps even a book of personal correspondence between herself and Dr. Rice—who wrote daily when he was absent. One or two of his daughters are also interested in writing personal biographical sketches which would, beyond question, be of great interest to the general public.

*May God, in His grace, raise up an entire generation of men possessing the high caliber, the unwavering biblical convictions, and the holy character of John R. Rice.*

John R., baby George, Gertrude and Ruth. There were also three half brothers—Jesse, Joe and Bill; and one half sister—Jimmie.

# Table of Contents

*Chapter 1*

# Born to Preach

*Then the word of the Lord came unto me, saying, Before I formed thee in the belly I knew thee; and before thou camest forth out of the womb I sanctified thee, and I ordained thee a prophet unto the nations.*—Jeremiah 1:4,5.

JOHN R. RICE, like Jeremiah the son of Hilkiah, was ordained by God to preach even before he came forth out of his mother's womb. His mother, Sallie Elizabeth LaPrade Rice, could say with Hannah of old, *"For this child I prayed; and the Lord hath given me my petition which I asked of him: Therefore also I have lent him to the Lord; as long as he liveth he shall be lent to the Lord"* (I Sam. 1:27,28). John Rice was born to preach!

One of the tenderest of all the many moving tales this famous editor and evangelist told about his life pertained to his accidental discovery of this truth. When he was teaching at Wayland College in Plainview, Texas, he visited his mother's sister, Mrs. Esse McLaughlin, at Amarillo. He was looking, teacher fashion, through some of the books in his aunt's library when a letter dropped out of one and fell to the floor. Picking it up, he remarked, "This looks like my mother's handwriting. I've seen some of her love letters to my father and this looks the same."

"It is," Mrs. McLaughlin replied. "Would you like to read it?"

The letter had been written by his mother when he was five years old, while they were living on a farm near Pleasanton, in

South Texas, below San Antonio. His mother had said in the letter to her sister, "It is very hot here. The fields are dried up and we will not make much crop this year, I am afraid. Willie [Dr. Rice's father] is not well."

Then in typical mother fashion she began to talk about her children. "Gertrude is lots of help to me now," she said. "She looks after the baby, dries the dishes, and assists me in many ways. Ruth is the quietest little thing you ever saw, very sweet and lovable. George is into mischief from morning till night." Then she said, "Let me tell you what my preacher boy did the other day."

He stopped reading and looked up in astonishment. His mother had named all three of the other children, and then spoke of a "preacher boy." He said to his Aunt Esse, "Mother wrote of Gertrude, Ruth and George, then she speaks of her 'preacher boy.' Did she call me her preacher boy?"

"She never called you anything else!" assured his Aunt Esse.

When he later had occasion to go to Decatur, Texas, he remarked to his father, "Dad, I saw a letter the other day written by Mama before she died twenty years ago, and in it she called me her preacher boy. Would you tell me about it, please?"

The elder Rice replied, "Yes, when you were born your mother and I gave you to God and prayed that He would make you a preacher. We already had Gertrude, and when you came she was so happy that we had a boy now who could preach the precious Gospel of our Lord Jesus Christ."

The young college teacher exclaimed, "Dad, why didn't you tell me long before! I feel like I have been wasting time!"

"We wanted God to tell you, Son," he said. Just a few months after the incident the classroom was abandoned for a pulpit; and he felt clearly led to give himself to the gospel ministry following what, he is convinced now, was the call of God which had somewhat influenced him ever since babyhood.

John R. Rice came from good, hardy pioneer stock. His great-grandfather Rice had a large plantation in Missouri and lost about ninety-five slaves when they were released during the Civil War. His grandfather Rice served as a captain in the Confederate

Army, and during that time the great-grandparents moved from Missouri to Texas. However, it was in Missouri in 1857 or 1858, that William H. Rice made his debut.

At the age of 18, when the family was living at Bonham, Texas, it was discovered that William had galloping consumption, or, as we call it today, tuberculosis. Following the doctor's advice to sleep out of doors in open air, he went farther west and took work on a cattle ranch. Those were the days before there were any barbed-wire fences and one could ride all the way from Fort Worth to Denver without going through a gate or coming to a fence. The only fenced land of those times was in the infrequent wooded areas where it was possible to have rail fences. Rice worked some years there, then later moved back to Gainesville, Texas.

It was in Gainesville as a young man of about thirty that Will, as his friends affectionately called him, attended a few services of a local revival meeting. To his acute embarrassment, a cowboy companion slipped up during the invitation one night, threw an arm around his shoulder and softly whispered, "Will, I'm praying for you. I am anxious about your soul. God has saved me and I would like you to take my Saviour, too."

The cowboy drew himself haughtily erect and sharply responded, "I'm a grown man and I know what I want to do without anyone telling me. I came to enjoy the sermon; but if I have to be disturbed and embarrassed by people coming to me publicly, urging me to become a Christian when I am not ready, then I will not come to the meeting any more. If anyone talks to me again, I will never come back."

The Christian friend left, resolving not to disturb him again; but a few nights later the urging of the Holy Spirit was so strong in his heart that he approached the lost cowboy the second time, saying, "Will, I didn't intend to come back, but something compels me. I am so burdened about you. I cannot get any peace and I am so anxious for you to be saved."

Will threw down his song book, grabbed his big Stetson hat, angrily turned to his friend and said as he stomped out, "I told you that if you did not leave me alone I would never darken the door of this church again as long as I live! Perhaps it will give you some pleasure to remember that you have driven me from the house of God!"

At the time, Will was rooming with his brother and sister-in-law. Arriving home before the others, he went directly to his room and retired for the night, but could not sleep. For hours he tossed upon his bed without relief. He would get up, smoke, pace back and forth across the room, then return to his bed; but slumber simply would not come. The long hours of restlessness were accompanied by increasing, deep conviction of sin. Eventually he said to himself, "What a fool I am! The best friend I have in the world came to me because he loved me, wanted to see me saved and keep me out of Hell; and I, like an ill-bred wretch, insulted him and drove him away. Now no one else will speak to me and it will only serve me right if I end up in Hell!"

Finally, at four o'clock in the morning, he fell on his knees beside his bed, confessed his sins, and cried out to God for mercy and salvation. Sweet peace instantly came into his heart and he found the rest he sought in Jesus Christ. When the janitor arrived at the church the next morning at five o'clock to open the doors for the sunrise prayer service, he found Will Rice, the man who had vowed only the night before he would never return, sitting on the front steps waiting for the others to come so he could tell them what had happened!

Shortly thereafter Will felt called to preach. He spent about one year at the Baylor academy in Waco, Texas. Later he studied one year at the Southern Baptist Seminary of Louisville, Kentucky. He became a very successful preacher in country churches and was in much demand throughout most of his life. Eventually, however, he became so absorbed in business affairs and making a living that he did not preach regularly. No doubt part of his joy in his famous son's ministry was in the fact it fulfilled some of the dreams which were never realized in his own life. Aside from preaching, his principal business was raising cattle and horses and trading in real estate—which took much of his time for a good many years. While living in Decatur he ran for the Texas state senate and served in Austin one term during the governorship of the Honorable Pat M. Neff.

The subject of this book called his father "Papa" as a child, later changing it to "Daddy," and confessed he revered the memory of his father, who went to Heaven in 1930, all his life. Although Will was a stern disciplinarian who did not spare the rod, a deep bond of affection existed between father and son. In an unpublished summary of God's leading in his life, Dr. Rice wrote: "I remember that I kissed my father goodnight every night before he went to bed, until I was 15 years old; then I grew a little timid and embarrassed perhaps." He said his father was "a dominant influence" in his life until he was at least twenty-five.

A little of the love, respect, and influence Will Rice had in his son's life and ministry is evidenced by the following paragraph in Dr. Rice's book, *The Home—Courtship, Marriage and Children:*

> I remember with joy the reverence I had for my own father and my unbounded trust in him. I felt he was about the bravest man who had ever lived. I asked him the most unheard-of questions, and I took, without a grain of doubt, his answers as being absolute truth. When my father sometimes said, "I do not know, Son," I had a feeling that if he would think awhile on the matter or give it a little attention he soon *would* know. If my father said a thing was right, I felt it was right; if he said it was wrong, then certainly for me it was wrong. I thank God that I have had few occasions even yet to believe my father was essentially wrong, now that he has been in Heaven for a number of years. In his affection, in his providing, in his punishment of our sins, in his kindness, in his counsel, my father was to his eight children the best earthly image we ever saw of God.

It was at Custer School Community near Gainesville that Will Rice met and courted Sallie Elizabeth LaPrade. LaPrade is a French name and the ancestors may have been Huguenots, but it is not certain. At any rate, the LaPrades were solid citizens in Cooke County, Texas, when Will and Sallie discovered they were in love. In 1893 she became his second wife, his first wife having died some years previous.

It was on December 11, 1895, that the second fruit of this

union, John Richard* Rice, saw the light of day. The birthplace was in Cooke County a few miles from Gainesville and the family continued living there for some years while the father pastored a country church. The mother's desires and prayers have already been noted, but perhaps it would be well to observe here that the grateful father went to his Bible and heavily underscored in Luke 1:63 the words of Zacharias concerning the birth of his son, "His name is John." He, too, trusted that his John would be a preacher in the spirit and power of Elijah, filled with the Holy Ghost throughout his ministry!

As a little lad of four years, whenever people would ask the one who was destined to become a world-famous evangelist, "Sonny, what is your name?" he would answer, "I'm John the Baptist preacher!" Little did anyone suspect the prophetic significance in that childish reply, or of the marvelous way in which the utterance would be fulfilled in an even more fruitful manner than manifested in the ministry of the original John the Baptist.

The little country place where they lived was called the Vilot Community, and the church where Will Rice pastored met in a little building at the crossroads, with a blacksmith shop on the opposite corner. Reminiscing in one of his sermons, Dr. Rice said:

> I remember where the washpot was, and where the cowpen was when I would go and sit on the fence with a tin cup in my hand, and my dad would milk the cup full of foaming milk for me, and I would drink it down. A young cow Dad was milking one day ran around sideways and knocked me over. My dad thought it was so funny. I remember when I went down into the old cellar to see the goose and the eggs she had down there, and the old gander came down and got me by the palm of my hand with his bill and led me out! I was yelling bloody murder!

Many happy experiences undoubtedly took place in that home where the family eventually grew to number seven. Then Mrs. Rice's health broke and doctors advised a long journey to find a more beneficial climate.

The family sold the farm and traveled throughout the Panhan-

---

* Dr. Rice was uncertain whether the "R" in his name stood for Richard or Robert, although he believed it was in honor of his father's good friend, Rev. R. R. Gaines. I told him I would "name" him Richard in honor of my eldest son. Since then others have felt the "R" was for Robert. Perhaps so.

dle of Texas, spending long weeks in hopes of noting some improvement in Mrs. Rice's health. Failing in this, they moved down below San Antonio where they stayed for a year. Finally, with the mother desperately sick and all their money gone, the pitiful family moved back to Cooke County and were welcomed into the home of Will Rice's sister, Mrs. Tom Allen, on a farm near Red River. It was there, in September, 1901, that Sallie Rice died, just a few months after her fifth baby, Porter, had been called to Heaven.

Will Rice had just bought his boys a little wagon and his girls new dolls, and they were playing down in a ravine with dolls and wagon when Cousin Georgia came to call them, saying, *"Hurry, come to the house quickly!"* When they began to gather the dolls and playthings and put them in the wagon, she said, "Never mind those things; we'll get them later. *Come now!"*

They went immediately; and outside the plain box house the older half-brother, Jesse, a son by Will Rice's first marriage, fifteen years old, leaned his face upon his arms and sobbed. Young John, hardly six at the time, did not understand why. They went into the room where the mother lay; and around her bed had gathered Uncle Tom, his wife Nannie, their three children, and the husband, Will. All were weeping except Mrs. Rice, who was making everyone promise to meet her in Heaven. Turning to Cousin Georgia, she requested, "Georgia, will you play and sing for me?"

"What should I sing, Aunt Sadie?" asked Cousin Georgia.

And the dying saint said, "Sing *How Firm a Foundation!"*

So Cousin Georgia went to the little cottage organ and played and sang with choked voice while others tried to join in singing those blessed words,

> **How firm a foundation,**
> **Ye saints of the Lord,**
> **Is laid for your faith**
> **In His excellent Word.**

Mrs. Rice rejoiced and clapped her frail hands while everyone else wept. Her feet were on the Rock of Ages and it did not tremble in her dying hour! Yea, it was a soft pillow for such a saint of

God who faced her Homegoing to be with the Lord! Lifting her hands high and gazing as if seeing through ceiling and roof to the far-off Heaven, she said, "I can see Jesus and my baby now!" Then her hands fell across her breast, she smiled, and was asleep in Jesus.

Dr. Rice said to me, "That scene was so engraved on the mind of a boy less than six years old, that I remember a hundred details. I could go back into the same room and I'd know exactly where the bed was. I can still see the long, black, braided hair by her side on the pillow."

Describing her death and Homegoing in his sermon, "What Will Happen When Jesus Comes?" he said:

> I remember the November day when we laid her body away. My father knelt beside the open grave. There was no white muslin to hide the raw dirt of the grave—like a wound in the earth. No fake, man-made carpet of grass was thrown over the clods. My father put one arm around his two little orphan girls, and one around his two little boys, and watched as they lowered the precious body in its dark casket into the bosom of mother earth. The rain beat down upon us, and a friendly neighbor woman held an umbrella over our heads. O death! *death!* DEATH! All the years my lonely heart has known the reality of death.

Later in the same sermon, he said:

> Some years ago I stood by the grave of my mother in a little country cemetery at Callisburg, Texas, in Cooke County. I talked to my mother as if she could hear me, and I think she could. I have no doubt that she knows about the long, hungry years I have spent without her. And I said, "Mother, it won't be long until I will see you again, for Jesus is coming. You will come back to this body, and it will be raised and glorified; I will be changed, and together with all our loved ones we will meet the Lord in the air and ever be with the Lord."
>
> Yes, I will see my mother again. And she will have a real body of flesh and blood and bones. I will feel her arms around me again and her hands upon my face. She will not be wan and pale as she was when I told her good-bye many years ago; no, she will be glowing with health and beauty, like a bride, I believe. I think her hair will be as long and black as it was the day she left us. But in every detail she will be real and will be

my mother, and we will love one another. She gave me to God when I was born, called me her preacher boy and prayed that I might preach. In that glad day when Jesus comes, I will make my report.

As was previously mentioned, one son, Jesse Rice, was the fruit of Will Rice's first marriage. He never had much education but was a man of genuine character and a noble Christian with much of the charm and friendliness of his father. He worked on a farm and in the oil fields until his death a few years ago. A daughter of that marriage, Jimmie (Mrs. Dave Thomas), lived at Oklahoma City, a lovely Christian, greatly loved. She is now with the Lord.

Gertrude was the first child of that second union. She was a very attractive and popular girl. Finishing one year at Baylor academy, she took examinations and taught in village schools of West Texas before her marriage to Mr. Rufus Nutting. Always very active in Christian work, she was a good soul winner, an earnest Bible student and teacher. After assisting her husband in various retail stores, she moved to Wheaton, Illinois, where she worked first for *The Sword of the Lord*, then with Wheaton College before her retirement. She and her husband lived at the Bill Rice Ranch near Murfreesboro, Tennessee, until her death several years ago.

John R. Rice was the second child, born about sixteen months after Gertrude. Next was Ruth Rice, now Mrs. Millard Martin of Nederland, Texas, a retired schoolteacher with an earned master's degree, an active and cultured Christian woman.

George H. Rice was the next addition to arrive at the Rice household. He graduated from Decatur Baptist College and Baylor University, where he earned his master's degree. The major part of his life was spent in West and Southwest Texas, serving as teacher and high school principal. Greatly loved, he died in the early 1950s.

Porter Rice was the baby of this union and died in infancy, preceding his mother to Heaven by just a few months.

Soon after Mrs. Rice died, the family moved to Gainesville; and a good housekeeper, Mrs. Byron, was hired to help with the children. She took care of them for several years until, in 1905, when John Rice was nine years old, his father took them from the home in Gainesville to his brother's ranch in West Texas, six miles out of Dundee. Not long after, he married again, this time a woman from a neighboring ranch by the name of Miss Dolous Bellah. They were very happy together and two sons, both preachers, resulted from the union. The older, Evangelist Joe B. Rice, lived at Edmond, Oklahoma, and was a very earnest, humble, serious preacher, greatly loved. He died suddenly on the street from a heart attack in 1958 as he returned from a revival in Michigan.

Next was Evangelist Bill Rice, a very colorful and popular evangelist. He and his wife Cathy founded the Cumberwood Christian Retreat, now called the Bill Rice Ranch, near Murfreesboro, Tennessee. The Bill Rice Ranch is the world's largest camp for the deaf and the South's largest independent conference ground. Dr. Bill also served as co-editor of *The Sword of the Lord.* He suffered a massive stroke on June 25, 1976; then, about two years later, on May 29, 1978, he lay down for a nap after lunch and his heart simply stopped beating.

Until John Rice was nineteen and left for Decatur College, this large and happy family continued to live in and around the little town of Dundee—population about two or three hundred—in the cattle country. However, it was while still at Gainesville as a lad of nine that the most important event in the young Rice's life took place.

## Chapter 2

# Saved for Certain

*And this is the record, that God hath given to us eternal life, and this life is in his Son. He that hath the Son hath life; and he that hath not the Son of God hath not life. These things have I written unto you that believe on the name of the Son of God; that ye may know that ye have eternal life, and that ye may believe on the name of the Son of God.*—I John 5:11-13.

EVEN ONE who had been born to preach, dedicated to God with holy resolves and earnest prayer by spiritual parents, must be converted! John 1:13 reminds us that this new birth, so absolutely necessary for eternal life, is "not of blood, nor of the will of the flesh, nor of the will of man, but of God." John Rice had noble, earnest, spiritual, godly parents; but *that* did not make him a Christian. His father and mother had given him to God in humble dedication, but neither did *that* make him a Christian. He, like Nicodemus and every other individual born of the flesh, must also be born of the Spirit if he hoped to see and enter into the kingdom of God. And enter the kingdom he did—at the tender age of nine—another living illustration of the Saviour's sweet invitation, "Suffer the little children to come unto me, and forbid them not: for of such is the kingdom of God" (Mark 10:14).

The Holy Spirit began very early speaking to this lad's heart "at sundry times and in divers manners." In one of his sermons he said:

Though I was saved so young, I remember a long series of incidents through which God spoke to my heart and convicted me of my sins. I remember the Sunday school lesson when we learned about the baby Jesus' being born in a stable because there was no room for Him in the inn. I was not more than four years old at the time, but I kept that little pictured Sunday school card and felt guilty in my heart that human beings like me had no room for Jesus!

When I was not more than five, I was deeply moved by a song my mother sang, "Turned Away From the Beautiful Gate." I seemed to have known that it was by their own sinful rebellion and rejection of Christ that men miss Heaven. I remember some unrest of soul about it. About the same time my mother, after I had told her a lie, talked to me with tears of how God hated a lie and what a sin it was. The occasion was burned on my memory, and I know that I felt I deserved the just condemnation of God. Surely that was God speaking to me through His Holy Spirit!

When my mother lay on her deathbed, she talked so of the Saviour as she had us all promise to meet her in Heaven that I felt myself under the spell of her dying smile and testimony until the time I trusted Christ as my Saviour. After Mother's death, I remember the tears and the exhortations of my Sunday school teacher. I remember the godly pastor who told the story of the prodigal son, told how he himself had once been a prodigal, how he ran away from home and came to want and trouble and how he was forgiven on his return. How strange, but it seems that God must have been calling from the first day I knew anything about good and bad, from the first time I ever had a sense of moral responsibility to God.

That deepening conviction came to a head one Sunday as the young lad sat in the morning service of the First Baptist Church at Gainesville, Texas, and listened to the faithful pastor, Rev. A. B. Ingram, preach a moving message entitled, "The Prodigal Son." The realization was strong in his heart that he, too, was a prodigal son who had broken the laws of a holy God and had chosen his own way of sin in preference to God's way of righteousness. At the same time he sensed there would be welcome for him, like the young man of the text, if he would only arise and go to the Father. With holy, determined resolve he slid off his seat and walked down the aisle to take the preacher's hand in an open, public profession of faith in Jesus Christ as his personal Saviour.

However, when he got to the front the minister was urging others, grown people, to come; and he seated young John to one side. No one showed him any Scripture or gave him any solid foundation on which to rest assurance of his salvation; so it was several years before he came into the definite, sweet, positive conviction that Christ was his and he was Christ's.

In his booklet for young Christians, *Seven Secrets of a Happy, Prosperous Christian Life,* Dr. Rice told about the sad, troubled years from the time he was saved until that positive assurance came. He said:

> They did not take time to teach me any of the Word of God. Perhaps they thought I was too young. I went home so happy that day and asked my father if it would be all right for me to join the church and be baptized since I was now a Christian. He said, "Well, Son, when you are old enough to know you are a sinner and honestly repent of your sins and be regenerated, then it will be time enough to join the church."
>
> I sat stricken and silent before my father. I did not know what all those big words meant—repentance and regeneration and more. I simply knew my father did not think I was saved! Well, I thought my father was the wisest man in the world and a preacher, besides; and if he thought I was not saved, I supposed I was not. Sadly I gave up the idea of joining the church and hoped the time would soon come when I would be old enough to be saved so my father would know that I was saved.
>
> The next morning on the way to school I stopped under a willow tree down on Pecan Creek and prayed. I asked God to help me to be a good boy and asked Him to save other people, since my father thought I was too young to be saved.
>
> I wish I could tell you all the sadness and disappointment of the next three years. I often prayed. We moved out to a ranch in West Texas and then to a little cow town. The company was not always the best. My mother had gone to Heaven, and I was a motherless boy. I did not get much instruction in the Word of God. I got no assurance about salvation. Again and again I prayed for God to save me. Once I asked a godly preacher to pray for me, and he asked me to pray for myself. So that night when I went home from the little church, I went out into the horse's stall, knelt down and asked God to save me. Then I

prepared for bed and knelt by the bed as I usually did for a good-night prayer and asked God to forgive my sins and save me. I felt no change. I did not have any glorious experience. I did not see any light shining round about me. I did not hear the flutter of angels' wings. No electricity came in at my head or went out at my fingers and toes! So I sadly went to bed without any assurance of salvation. Then I thought, "Well, I had better settle this thing for good some way or other"; so I got out of bed and prayed again. There on my knees I thought how strange it was that when I realized I was a sinner and that there was nothing I could do to earn salvation and when God had promised so plainly that He would save people and that Jesus had died to pay for our sins—how strange, I thought, that God would not save me! I decided I would leave the matter in the hands of God the best I knew how and go to bed.

I offered myself for membership in the church. I could not feel any great conviction for sin, yet I did not know that I was saved. When, in that little West Texas church, they asked me to stand and give my "experience," give my testimony before being received into the church, I simply said that I had thought about the matter a great deal, that I did not want to be a Methodist, so I had decided to be a Baptist! I was a trembling, inexperienced boy, twelve years old. I was frightened at speaking before the people. And they someway had more confidence in my salvation than my testimony would have warranted, and received me in the church as a candidate for baptism!

When I was baptized, I was strangely happy. Yet even then I could give no clear testimony as to when I was saved or how. Oh, I wished that I knew just how and when I was saved and could know for sure that it was settled for good! But when others gave the very date and place when they were saved and told how happy they had been, I could not give any such experience.

Then one glad day I began reading the New Testament and came upon those wonderful promises in the Gospel of John, like clusters of ripe fruit on a beautiful tree!

*"As many as received him, to them gave he power to become the sons of God, even to them that believe on his name."*—John 1:12.

*"He that believeth on the Son hath everlasting life."*—John 3:36.

*"Verily, verily, I say unto you, He that heareth my word, and believeth on him that sent me, hath everlasting life, and shall*

*not come into condemnation; but is passed from death unto life.*"—John 5:24.

Oh, that last wonderful promise! I found that when I heard the Word of God and put my trust in the God who had sent His Son to save me, I then and there received everlasting life. I had often tried to remember that incident or that experience when I was nine years old and came to claim the Saviour publicly. I could not remember how I felt. I wondered if I had been as deeply moved as one must be to be saved.

I recalled that a twelve-year-old boy who came the same day had been weeping, and I had shed noₜ a tear! Many a time I had thought, "If I were really saved, I would not do some of the things I do." But now I saw, praise the Lord, that when I had put my trust in Jesus Christ, then and there I received everlasting life! My doubts and fears were gone; gone, thank God, forever!

From that day to this I have never doubted for a moment that I am God's child. I know one thing beyond any doubt: when I trusted Jesus, depended on Him to forgive me, He did! The Word of God says so and that makes it so. On these promises I have hung the eternal welfare of my soul, and how sure, how unchanging is that blessed foundation for my faith!

Dear reader, do you have that same sweet assurance? God is no respecter of persons, and the promises in His Word guarantee that if you will honestly put your faith and trust in Him for salvation, then you, too, will have everlasting life *right now,* will *never* come into condemnation, but will have already passed from the death of sin into the life of salvation! How great, good and gracious is God to sinners such as you and me! No wonder the Bible refers to this as a "so great salvation" (Heb. 2:3).

John Rice was *certainly saved* at the age of nine.

He was *saved for certain* at the age of twelve.

*Chapter 3*

# Early Life on the Texas Prairie

*Rejoice, O young man, in thy youth; and let thy heart cheer thee in the days of thy youth, and walk in the ways of thine heart, and in the sight of thine eyes: but know thou, that for all these things God will bring thee into judgment.*—Ecclesiastes 11:9.

AT THE start of one of Dr. Rice's most popular revival sermons, "Home, Sweet Home," is the heading:

*The Dearest Place on Earth,*
*The Nearest Place to Heaven*
*Is a Happy, Christian Home.*

The home of young John Rice was that type of a place! In the same sermon he wrote:

At our home as a boy (it is one of my happy memories!) we always expected to go to church. My father, my stepmother, the whole family (too many to ride in one carriage!) went to church. We went when it was cold; we went when it was hot. We went when it rained; we went when it was dry. It was rare indeed that any were so sick they could not go; and if that were true, the rest of us went to church; and just one stayed home to take care of the sick, if necessary. We went to church and Sunday school on time. We went to prayer meeting. I thank God for the happy memories that proved to me the sincerity of my father's faith in God.

Not all the memories of that poverty-stricken boyhood are

pleasant, however. The Rice family was large; the land was poor, and money was anything but plentiful. Perhaps the reader can best picture the situation if I quote a paragraph from another of his sermons:

> When I was a small boy in West Texas, the entire community would have a Christmas tree at one of the churches. There nearly everybody would bring their presents for children, for parents, for sweetheart, for friends. Those were exciting days. We could hardly wait until the program of songs and "recitations" and speeches was over and "Santa Claus" would begin to read the names on presents taken from the tree one by one and handed out by his helpers to boys and girls.
>
> What anticipation! What thrills! I sat many a time hoping against hope. Could that air gun be mine? Was that the ball and bat and glove that I had wanted so long? A thousand hopes and fears made the suspense almost unbearable, and we waited breathlessly each for his name to be called. The packages, mysteriously wrapped, might be almost anything glamorous and fine!
>
> But my father was poor and we never spent much for Christmas. Year after year I saw the finest presents handed out to others, and I waited while hope ebbed slowly away. If the last present was given and my name was not called, then the mock Santa Claus would reach under the tree, get some little bag made of netting holding hard candy and perhaps an orange; and these would be handed out to any children who had gotten no presents, and sometimes to all alike.

Their home was a plain box house in the country. The land was dry and arid, not at all conducive to plentiful, fruitful crops. Since they had no wells, it was necessary to build the earthen tanks and ponds, so numerous in that country, to obtain water. Some of that water was, in turn, hauled to the cisterns at the house. Old oaken rain barrels sat at the corners of the house to catch rain water for washing clothes and shampooing hair.

As can well be imagined, the days were long and the hours filled with hard, backbreaking toil, even for a young lad, on the Rice ranch. They would hitch four horses to a double-disc plow able to cut fourteen to eighteen inches of soil in width and about six to ten inches deep. Then from sunrise to sunset it was necessary to plow across the open field under the broiling heat of the

Texas sun. The plow jolted and tugged while breaking the huge clods of hard, dry dirt. The plowing was followed, naturally, by harrowing and then planting.

Yet even that labor was not nearly as difficult or painful as was the "grubbing." All throughout the West Texas area, as is true also of the entire Southwest, the farmer is plagued with a shrub-like tree known as the "mesquite tree." A native of subtropical and tropical regions, its fruit is an edible and highly nutritious pod which is very valuable as fodder for livestock. However, since the seeds are carried in the alimentary tracks of cattle, then are deposited on the soil with the manure, it spreads very rapidly, sometimes completely crowding out the grass. The tree never grows very high above the ground, but what it lacks in height it seems to make up in depth! Its deep, spreading roots often reach twenty-five feet down into the earth and spread over a radius of seventy-five feet. As an added problem to the farmer who wants to grow grain or cotton, the wood is very hard—in fact it is so hard it is frequently called *ironwood.*

Understandably, it would not be sufficient to merely cut down the tree and burn the stump since the long hard roots would break the plow. Then, too, if any piece of root is left in the soil, sprouts quickly shoot out of the ground and a new mesquite tree is formed—and it is one of the fastest growing trees known to mankind! Since cultivation of the soil would be foolish and useless as long as any of the dread enemy remained in the field, the Rice boys were sent out to do the "grubbing." This meant digging with a *mattock*—a pickax which has flat and sharp ends on the sides of the head iron—after the team had already pulled the big portion of the stump out of the ground.

Even when the type of labor called for sitting down—for much of the work in that cattle country was done on a horse—it was anything but a Sunday school picnic! In one of his messages on prayer he gives us a picture of what those days were like, saying:

> Once after a long, heavy day it was far into the night when I, wearied to exhaustion, turned my sorrel horse homeward. As he followed the long road across a ranch pasture, I sat upright in the saddle, sound asleep. When he came to the gate and

stopped, I awoke. When I had opened the gate, gone through and closed it, again I slept in the saddle until the tired horse stopped at the corral gate. My muscles did their accustomed work of years when my eyelids shut and I slept. But part of me was conscious of my horse, my feet in the stirrups, and the accustomed motion; and I awoke instantly when the horse stopped.

It was during those days on the West Texas prairies that John was an unwilling participant to a runaway. A quartet of animals—two mules and two horses—were hooked to a big double-disc turning plow, ready to begin a hard day's work. As he was driving them onto the field, before he had the plow in the ground, the young mules got excited and bolted. The horses and the boy, of course, were dragged along behind. As soon as he recovered presence of mind sufficient to do so, he raised the lever which lowered the disc deep into the soil. The wild mules soon decided they had had enough as they zigzagged across the field doing the work it ordinarily took all four of the team to accomplish.

These experiences only acted to help mold and develop the strong, sturdy physique and hardy, determined character which assisted greatly in the long, hard work habits of the farm boy who became pastor, singer, evangelist, radio director, author and editor. It was the Lord Himself who said, "It is good for a man that he bear the yoke in his youth" (Lam. 3:27), and it is so, of course.

On another occasion an incident took place which proved young John to be considerably short of perfection. As a nine-year-old boy on his father's 6,000-acre West Texas ranch, he had the man-sized chore of planting seed in a field a mile square, driving a long grain drill behind a big six-mule team. He was not large enough at the time to harness the team alone; but once someone else had harnessed them, the job was his alone for the day.

This particular event found him driving "boyfully" behind the team, watching to make sure the wheels overlapped the track of the previous round, yet dreaming lazily of the wonderful things he would do in the future. So enthralled did he become in his world of fantasy that he completely forgot to check and refill the big seed box in the grain drill! When he finally returned to reality with a start and stopped the team to check the box, he found it completely empty. Since he had no idea how long he had driven without seed, he made a wild guess, filled up his seed box, then went over much of the land the second time. It proved to be a mighty poor guess; and when the grain came up, there was a desolate, barren strip of cultivated ground approximately a mile long and fifty feet wide! Ranchers in that community enjoyed considerable merriment at the frustrated young farmer's expense; and he learned an early, unforgettable lesson in the realm of responsibility and duty.

Many other spiritual lessons were learned and numerous victories won on that West Texas farm long before he ever entered a theological seminary or sat in a Bible class at a Christian college. It was there he learned to pray in his own "secret closet" under a chaparral bush in a ravine, and it was there he also joyfully discovered the truth that God wants us to pray definitely.

Once, when he was still just a young teenage Christian, a country preacher by the name of R. H. Gibson invited him to go to the Black Flat schoolhouse in a rural area to assist in revival services. On the first Monday following the opening of the meeting, they arose early to go out and pray together. After reading a few verses from the New Testament, the preacher asked, "Can we agree on something definite to ask God to give us in the service tonight?" They discussed the matter thoughtfully and prayerfully for some time and were finally convinced they should pray for five souls to be won to Christ that Monday night. They definitely prayed for that number to take a public stand, and that night there were five public conversions.

The following morning they met again for prayer and rejoiced over the answer of the previous evening. That day they felt impressed to ask for three public conversions, and again that night their prayer was answered as three people openly professed faith in Christ. As the meeting progressed they began to pray for specific people to be saved in the services of a certain evening. One morning they prayed for Bill Palm, who was later John's roommate in college, to be saved; and he trusted Christ that night.

It was also on the farm in West Texas that he went one day past the woodpile, across the pea patch, squirmed through the barbed wire fence, knelt under his chaparral bush in the "brakes" and laid everything on the altar for God. He had the challenge of Malachi 3:10, "Prove me now herewith," fresh on his mind, and he promised God he would tithe. From that hour he had a holy boldness about expecting God's provision, and he happily proved the reality and trustworthiness of that promise many thousandfold. John Rice, the man, was able to trust God for hundreds of thousands of dollars later in life partly because John Rice, the boy, learned to trust Him for his daily needs as a faithful teenager.

It was also as a fifteen-year-old West Texas lad that he won his first soul to Christ. They were in the midst of a blessed revival campaign in the little cow town where he lived, and he had been meditating for several days upon the second chapter of Acts. Over and over again he had read and reread its thrilling account of three thousand people being saved in a single day. Reports which he had been reading in the *Baptist Standard* of revivals all over Texas helped to kindle the flame. He began to pray passionately for the power of the Spirit of God to win souls. One day the visiting preacher earnestly appealed in his message to the unsaved who were present in the little church at Dundee, Texas. After the message he asked the people to bow their heads, then requested those who were desirous of knowing Christ as personal Saviour to raise their hands for prayer.

On the seat in front of the young Rice boy was Albert, an unconverted lad of fourteen. John leaned over and whispered in his ear something like this, "Don't you want to be saved? If you do, then hold your hand up now." When the boy hesitated, unsure and timid, he urged him, "Hurry; you know you need to be saved. The preacher will pray for you. The Lord will save you right now, so hold up your hand if you want to be saved."

Timidly the boy raised his hand; the preacher noted it and then prayed for him but strangely gave no invitation for the lad to come forward and make a public profession of faith in Jesus Christ. Neither did he approach the boy after the service to talk to him.

As a result, Rice took the boy outside, and there, in a private conversation beside the church building, he encouraged him to take Christ as his Saviour immediately. The boy agreed to trust Him, and they shook hands as an outward symbol of inward surrender. Then John took the boy inside to the preacher, a Brother Hodges, to tell him about the transaction which had just taken place between the boy and the Saviour. It was the first time John Rice had ever won a soul to Christ, and it was a tremendous blessing and thrill. Both boys were very happy about the decision, and the older one never forgot how the younger one loved him for helping him find salvation through Christ.

One day when both were grown the preacher went back to that little cow town for a special service. After the message a tall, strong man walked to the front of the church and questioned, "John, do you remember me?"

The surprised preacher replied, "Albert, is it you?"

*It was!* After a joyful reunion the man introduced to his wife and children the one who had won him to Christ in youth. That first taste of the joy in winning men to Christ never departed from the heart and soul of this one whom God used to move tens of thousands to salvation. As a matter of fact, he had already won hundreds of souls to the Saviour before he ever preached his first sermon from a pulpit!

Not every effort he made to win others to Christ was a success, of course. On another occasion, in the same little cow town of Dundee, in the same church, he felt impressed to speak to an older youth. He slipped up to him, placed his hand on the young man's shoulder, and said, "Roy, this is the time for you to go. God has spoken to your heart; and if you will come to Christ, friends of yours will probably come, too. Won't you come?"

Roy responded, "That may be so, but, nevertheless, I am not going. I am not ready yet. I am not going now." Further urging proved of no avail.

The following Saturday afternoon, just one week later,

someone sailed a Stetson under Roy's horse which he had hitched to a cart; the animal bolted, and Roy fell from the cart to the ground. He got up, brushed the dust off his clothes, laughed with others about the joke, and later that afternoon started for home. He never arrived. They found Roy where he had fallen from the cart the second time with internal injuries, and in a few hours he was dead.

On another occasion a godly Sunday school teacher asked her class of boys to pray for her unconverted son to be saved. John was a member of that class, and on the first Sunday morning of a revival in the local Methodist church, he approached the son and said, "Clyde, your mother and the whole Sunday school class agreed to pray that you would be saved in this meeting. It is time to be saved, Clyde. All of us are praying for you. Won't you come today?

The boy gripped the back of the seat in front of him; tears flowed down his cheeks and dropped on the pine pew before him, but with trembling lips he said, "John, I am glad you are praying for me and I want you to keep on. And I am going to be saved, too. I am not quite ready, but I sure am glad you are praying for me."

The meeting ended with Clyde still unsaved. A year later another revival was in progress at the same church, and the second time John went to deal with him. This time the lost youth did not weep. Politely he thanked Rice for talking to him but insisted he was not yet ready to be saved. He did not surrender during that meeting.

Another year or two went by and another revival was in progress. Clyde now sat with the rough crowd of unconverted men in the rear of the auditorium, but for the third time young Rice went to plead with him for Christ. This time without tears, without politeness, but boldly and sarcastically he spit out, "Don't you think I have sense enough to know if I want to go, without anybody telling me? *I'm not going!*" When Rice insisted that he ought to be saved, he finally turned and spoke aloud so that all could hear him, using profanity to emphasize that he

would not surrender to Christ. The years passed on and both
marched off to World War I. John Rice never saw Clyde again.

I do not mean to imply that young Rice was always on a
spiritual mountaintop, for such was not the case. Just as any
teenage Christian, he had his temptations, trials, tears, and
testings. Sometimes he fell into sin and lost the joy of Jehovah's
salvation. In his sermon, "The Backslider," he describes his experience:

> My mother was dead, and my boyhood companions in the
> West Texas cow town were rough and wicked. And one day it
> dawned on me that I had drifted far from God in my heart. I
> had grieved Him in my life. I had gotten to where prayer was
> not a joy, the Bible was not sweet.
>
> I was attending special services in a little Presbyterian
> church. Many young people found Christ, and many Christians
> had their joy restored, and I alone seemed left without a bless-
> ing. How sweet was the singing! What a light on the faces of the
> happy people! And one night as they sang,
>
> **Pass me not, O gentle Saviour,**
> **Hear my humble cry,**
> **While on others thou art calling,**
> **Do not pass me by.**
>
> I cried out, "Lord, is everybody going to get a blessing but
> me? Do not pass *me* by!" And, thank God, all the joy came
> back, and peace flooded my soul! I knew that my failures and
> my sins had been forgiven. It was as definite as if my Father
> had taken me in His arms and kissed away my tears and told
> me so!
>
> That night as I walked home across the prairie and looked up
> at the stars, I made a vow to God. I said, "O God, I will never
> fail You again! I will never forget my prayer time; I will never
> give way to temptation and sin!" You may well smile; I think
> that maybe a loving and kindly God smiled at my great
> promises that night. How well He knew my sinful nature, my
> frailty and sin!
>
> It was not more than two weeks before I had sinned in a way
> that shocked me terribly, though I do not now remember the
> details. I found my joy gone. And when I went to God in prayer
> to confess my sins, again I made great promises. "God, I failed
> You this time; but if You will give me one more chance, I will
> not fail You again. I promise You I will be more faithful. I will

be true this time, if You will only try me once more!" How little I knew that God wanted trust instead of promises, and that He wanted me to depend upon Him instead of myself. But He gave me sweet peace again.

But the tragic story was repeated until in despair I felt I had lied to God, had failed Him, and that He must be so disappointed in me He would never trust me any more, and would never give me back the joy of His presence. And then at long last I learned the lesson that I have an evil nature as well as a new nature which is from God.

Like every child of God, I am two persons in one. I am the old man I was before I was saved, with a human body and human frailty and a human tendency toward sin; and I am also a new creature in Christ who loves the Lord and hates sin. And I learned that God knows all about me, and that what He wants me to do is to come regularly to confess my sins and earnestly turn from them, depending on His never-failing mercy to forgive and cleanse, as He promised to do.

Another incident happened while the Rices lived in Dundee which made a profound impression upon the boy, John, then about fourteen years of age. Doctors told Will Rice the long strain he had passed through had so seriously affected his body it would be necessary for him to get away from all his business and rest for several months in the mountains. When the physician's advice was ignored, the inevitable breakdown came; and they despaired of his life. Two doctors agreed the case was hopeless and that he could not live through the night.

Without knowing what the Bible taught with reference to healing, young John knew and believed God had promised to answer prayer. Immediately he started for his "secret closet." On the way he passed the buggy shed and heard his older sister, Gertrude, crying out to God to spare the father's life. John stopped off at the barn, fell on his face in the horse stall, and begged God to intervene. When he went back to the house, he heard noises in the front room and went in to discover his stepmother crying to God for the same thing. The boy went to bed and dropped immediately off to sleep without any distress or turmoil, confident his father would live in spite of what the doctors had declared.

In his book, *Prayer—Asking and Receiving,* he describes what happened the following day.

> The next morning my father opened his eyes and looked around him strangely. He had for days, as I recall, been either half conscious or delirious. Now he sat up in bed and said, "Where are my pants?"
>
> My stepmother, half laughing, half crying, said, "What do you want with your pants? You are sick; you must stay in bed."
>
> "I am going to town," he said. "I am all right." And he would not be denied. He got up, dressed, and went to town, while my stepmother frantically called the doctors. After he returned to the house, the doctors saw him and marveled, said it was simply unreasonable, and went away dumbfounded!
>
> Later my father went again to the specialist in Fort Worth and told him about the whole case. "Who was your doctor?" said the specialist. "Why, a country doctor, Dr. Robinson," my father answered. The specialist then said my father was the luckiest man alive to have happened on such a physician, that not one doctor in a thousand could have done what that country doctor did; that if he ever had similar trouble he must go to that doctor, wherever he might be! But I know it was not that country doctor, it was the Great Physician Himself who healed my father in answer to prayer.
>
> It now seems to me most remarkable; then it seemed to me the most natural thing in the world that God should answer such prayers. In those days, with the people I knew, evolution was a joke; a man who doubted the Bible was a fool, and God was real. I do not remember that I told anybody about our prayers; I think God let me hear my sister's and stepmother's prayers because He planned for me to tell it. How warm it makes my heart now to remember it! My father lived nearly twenty years longer to the glory of God.

It was about eighteen years later—while conducting a revival campaign in Louisiana—a telegram reached him saying his father had just suffered a stroke, that he was to come immediately if he wanted to see him again on this earth. He went at once to his father's bedside, but God in His mercy allowed him to recover sufficiently to live another two years before going Home to be with the Lord and his loved ones who had preceded him to Glory.

During the days of his youth John Rice had no idea the things which were falling out unto him were helping shape and mold his life into an instrument of blessing for sin-darkened souls all over the globe. But our great God, who uses a master plan for each life completely free from any mistake, was overseeing every detail. This was true not just in the life of the boy on a Texas farm, but in the preparation of the young man's schooling, as we shall see in the next chapter.

*Chapter 4*

# Shaping the Vessel

*Then I went down to the potter's house, and, behold, he wrought a work on the wheels.* —Jeremiah 18:3.

*Nevertheless the foundation of God standeth sure, having this seal, The Lord knoweth them that are his. And, Let every one that nameth the name of Christ depart from iniquity. But in a great house there are not only vessels of gold and of silver, but also of wood and of earth; and some to honour, and some to dishonour. If a man therefore purge himself from these, he shall be a vessel unto honour, sanctified, and meet for the master's use, and prepared unto every good work.* —II Timothy 2:19-21.

IN THE wild, woolly, West Texas prairie days of John Rice's boyhood, the amount of education received depended almost entirely upon the initiative of the youth. The school at Dundee had only three teachers, and the students never graduated from high school. They simply took whatever courses were available and eventually dropped out. After taking all the subjects the school offered, Rice decided to study for a teacher's examination. With what little help he could get from various textbooks, he first studied and then took the county teacher's examination for a second-grade certificate. Eventually he took and passed the examination for a first-grade teacher's certificate, allowing him to contract to teach in any school in Texas.

It was when he went to Archer City to take one of those county teacher's examinations that an incident happened which gives an insight into the character of the man who was his father and who helped develop the same type of character in him. Some time previously a very distinguished professional man, Judge Walker, had moved with his family from Dundee to Archer City. To the amazement of the Rice lad, the judge looked him up in that strange town where he did not know anyone and insisted he be guest at their lovely home during his stay in the city. The Walker family showed him every kindness. They gave him the best room in the house, served him delightful meals, would not let him spend any of his own money, went out of their way to please him and treat him like a king, and made his every wish their command. He was amazed that such distinguished people would treat so royally a poor, country lad of only eighteen.

A long time later he learned why the judge almost wept in begging to be allowed to do something for him. In his sermon, "The Seamless Robe," Dr Rice gave this explanation:

> This family had a prodigal son. One day, after he had long been gone from home, my father saw him in a certain Texas city. He was unshaven, filthy, in rags. My father recognized him and called him by name, "Bruce! What are you doing here?"
> The shamed young man told a sad story. He drank and gambled until his money was gone. Then he slept in a flophouse. His clothes became dirty. He had no money for a shave or haircut or bath, no money for clean clothes. He was too ashamed to go home as a ragged and disreputable bum.
> My father took the young man to a barber shop where he got a haircut and shave and a bath. Then my father took him to a clothing store and bought him a suit, shirt, underwear, hat, and shoes. He outfitted the prodigal son of his old friend, then took him to the train and bought him a ticket home.
> Now, months later, I was entertained as the darling guest in that home. My slightest wish was law. They treated me as if I had been the most distinguished guest. Everything in the house was at my disposal. All of it because my dear father had earned it for me by kindness which the family could never, never forget! Because of my father's righteousness I was received and loved in a strange home.

And Will Rice's tender heart beat in the breast of his famous son. Only eternity and the judgment seat of Christ will reveal the multifold acts of human kindness and material help given by this humble man of God to those in need and distress. To him, such biblical exhortations as "Be not forgetful to entertain strangers: for thereby some have entertained angels unawares" (Heb. 13:2), and "Whoso stoppeth his ears at the cry of the poor, he also shall cry himself, but shall not be heard" (Prov. 21:13) were a very vital and important part of the Word of God to be followed just as closely and carefully as Malachi 3:10 or John 3:16.

After obtaining his teacher's certificate, Rice taught in a one-room country school fifteen miles from his home, handling pupils up to and through the eighth grade. Every morning he would write a Bible verse on the blackboard and have each student memorize that verse for the day. The school was only open four months of the year and his $55 a month salary gave him a gross income of $220 for the entire year. Naturally, he was not able to save much money from such a meager revenue.

More and more, however, he felt an increasing burden to continue his schooling and broaden his education. On one occasion he went thirty miles to hear Dr. J. L. Ward, president of Decatur Baptist College, and Dr. George W. Truett of the famous First Baptist Church in Dallas, when they were speaking at the First Baptist Church of Wichita Falls, Texas. Again he was deeply stirred about his need for further education.

Back at home he continued to pray much about the possibility of going to school. He had been reading the little book by Dr. R. A. Torrey, *How to Pray,* and one day in January, 1916, when he was just barely twenty years of age, he went out to his secret "prayer closet" to wrestle the thing out with God. He acknowledged to the Lord that he had come to the end of his own resources. He reminded Him how he had tried to borrow money at the bank, had tried to get loans from two of his prosperous friends, had tried to sell his horse, but the depression days of the time prohibited borrowing the money or selling the horse.

Describing that holy experience later, he said:

> I remember that on the thirteenth day of January, as a cold mist was falling, I went out by the woodpile, through the pea patch, crawled through the fence and walked over the hill to a place of prayer I had. It was in the brakes in a bare ravine under a chaparral bush. There I went down on my face and

prayed. I told God that I would do anything He wanted me to do: I would preach the Gospel, or I would be a gospel singer, or anything else that He should clearly lead. I told Him I would give carefully a tenth of my income besides free-will offerings through the years. Then I told Him that since this burden was on my heart it must be from Him, and I must ask Him to give me the means to go through college. I promised Him I would go, and I would look to Him to open the way before me.

Having won the victory in his own soul under that chaparral bush on his knees before God, he went to the house and told his father what he planned to do. He packed his clothes in a little old wooden trunk his mother had left him when she died, gave instructions to his father as to when to ship it, then saddled his sorrel cowpony and started off through the rain toward Decatur Baptist College at Decatur, Texas, approximately 125 miles away.

In his pocket was $9.35, his total life savings! How the God of miracles opened the door and provided for him is described graphically and pungently in his book, *Prayer—Asking and Receiving:*

On the way I talked to the Lord and told Him I would try every way to borrow money on my horse or to sell the horse for the money for the first tuition. I rode twenty-five miles and the next day walked into the Power State Bank at Archer City, Texas. Speaking to the cashier I said, "Mr. Power, I would like to borrow some money on my horse; I am going to college." He did not even look at the horse, but reached for a bank note and said, "Mr. Rice, how much money do you want?"

That stumped me! I hadn't ever gotten that close to getting the money before! But I said, "Well, I would need to get $60 for the first payment on tuition."

"How long do you want it?" he asked, waiting to fill in the due date.

"I could pay it back in six months, I think, when I am back home in the harvest," I said. So he made out the note for $60, payable in six months, and I signed it.

A man standing at the window spoke up and said, "Mr. Power, you told me you couldn't let anybody have money for longer than three months in these hard times!"

"But this young man is a friend of mine and did me a special favor once," the cashier said. The favor was that I had once taken ten minutes to show him what I had learned from a book about grafting high-grade peach branches onto old trees for his orchard!

After leaving the bank, he rode on until he came to his brother's farm in Wise County, near Decatur, where he left his horse and went by train the remaining distance. They offered him absolutely no encouragement at the school, explaining that it was the middle of the year and all the student jobs were taken. Not at all daunted, he replied, "I am certain there will be some work for me to do. I will see you again tomorrow."

When he returned the next day, the president, Dr. J. L. Ward, told him a little impatiently he was sorry, that all jobs were taken, and he did not know when there would be anything open. Again the farm boy from Dundee cheerfully thanked the astonished prexy and said he would see him the next day. When he went in the following morning, Dr. Ward said, "I have been thinking about you and I feel that Joe Owens ought to leave the college dairy. He is a senior. He waits on tables and that is enough for a senior. Could you milk the college cows?"

Rice replied to the effect that they would be surprised at how good a milker he was! He got the job! Later he was asked to be one of the two waiters who served about eighty people in the college dining room. So well did he do it that they eventually gave him the whole job of waiting tables, letting the other waiter go. Still later he was called into the president's office again and Dr. Ward, who was a great blessing to him during his days at Decatur, said, "We have some fellows here who need some coaching in arithmetic before they can do the other math courses. Do you think you could coach them on arithmetic?" John assured him he had taught arithmetic in the country school the preceding year and would be glad to do it. With all these things added together, he managed to make enough to pay his bills and get by the first year.

However, what few clothes he owned began to get rather ragged. He patched the seat of his trousers more than once and eventually it got where he felt like holding his cap behind him when he walked. One night, turning to his roommate, Riley

Whatley, he said, "Unless God makes some way for me to have some new clothes, I don't see how I can stay on in school."

His godly roommate said, "Let's pray about it."

They fell on their knees and earnestly petitioned God in His mercy to let him have some way to buy enough clothes to dress decently. That was on Friday night. Sunday afternoon from the girls' dormitory, where the only phone in the college was in the president's office, there came a message, "Long distance wants John Rice."

When he answered the phone, he discovered the call was from his uncle, George Rice, who lived at Gainesville, Texas. The very first words his uncle said were, "John, how much do you need for a new suit of clothes?"

"What makes you think I need a suit of clothes?" the destitute student questioned.

"Well, I thought a boy would always need clothes going to college," his uncle answered. They talked on for a little bit, and the boy with the patched trousers told his generous and godly uncle he thought he could buy a suit of clothes for fifteen dollars, if he wanted to lend him that much.

On Tuesday morning there came a check for twenty dollars. John took down a Sears & Roebuck catalogue and ordered a blue serge suit, a blue cap to match, and other vitally needed accessories. He eventually paid back every penny to his uncle, as well as some money he had borrowed from Dr. Ward to give to the Lord.

When school dismissed in the spring, he sold his horse and paid off the loan at the bank in Archer City. Then he worked in the harvest throughout the summer months and made a little money. In the fall he returned to Decatur and worked his way through two more years of college.

It was in that fall of 1916 that he saw his first football game when one Saturday the little Decatur Baptist College played another junior college. The following Monday in a chapel the teacher-coach urged more fellows to try out for a position on the pitifully understaffed team.

The idea of football with its rough and tumble bodily contact

appealed strongly to the lad from Dundee. He was used to breaking horses and mules, had spent long hours at hard and rough
work, so football did not seem overly tough or dangerous to him.
That very Monday afternoon the big raw-boned farmer applied
for a suit, assuring the teacher-coach he was willing to do or die
for dear old Decatur. When they asked him what place he played
on the team, he replied to the effect he did not know what position to apply for. They asked him where he played the previous
year, and he told them he hadn't played.

"Where did you play in high school?" was the next question.
He assured them that when he went to high school there were not
enough men in the whole town to make a good football team and
that he had never seen a game before the preceding Saturday!
With some astonishment and smiles of tolerant amusement, they
suggested he just come out in his overalls for a while to see if he
liked the game, explaining there were not many suits; and they
couldn't furnish one to just anybody. Actually, they thought the
sport would be a little too rough for this rookie who had seen only
one game in his entire life.

*What a surprise they were in for!*

He went out on the field in his overalls, just as he had been instructed, and confidently asked, "Where do I play?"

"Over there with the scrubs, of course," he was rather scorn-
fully directed.

"But what do I do?"

When they told him to buck the line, he patiently explained
that he didn't know what all those terms they were using meant
and asked if they would please explain to him more in detail.
Then the acting coach said to him, "Do you see that line-up?
That is the first team. The man in the middle is called the
center. He has the ball in his hands. When he throws it back
between his legs it goes to the quarterback. Do you see that
quarterback? Well, when the center snaps the ball, you break
through there, knock this man out of the way and ram your head
into the quarterback's belly!" He laughed a little as he said it,
but the rookie from Dundee got the idea.

They lined up and the ball was snapped. John Rice brushed

aside the big guard and, sure enough, he rammed his head into the quarterback's belly. The ball went squirting out of the back's arms, but Rice didn't even know he should try to recover the fumble. The quarterback was knocked cold; and when he came to, he remained groaning on the ground until he could get breath enough to get up again.

Rice thought to himself, "I have certainly ruined it now! They'll kick me off the grounds for playing so rough." Imagine his surprise when Joe Owens, the quarterback, got to his feet and said, "Who hit me?" And when they told him it was John Rice, he came and whacked him on the back saying, "Go to it, old fellow!" The next day they started teaching him the signals for the first team.

He played the next Saturday at guard, just one week after he had seen his first football game. Then they switched him to tackle where he played all that season and the next season as first-string right tackle for the Decatur Baptist Junior College. He played every quarter of every game, was never knocked out and never taken out.

About his football days, he said in his sermon, "Spectators in the Heavenly Grandstand":

> I remember in one game when the other team was about to kick, our cheering section cried,
> > "Block that kick!
> > *Block that kick!*
> > BLOCK THAT KICK!"
>
> If you made that much noise about the Lord, you would be a fanatic or a Holy Roller, or too emotional; but about a game it is all right! They said, *"Block that kick!"* and I broke through that line by good fortune, got through the guard and tackle, blocked the kick, and fell on the ball six yards behind the line! The ball was ours!
>
> That night when I left the boys' dormitory and went across the campus to milk the college cows—you didn't know cows went to college, did you—I wouldn't say I didn't limp more than was absolutely necessary! I remember how on the second floor balcony of the girls' dormitory the girls gave fifteen "rahs" for me. It matters a whole lot about the grandstand!

When he went to Baylor, he was invited to the pre-season football training for two weeks. However, with working his own way and the heavy courses he planned to take, he found himself saddled with more than he could do, so he begged off. The coach called him some hard names for quitting; but he felt he could not take time for college debating, for voice lessons, for expression lessons, for literary society, do enough work to make a living, and still have time left to play football. The result was that he sacrificed what he considered the least important and left off football.

He graduated from Decatur Baptist College in the spring of 1918 and at the start of the commencement week exercises was drafted into the army and sent to Camp Travis at San Antonio, Texas. A United States flag was draped over his empty chair by the college for the commencement exercises. He served in the United States Army for eight months, until the close of World War I. The God who acts wisely, and always with the best interest for each of His own in mind, allowed him to have an attack of mumps which put him in the base hospital at Camp MacArthur, Waco, Texas, preventing his being shipped overseas with the Seventh Division. By the time he had recovered, the Division was overseas. As a result, he was placed on guard duty, then assigned to the Dental Corps where he was when the Armistice was signed. In January, 1919, he was discharged.

Immediately he enrolled at Baylor University, a Southern Baptist school located at Waco, Texas. Since he entered at the start of the second of three quarters, by making up some extra credits and with some military credit, he was able to graduate from Baylor with his B.A. degree in 1920, after only a year and a half in Waco.

He did not understand at the time, of course, but the subjects he selected for study were ideal in preparing this vessel for the right ministry his Heavenly Father had planned for him. He entered literary society work. He became active in intercollegiate debates and with his partner debated and won against Hardin Simmons University. Later he was also in the famous Connelly debate between societies. He won the Erisophian Oratory Contest and a scholarship which went with it. He also was awarded the "1914 Class Scholarship," a scholarship donated by that class and presented each year to some student who by good scholarship, student leadership, and worthy character would be selected by the faculty for that place. So he turned down the Erisophian scholarship to accept the 1914 class scholarship.

It is not difficult to understand why John Rice did not have time for football. He was up every morning at 5:20 to carry the mail from downtown Waco to the Baylor University sub-station. Then he went to milk the Baylor cows. After the milk was carefully strained and put away, he went to earn his breakfast by drying the dishes at the girls' dormitory. In addition, he worked at the university bookstore and served as janitor for the Seventh and James Street Baptist Church. He also conducted a little mission Sunday school for the Seventh and James Street church; and by pooling the income from these sundry sources, along with some small loans, he was able to make his expenses and pay his way through college.

He made acceptable but not outstanding grades. He simply did not have the time to do the studying necessary to lead his class scholastically. He was elected president of the University Christian Association and thereby served as the Baylor University director of the Seventy-five Million Campaign. He led his fellow students in this effort to raise cash and pledges for the Southern Baptist denominational fund, and they successfully reached their goal of $75,000 at Baylor under his leadership.

Even in college he gained considerable reputation as a speaker. He gave commencement addresses in high schools and spoke frequently as a layman to church and young people's groups. He sometimes helped conduct street services and preached in the jail at Waco. Although he then had no idea of becoming a preacher, he was generally considered with the ministerial students by the faculty and student body alike. On one occasion Dr. J. B. Tidwell, the noble head of the Bible department, remarked to one of his classes (where, incidentally, the future Mrs. John R. Rice was enrolled), "If any girl does not want to marry a preacher, she had better not marry John Rice."

How he did get the girl is another story. . . .

## Chapter 5

# Finding a Good Thing

*Whoso findeth a wife findeth a good thing, and obtaineth favour of the Lord.*—Proverbs 18:22.

*Who can find a virtuous woman? for her price is far above rubies. . . .Favour is deceitful, and beauty is vain: but a woman that feareth the Lord, she shall be praised.*—Proverbs 31:10,30.

LLOYS McCLURE COOKE was a beautiful, gray-eyed brunette with a very sweet tooth. Her principal delight in this realm consisted of a golden, three-deck box of expensive candy called "King's Nut Trio." It contained an assortment of Brazil nuts, almonds and pecans dipped in the richest chocolate—and retailed at $1.50 per pound, a goodly sum in that turbulent World War I era! The fellow student who determined to win her hand was working his way through school, often limiting his lunch in the school cafeteria to buns, potatoes and gravy, sometimes wearing patched clothing to classes; *yet the lovely Miss Cooke never lacked for her favorite delicacy.*

When John Rice returned to Decatur Baptist College in the fall of 1916 he was already a very busy man on the campus, both as a part-time member of the college staff and as an active reader for the Erisophian Literary Society. One of the new girls enrolling at Decatur that fall was Lloys McClure Cooke. She was from a well-to-do home and her father, who owned a farm north of Muenster in Cooke County, brought her to college in a Maxwell car, really something in those days.

John and Lloys met the first time at an open house for the

Lloys McClure Cooke who was married to John R. Rice September 27, 1921. Picture taken in 1920.

Erisophians and its companion girls' literary society, the Palla-
dians. They saw each other frequently after that, and whenever
there was a "suspension of the rules" allowing students to have
dates on Friday night, they walked together to a play at the local
high school or to some meeting at the First Baptist Church.
Those dates consisted of walking in a long line of other dating
students, chaperoned very primly by one of the college professors.

The sweethearts took the same classes in German and
otherwise managed to see each other occasionally in spite of
strict college rules. Miss Cooke's piano practice rooms were in
the basement near the dining hall, and when young Rice went for
his meals he not infrequently stuck his head in for a few words!
They went together more or less regularly that year, saw each
other informally at society functions or at croquet games on
Saturday, and by the second year they counted themselves informally engaged.

Before he entered the army in the spring of 1918, the college
president's wife, Mrs. Ward, was greatly distressed because it
seemed his draft call would come before he could have the
pleasures of commencement week, the regular dating of good
friends, and the honors which go with graduation time. So she
suggested that John and Lloys be permitted to study their lessons together each night in the parlor of the girls' dormitory.
Thus, for the entire week preceding the commencement activities, they did nearly all of their studying together, although it
must now be confessed that they did not study all the time! He
did get to stay for the first few days of commencement events,
but the day before he was to receive his diploma, the call to the
colors came and he was shipped out to an army camp. His Lloys
sat beside his empty chair—one draped with an American flag—
and he got his diploma from Decatur Baptist College in absentia.

During the eight months he served in the army, Uncle Sam
received considerable revenue from the steady flow of correspondence which passed between the separated lovers. Regular
letters went each way six times every week with only the fact
that neither could receive mail on Sunday preventing a seventh

missive. When Lloys was finishing her last year at Baylor University and John was on the field teaching at Wayland College, they continued their letter writing every day except on the one day their letters could not be received.

The sweetness and hallowedness of that long romance is described in his sermon, "The Master Is Come and Calleth for Thee."

> I can remember so well those four years—how long they were!—when Mrs. Rice and I were engaged. We felt I must finish college. I had big plans ahead of me, yet the road was so long. How I longed to make her happy and to let her know how I loved her!
>
> When the spring came around, I looked for the first flowers that I might take them to her. Why, I could hardly enjoy anything that was pleasant without her enjoying it, too. When I read a good book, I marked it; I underlined favorite passages, and then I sent her the book to read!
>
> I well remember how I watched the peaches slowly ripening on the trees, eager that I should be the one who would first take them to her. It seemed that my heart would burn itself out, seeking ways to let her know how I loved her! And I love her still and rejoice to make her happy.

In another message, "The Banquet Invitation, R.S.V.P.," he describes this incident in their courtship:

> Once, when I was a senior in Baylor University at Waco, Texas, I received a large, beautifully engraved invitation to the Junior-Senior banquet in the Gold Room of the Raleigh Hotel for February 22, 1920. The juniors were to entertain the seniors; and as a senior, I was invited as an honor guest. Enclosed in the envelope was a small card with the name of my sweetheart, Lloys McClure Cooke. And down in the corner of the beautifully engraved invitation were these four letters, "R.S.V.P." I found those letters represented the French words, *Repondez s'il vous plait.* And those words mean, "Answer if you please."
>
> In that beautiful Gold Room of the Raleigh Hotel, the seniors would be there and the juniors, my classmates and friends. We would soon be saying goodbye after our years of college were over. And I would be long, long months away from my sweetheart. Now I was invited to be present. But if I could not go, or would not, another must be invited in my place. There must be no empty place at the banquet.

So I answered right away! I wrote a note accepting the invitation and telling the girl I loved I would gladly go as her escort and guest. Then I cut across the campus to meet her as she came from an English class at 11 o'clock to make sure that I could say informally what I had already written formally.

Poor as I was, working my way through the university, up at 5:20 every morning, with barely enough money to get by, and wearing patched clothes, I bought beautiful, long-stemmed, hothouse roses for my sweetheart. I dressed in my best, and we took a taxi to the banquet. I found a place with my place card, and just beside me, one for my dear sweetheart. And we sat together at the banquet.

Lloys went through her last year at Baylor University and graduated in 1921. They had talked of marrying in the early summer following her graduation, but he soon had dates to sing in revival campaigns, and they decided to postpone the wedding until he could register at the Southwestern Baptist Theological Seminary in the fall. In September, the prospective bridegroom went to Fort Worth, rented an apartment and called by telephone to suggest, "Let's get married Monday morning," which was one week earlier than they had planned.

She answered in the traditional, "This is so sudden!" but he got the wedding ring, the license, and made the necessary arrangements. On September 27, 1921, John Richard Rice and Lloys McClure Cooke were united in the holy bond of matrimony at her father's farm home near Muenster, Texas. Rev. R. R. Gaines, a long-time friend of the groom's father and greatly used as a country Baptist preacher, performed the ceremony. Then, since no one came to offer them congratulations and best wishes, they went around to the bride's weeping mother, father and brothers, attempting to comfort each one. The groom turned to his own father, whose features appeared very gray and shaken, to say, "Dad, I believe you were worse scared than I was." He replied, "Son, when you've been married as long as I have, you'll be scared, too!"

After the ceremony they were driven twenty miles to Gainesville and from there took a train to Fort Worth. There they entered the little two-room apartment rented for $15 a month in the Crowder House on Seminary Hill and started married life. There was a bathroom off the back porch with a sheet-metal tub for bathing. It was necessary to heat water in a tea kettle and pour it into the tub when they wanted a bath. They purchased about $100 worth of secondhand furniture with $19.75 down, paying out the balance by the month. Limited funds caused them to buy only one pint of milk every other day, and they managed to live on five to eight dollars *a month* for groceries!

Perhaps a true picture of those early marriage adjustment days cannot be realized without remembering that Lloys and John were from entirely different backgrounds. His poverty and deprivation have already been described in detail. Her father owned a thousand acres of black land; and when she went off to college, he gave her a checkbook with unlimited privileges of writing drafts to buy whatever she wanted. Once when they were in Baylor University and had a date, she said to John, "I need advice." He immediately assured her that advice was his strong point, and she should simply tell her problem to him, and he would have it settled in no time.

She replied, "I want to buy a new hat and there are two I like. One is blue and it turns up on the left front corner and has a rose underneath and a ribbon on top. It is $15. The other one is pink. . . ."

At that point the impatient suitor interrupted to exclaim, "Don't buy either one of them! No wife of mine is ever going to pay more than $5 for a hat, and I don't want you to get started paying that kind of money!" When they finally did marry, she had plenty of clothes, fortunately, for it was another two years before they were able to buy her anything new, they were so poor.

The young Mrs. Rice enrolled in the seminary along with her husband, and he recollected with a warm, wry chuckle how her grades in Hebrew were superior to his. Times were hard and money was scarce, but God was with them and those were very happy days.

The enthusiastic bridegroom never got over what "a good thing" he had obtained from the Lord. When his first clothbound book was printed, a volume of sermons released by Zondervan

Publishing House in 1939, he dedicated it: *"To my beloved wife, Lloys Cooke Rice, who for more than seventeen years has been my constant encouragement and help in revivals. Although burdened with the duties of home as the mother of six children, she is an ardent and successful soul winner, a diligent Bible student, my best critic, and my constant inspiration in revival efforts. She never said 'stay' but always 'go.' Her husband's preaching is always fresh to her, and her joy in revivals never fades."*

He never lost that complete devotion to his mate; and, at the end of the trail—just weeks before his fatal stroke—in the wee hours of the morning, he dictated the following letter:

"Dear Mother:

"We have had a wonderful life together. God's mercy has been extended to us over eighty-five years. These last two months, since I was in the hospital, have been a revelation to me. How kind you have been, constantly seeing that I was covered at night so that I did not get cold. And you have prepared for me the very finest of things to eat. How patient you have been and how wonderful.

"You have been a wonderful, wonderful wife and wonderful mother. You have loved the Scriptures, and you have helped me, to make them a blessing to me.

"You have a good name among the people of God, and you have deserved it. I hope the remaining years, whether few or many, will be very happy. I rejoice with you and our wonderful children. Your prayers have held them up and those of the grandchildren, especially those called to preach. I rejoice with you in the great work they will do.

"I greet you with a heartfelt kiss of love. You have been a wonderful partner and wife to me. We will sing at the last, 'On Christ the solid rock I stand, all other ground is sinking sand.' The dear Saviour will make you happy and care for you all the way."

God's loving favor was surely in the life-long companionship of this virtuous woman.

Chapter 6

# The Great Surrender

*Also I heard the voice of the Lord, saying, Whom shall I send,
and who will go for us? Then said I, Here am I; send me. And he
said, Go, and tell this people. . . .*—Isaiah 6:8,9.

APPARENTLY the very last one to realize that God wanted
John R. Rice to preach was John R. Rice! He, like any other
youth, had great plans and ambitions relative to the success he
would be in the profession of his choice. After graduating from
Baylor University in 1920, he worked throughout the summer as
field secretary for Wayland Baptist College at Plainview, Texas,
then taught English in the college during the fall and winter
quarters. While at Wayland he coached the football and basketball squads, as well as the girls' and boys' intramural basketball
teams. In the spring quarter he attended the University of
Chicago, taking work looking forward to a master's degree in the
department of education and psychology. He had already signed
to teach the following year at a senior college in New Mexico. He
dreamed of climbing the educational ladder until he became a
college president and then, perhaps, a senator, then possibly
even—who could tell—*President of the United States!*

It was not that he was unwilling to become a preacher, but he
felt he had never experienced the kind of emotional call necessary which, in his mind, he expected a man of God to receive.
However, we have already related how his mother and father
gave him to God before he was born, how his mother called him
her "preacher boy," how his father underscored in his Bible the
words of Luke 1:63, "His name is John," and how Dr. Tidwell

had publicly stated, "If any girl does not want to marry a preacher she had better not marry John Rice." It was pretty well a foregone conclusion among all his boyhood and young manhood friends that he would be a preacher, and others recognized it long before he did. All through the years there was upon him the call of God.

Even though he did not claim to be a preacher or expect ever to become one, he did personal work in revivals. He often preached on street corners with preacher boys from the school. He helped conduct services in jails and openly delighted in revival meetings. He did the work of a gospel singer in a good many such campaigns and not infrequently he would personally win as many people to Jesus Christ as all the church members, pastor and evangelist would win together. Though he did not recognize it then, he later knew that there was a moving of God's Spirit upon him and that this was some kind of evidence God intended for him to preach.

The event of his actual surrender to God for the ministry took place while he was doing graduate work at the University of Chicago. One night he took off from his studies to attend services at Chicago's famous Pacific Garden Mission where Billy Sunday, Mel Trotter, and thousands of others have found Christ. He heard a plain-speaking, Spirit-filled preacher, Rev. Holland Oates, address the men from the familiar text in Romans 12:1 and 2. Oates stressed heavily that night the call of Isaiah and how Isaiah volunteered his services to Jehovah, saying, "Lord, here am I, send me." He told how he, a drunken stone mason, had been converted, then with only a fifth-grade education had surrendered to preach the Gospel or do anything God wanted him to do. That dear man butchered the king's English, but the power of God was obviously upon him, and John Rice felt led to cry to God in his own heart, "Lord, I am a college English teacher. If You can use him, why can't You use me?"

That same night he went to the altar, knelt beside a poor drunken bum, put his arm around his shoulders, opened the Word of God and showed that lowly lost sinner how he could experience God's "so great" salvation. God moved John Rice's heart that night as never before as he saw the light dawn in that bum's soul, saw the changed expression on his face, saw the evidence of peace in the troubled sinner's breast, and beheld the new-creation kind of transformation take place. In a single moment all the glamour and glitter wrapped around his ambition to be a great educator or politician fled away. He lost all his taste and enthusiasm for college classrooms or political platforms. God showed him in that hour the worth of a soul and the eternal dividends to be received by one who gives himself wholeheartedly and unreservedly to the Father's business.

Describing that experience in his sermon, "Outside the Gate With Jesus," he says:

> I got up from my knees beside this poor, dirty, unshaven, but now converted bum and found that all my ambitions for college teaching were gone! I wanted nothing better than to win souls and to have welling up in my heart continually the glad joy I felt at that moment. I looked through the vista of future years and saw the time when "they that be wise shall shine as the brightness of the firmament; and they that turn many to righteousness as the stars for ever and ever" (Dan. 12:3). I gave up my graduate work, gave up my contract, started revival work, then entered the seminary for ministerial training.
>
> What I did then, I have since done a hundred times, a thousand times. I have said good-by to good friends for Jesus' sake. I have laid on the altar the dearest things a man can know in this world, save the love of God and the presence of the Holy Spirit and eternal blessings. I have loved those who did not love me. I have helped those who did not thank me. I have through the long years willingly paid whatever price God would help me pay to help bring back revivals. I have been unknown when I could be known. I have been despised when I could have been honored.

After he made his decision, he wrote to his former pastor at the Seventh and James Street Baptist Church in Waco, Dr. W. W. Melton, who had at one time invited him to become his assistant pastor, and told him that if God would use him, he would enter some form of Christian work. The good brother wrote back immediately, saying, "Why don't you just say you are going to preach and go to it?" *So John Rice started out to preach!*

When he told his old friend, the president of Decatur Baptist

College, Dr. Ward, that he felt he must preach, Dr. Ward replied, "My wife and I have known that for a long time."

Yet his actual decision to preach was primarily a step of faith. He had volunteered his services according to the *command* of God in Romans 12 and the *question* of God in the sixth chapter of Isaiah. One time in Texas, after he had described how he had *volunteered* his service to God, told Him he would do anything He wanted him to do, then began preaching, one brother said to him, "Is that the only call you have?"

"I suppose it is," he replied.

"Then you are not called to preach," said the pastor.

He replied, "I don't care whether I am called or not, just as long as God doesn't stop me." But more and more he became certain that it truly was the will of God for him to proclaim the unsearchable riches in Christ Jesus.

As we have already shown in a previous chapter, God had been leading in a wonderful way throughout his college education, even though he did not know then he would be preaching. He took lessons in expression and lessons in speech at both Decatur and Baylor. *He worked hard at it.* He prepared orations, memorized readings, took part in literary society debates, in intersociety debates, and in intercollegiate debates. He raised money for the Red Cross and otherwise took places of leadership. As a layman, he was president of the University Christian Association of Baylor. He conducted, as a layman, a little mission Sunday school and preached in a mission for the Seventh and James Street Baptist Church at Waco. Although a layman, he joined the preacher boys in protesting the teaching of evolution by a sociology professor at Baylor. Long before he recognized the call of God in answer to his godly mother's and father's prayers, he had won hundreds of souls and had been used in a greater manner than many Bible preachers.

So after the surrender that night in the Pacific Garden Mission, he left work at the University of Chicago, went to Texas to lead the singing in revival campaigns throughout the summer of 1921, then borrowed $100 to get married and entered the

Southwestern Baptist Theological Seminary at Fort Worth. Today there are multiplied thousands of souls all around the world who are extremely thankful to God that John R. Rice was "not disobedient unto the heavenly vision" (Acts 26:19).

*Chapter 7*

# Early Experiences in the Harvest

*Jesus saith unto them, My meat is to do the will of him that sent me, and to finish his work. Say not ye, There are yet four months, and then cometh harvest? behold, I say unto you, Lift up your eyes, and look on the fields; for they are white already to harvest. And he that reapeth receiveth wages, and gathereth fruit unto life eternal: that both he that soweth and he that reapeth may rejoice together. And herein is that saying true, One soweth, and another reapeth. I sent you to reap. . . ."*
—John 4:34-38.

JOHN RICE stayed with his studies at the Southwestern Baptist Theological Seminary until he had completed two years' work, but his heart was burning within him to be out preaching all the time. Sometimes it seemed totally impossible and completely unbearable to postpone the work God had called him to do. During his seminary days he preached in jails, on street corners, and served as student pastor of rural churches in Cooke and Fannin counties. His summers were filled with revival campaigns.

Finally he felt he dared not wait longer to get into full-time work and so, without waiting for the third year to secure a Master of Theology degree, he accepted a call to join Dr. Harlan J. Matthews at the First Baptist Church of Plainview, Texas, as his assistant. Since then he has been given several honorary doctor's degrees: the Los Angeles Baptist Theological Seminary (now Northwest Baptist Seminary) conferred the Doctor of Divinity title upon him; Bob Jones College (now University) honored him with a Doctor of Literature; the Doctor of Sacred

Theology degree was given by the San Francisco Baptist Theological Seminary; and the Doctor of Humanities conferred by both Hyles-Anderson College and the Sioux City Community College.

Many valuable lessons were learned while working with that noble, godly pastor in Plainview; and throughout his life, in many of his sermons, he acknowledged Dr. Matthews' help. It was while there that he learned another lesson which influenced his ministry greatly. It seems that he was to preach on a Sunday evening, in the absence of Dr. Matthews, to a crowd of about six hundred people. Burdened about a fitting theme for his message, he said to an elderly minister, Rev. G. R. Brittain, as they walked together, "I don't know what to preach Sunday night." The elderly saint promptly responded, *"And don't you know where to go to find out?"*

Rebuked to the depths of his soul and sensing immediately his sin, he quickly answered, "Yes, I *do* know where to go to find out what to preach, and I am going there!" Then he went alone, fell on his face before God, crying out to Him for wisdom and leading. God wonderfully answered, gave him a message, then anointed him with His Spirit to preach it in power. From that time on he never lacked for a proper message to preach on any occasion.

After spending one year as assistant to Dr. Matthews in Plainview, he accepted a call to the pastorate of the First Baptist Church in Shamrock, Texas. At that time Shamrock was just a small town with unpaved streets, and the church was very small and cold, meeting in a humble 40 x 60 wooden tabernacle; but God gave them many blessed and thrilling experiences. In two short years' time the church had grown from 200 to 460 members, and a beautiful brick building had been built. An oil boom came to the surrounding country; the streets of the little town were paved, and the work of the church prospered under the merciful hand of their omnipotent God.

It was of his pastorate in Shamrock that he somewhat humorously and in a measure facetiously wrote in his booklet, *A Church That God Blesses and Why:*

Again I speak from a personal experience. I was pastor of a good church which endeavored to keep up all the organizations and activities required or suggested by denominational leaders.

We had a Women's Missionary Society with five circles. Every Sunday I had to announce where Circle No. 1, Circle No. 2, Circle No. 3, Circle No. 4, Circle No. 5 met, etc., etc. If the pastor did not get to attend a good portion of the programs himself, he was scolded, invited, pleaded with. Of course this W.M.S. had its "week of prayer" in which they did not pray but talked; its study courses, its socials. These good women were always in a stew about county-wide meetings, district meetings, and state meetings; about reports, and most especially about credit for all the money they gave or raised!

Then there were B.Y.P.U.'s, the B.T.S. (Baptist Training Service). We were supposed to maintain an Adult Union, a Senior B.Y.P.U., an Intermediate Union, Junior Union, and even a Primary Union! Of course, the little fellows had to learn properly all the machinery and red tape necessary to be a good loyal Baptist!

But wait, I forgot to tell you about the subsidiary organizations of the W.M.S. It was the ambition of these good women, egged on by their ambitious statewide headquarters, to supervise all the young people's work of the church. So, in competition with all the B.Y.P.U.'s, the women organized a Y.W.A. (Young Women's Auxiliary), a G. A. (Girl's Auxiliary), the "Royal Ambassadors" for boys, and a "Sunbeam Band" for little tots.

For some strange reason, probably because they never thought of it, the good women had no organization for old bachelors! Being a loyal Baptist preacher, and "for the whole cooperative program," of course I tried, though in vain, to make all these organizations, wheels within wheels, turn and whir.

But hold on, dear reader, for if you are flabbergasted, there is more yet to come. There was a Board of Trustees, Finance Committee, and a "men's Brotherhood" to deal with besides all the good women and young people!

To be sure we had a modern Sunday school with all the fixings. Had I not been trained as an educational director? We had superintendents, department superintendents, secretaries, and organized classes. Each organized class had to have three or four vice-presidents, as did each B.Y.P.U. and Missionary Society. Then there were the study courses, classes, lectures, seals, diplomas, and red tape.

I forgot to say that I had been moderator of the Baptist

County Association (such a "good Baptist" would be!),
organizer for the Baptist Conquest Campaign, and representative for the *Baptist Standard!* Incidentally, I was supposed to
rake up students for the Baptist colleges.

The Sunday school had study courses; the W.M.S. had study
courses; the B.Y.P.U.'s had study courses! Lunches were
served, examinations were given, "awards" given.

Then everybody had to give "programs." Leaders must be
"recognized" publicly. There were "installation" services.
There were 100 "officers" in a church of 300 members! Each
B.Y.P.U., each organized class, must be "A-1"—fit a standard
supplied by the Baptist Sunday School Board—and to do that
each one must have a "social," a party, at least once a quarter,
preferably once a month.

I had no time then for week-night Bible classes and home
prayer meetings such as we keep going all the time in our
church. No one had time to go from house to house to win souls.
In fact, we never even tried. We were keeping the wheels
turning! We were following the standards put up by men, not
the one set up in the Bible!

I wonder now how I ever got anybody saved! Actually I had
no time to study the Bible, had not been taught even that I
needed to study it much. I do not wonder that I developed few
soul winners and no Bible students or great "pray-ers" in my
church. Time would fail me to tell of "budgets," "drives,"
"every-member canvasses," etc.

Finally, in desperation, I decided to enter the ministry and
left the whole "kit and bilin" and went into evangelistic work!

Actually, it was in 1926 when he felt clearly led of God to enter
the full-time work of an evangelist. So, despite the protests of the
people who loved him, he moved back to Fort Worth, built a
pretty little brick house at 4422 James Street near the seminary
campus, and began his revival campaigns.

At that time it was not customary for revival work to go on the
year around. There were very few full-time evangelists among
Baptists in the South, and after World War I there had been very
few citywide revivals. He was deeply moved with a concern
about how he could keep busy in revival work and support his
growing family. Because of this, he made a solemn covenant with
God that if He would look after his business, he would look after
His. As a token to God of his faith and earnestness in his part of

the covenant, he gave up his $10,000 government insurance policy. On the same basis, he decided to renounce any form of a regular salary, and from that day on he never made any requirement—either as pastor or evangelist—as to what remuneration he should receive. Almost fifty-five years of personal experience abundantly proved God's gracious faithfulness in fulfilling His part of the agreement.

Commenting on this covenant with God in his book, *Prayer— Asking and Receiving,* he said:

> Praise His name, God has kept *His* part of that bargain! He has kept my growing family and supplied all our needs. He has provided hundreds of thousands of dollars for printing gospel literature. He has provided thousands of dollars for radio bills, and day by day, sometimes meal by meal, God has provided our needs bountifully; and we have lived a life of resting in God's faithfulness.
>
> I know a lot more about God than I did when I entered into that covenant. My faith is much stronger. Your faith, too, will grow, if you really take God up on His proposition, if you try Him on His promises, and promise to prove His faithfulness!

Many years later, in his book, *All About Christian Giving,* he gave further comment which I think will be a blessing to the readers of this book and an additional insight into his spiritual character.

> Some years ago as I got to meditating on these things and praying for the Lord's direction in my life, I said to God, "Lord, do You think that I meant business more in the days of my ardent young ministry than I do now? Well, I want to prove to myself that Thou art the same God, that I can trust You as safely now as ever. I do not want to feel that the God who answered prayer so wonderfully in my early ministry is now farther away. And I do not want to depend now on men, or on material things, where once I depended so clearly on God."
>
> So I decided to put God to a fresh test. I had recently come in from revival services. I had about $200 in cash after giving Mrs. Rice the grocery money. For two months ahead I had no revival services scheduled, no engagements from which I would expect any income. From the work of *The Sword of the Lord,* of which I am the unworthy editor, I receive no salary. Now would be a good time to prove God!

So I bought $50 worth of clothes for a ministerial student in Moody Bible Institute, a young black man whom some of us had brought from British Guiana, in South America, to study for the ministry. Then I bought a new suit for a ministerial student in Wheaton College. Then I sent $100 to Northwestern Schools in Minneapolis, which schools I had the honor to serve as a trustee.

When the family's needs were supplied for a week, I had no money left in the bank and only some coins in my pocket. I closed the door to my office and walked up and down with tears of trust and praise to God running down my face. I said to the Lord, "Lord, You see I am not afraid to trust You. I do not have to have money in the bank. You never failed me before, and I want to prove that You will not fail me now."

And, praise be to God, from unexpected sources, from people who had no reason to know of my need, gifts began to come in; and during the two months or so before I would have other income from revival services, our needs were completely supplied.

When he first began preaching the Gospel, he foolishly supposed it would be no different than the public speaking to which he was accustomed and in which he admittedly excelled. So he labored long over his sermons, working out every detail, thinking even he might memorize his message, preparing them in a cold, logical manner. But when he tried to preach them he discovered, unlike his debating experience, he would leave his train of thought for some illustration or new material he had not thought of before—and that he would often weep as he spoke.

Commenting about it in his book, *The Soul-Winner's Fire,* he said:

When I first began preaching, I remember how I wept from the beginning to the end of my sermons. I was embarrassed about it. This was wholly unlike the college debating, the commencement addresses and other public speaking to which I had been accustomed. The tears flowed down my cheeks almost continually, and I was so broken up that sometimes I could scarcely talk. Then I grew ashamed of my tears and longed to speak more logically.

As I recall I asked the Lord to give me better control of myself as I preached. My tears soon vanished, and I found I had only the dry husk of preaching left. Then I begged God to give me again the broken heart, the concern, even if it meant tears in public and a trembling voice. I feel the same need today.

We preachers ought to cry out like Jeremiah, "Oh that my head were waters, and mine eyes a fountain of tears, that I might weep day and night for the slain of the daughter of my people!" (Jer. 9:1).

After he moved to Fort Worth, he began regular radio services and God blessed this particular ministry. As the fight over modernism in general—and teaching about the book of Revelation in particular—became more pronounced, he was thrown more and more into the company of Dr. J. Frank Norris, pastor of the First Baptist Church in Fort Worth, and often supplied his pulpit. Then, because of Rice's opposition to some of the unscriptural practices and teachings of his own denomination, the doors of Baptist churches within the Southern Baptist Convention began to close to him, and he started conducting independent citywide campaigns throughout the Lone Star State.

Even though the denominational leaders were generally against him and he did not get invited into the best churches, he had built a big hearing with many, many friends over Oklahoma and Texas through his daily radio broadcast. So, with the help of friends in Fort Worth, he bought a secondhand tent about 60 by 80 feet in size and held several campaigns in the suburban areas of that city—where he could maintain his radio broadcast without difficulty.

After the campaigns in the Fort Worth area, he took his big tent to Decatur, Texas, where he had attended junior college and where his father then lived. Will Rice hitched his Chevrolet car on to a block and tackle to help his son raise the big 800-pound center poles. They built the seats with volunteer labor and got out handbills to announce the meeting. He stayed there preaching nightly ten weeks; the little county seat town was deeply stirred; there were hundreds of remarkable conversions, and a new church was organized.

He did not originally intend to organize a new church in Decatur, but the local churches fought the revival and opposed him. He had visited the pastor of the First Baptist Church and other leaders in the town but could not get their cooperation. As a result, there was no one to look after the new converts, and organizing a new church seemed to be the only sensible solution. They built a temporary baptistry right there at the tent and baptized the converts. Then they bought a piece of ground and built a large, permanent tabernacle. At the close of the ten-week campaign the membership numbered 500, so a pastor was called to the field full time with a starting salary of $200 a month—no little sum in that day. Not long ago that church, the Fundamentalist Baptist Church, was still considered the largest church in Wise County, and a host of young preachers had gone out from it into the Saviour's whitened harvest field. It was this author's joy to hold a blessed campaign there in 1951, when Rev. L. J. Power was the pastor.

Later Rice went to Waxahachie, Texas, and rented a large building—a former livery stable—and with volunteer workers built seats for about 1,200 people. Handbills announcing the meeting were printed, and the volunteer helpers sowed the town down with 10,000 copies at a time. Even though no local churches were sponsoring the campaign—nor were they particularly friendly—the crowds grew and grew. In no time at all they were having many remarkable conversions, and the campaign lasted for about twelve weeks. At that time a new church was organized with more than 300 members. During the Waxahachie revival he traveled back and forth to Fort Worth early Sunday morning and late Sunday night to maintain his touch with his radio audience.

From Waxahachie he went to Sherman, Texas, a town of about 16,000. The courthouse had been burned down in a riot over a lynching a year or two previously, so he got permission from the city council to use the now vacant courthouse square—right in the center of town—for the campaign. On the radio in Fort Worth he called for volunteers to meet him at a certain time to build benches and string light wires to the platform. Handbills were printed and spread door to door and placed in cars by the thousands. The meeting was advertised extensively in the local paper. Great crowds of people came; the blessed power of God was manifest, and the campaign continued for twelve or thirteen weeks. They organized a new church with more than 300 members, purchased a lot, built a big tabernacle 80 x 130 feet, and then called a pastor. The church is still in existence and doing a good work. Dr. Rice later returned for a revival meeting—twenty-four years after its organization.

He then held other blessed, fruitful campaigns in Wichita Falls, Bowie and Bridgeport. New churches were organized after each meeting, but he discovered the principal trouble with such campaigns was that they did not reach the other churches; and while they could get many people saved, teach many people the Bible, and organize a good new church, there was a real problem in getting adequate pastors. Not many men in those days wanted to be known as "independents" and lose their fancied influence and prestige with denominational leaders. Eventually he went to Dallas for a big independent campaign and stayed for seven and a half years as pastor of the work which grew out of that meeting. That story will be told in the succeeding chapter.

In addition to these independent, citywide campaigns, he held numerous meetings in local churches with many unusual incidents and remarkable results. For example, he says in one of his books:

> In 1931 I went for a series of revival services with the First Baptist Church of Peacock, a little town in West Texas. That midwest town was in the clutches of a terrible drought. It had not rained for months. Crops were utterly ruined. Even normally it was too dry to raise corn, but in that particular year even drought-resistant crops, such as milo maize and cane, were blighted and their tops were all sere, brown and dead. Water holes were dried up. The pastures were in some places almost as barren as a floor. Frequently as one drove down the lane, he would smell dead cattle, starved to death. Some farms were deserted and people had traveled far to get work and earn a little income to live on.
>
> As we went into the revival services, my heart got more and more burdened about the barren country. I felt that God wanted to show His power. So I promised God that just as soon as the Christian people began to be aroused and concerned over their sins and over their lost loved ones, I would call a meeting

of confession and prayer, begging God to send a rain, as well as a revival.

God's Holy Spirit took hold of the people; they began to have broken hearts, to seek God and to want souls saved. I took courage and called a meeting for prayer, telling the people I felt definitely led to pray for a rain. I felt that the Holy Spirit had put the matter in my heart. Many agreed to pray with me.

We publicly asked God to send a great rain and to send it within twenty-four hours. I announced to the public that we would expect a rain in twenty-four hours and that if it came after that time it would not be the one we were asking for and that we would not count our prayers answered. There was no evidence of any kind in the heavens that we should expect a rain.

The next day the sun beat down pitilessly on the barren land. In the morning service at 11 o' clock that weekday, we again prayed for rain, and begged God to send it by the night service so that all could know that God answered definite prayers. I announced that if the rain did not come within twenty-four hours, it would not be an answer to our prayers. God put it in my heart to pray that definite prayer, and I felt that He would hear it.

After noon my wife set about to wash some clothes and sent our little girl Grace, then five, to borrow a tub of a neighbor woman who had offered it. It was about 2 o'clock; suddenly black clouds began to roll up swiftly from the southeast. In a few minutes there came a mighty wind. Mrs. Rice had to rescue the little girl and catch the washtub, rolling across the prairie! The tabernacle where we had been meeting was blown off the blocks that supported it. Downtown in the stores the scoffers and the wicked had been saying, "Praying for rain may be all right in East Texas, but it won't work in West Texas. That fool young preacher will see; there will not be a rain by tonight." Suddenly the plate glass windows of a store were blown in and there came a flood of rain. The scoffers were scattered. Then there was a great downpour over the town and for about five miles in each direction. What a rain it was!

We had services that night in the Methodist church. People came, filled the seats, sat in the windows—all the building would hold. But they did not come in their cars; the roads were deep in mud; they came in farm wagons and buggies and on horseback and wading with rubber boots. God sent the rain. And we had a right to be definite and bold about it because the Holy Spirit had put it in our hearts.

Nor was that the only time God sent rain in answer to prayer. Once at Decatur, Texas, the area had been in the throes of a blighting drought for some time—so much so that the lake from which the city got its water supply was nearly dry, and local authorities had cut off all the water except for two hours a day. Many Christians knelt at the altar in fervent prayer, after confession of sin, and the evangelist led the earnest supplications to God for rain. God answered with a downpour lasting three days and three nights; the lake ran over, and they eventually called another prayer meeting to ask God to stop the rain so they could continue the revival campaign.

Not only did Rice see it start to rain in answer to prayer, but also stop. Once in open-air services at Dallas in 1932, without even a tent over them for protection, it started to rain. They prayed to God and He stopped the rain, although just two blocks away the water continued to fall. The same thing happened during services in Waterloo, Iowa—and in too many other places for it to have been an accident.

In a tent revival at Oklahoma City, he had preached for two weeks without any unusual results. Large crowds had come and a few had been saved, but there was no big break for which they were praying. One night he preached on the revival Elijah had at Mount Carmel and in his message said: "We will put no human fire on this altar. If God does not come to move and bless, we will go home without it. I promise you now and I promise God, I will never give another invitation in this campaign unless God begins to work without an invitation. I have pled and tried to get people to move, but I am not going to do it any more. God is going to move or the thing will go down in defeat." At the close of the sermon he said, "The thing is done. If anybody wants to be saved, you can be. We are not going to stand and sing. If anybody wants to be saved, you can stand to your feet."

Immediately a man rose and said, "Brother Rice, I am in torment. I must have this thing settled." The evangelist invited him forward and soon he had trusted Christ.

Then a woman stood and held two fingers high. He did not know what she meant until she showed him the yellow stain of cigarettes and said, "Twenty-two years. Will the Lord save a woman like me?" In a little bit she had the matter settled also.

Then another girl stood and came down the aisle weeping, still without any public invitation. All the way forward, weeping, her face covered with her hands, she was saying, "What will Mother say? She had such ambitions for me; what will Mother think? Oh, Lord, what does it matter what she thinks! What will Dad think? He has been holding me back; but what does it matter what he thinks? All my friends with whom I have been going out—what will they think? What does it matter what they think, just so my soul is saved!" By that time the crowd was deeply moved; the invitation was made public, and many got right with God. The pastor of the church, when I conducted revival services for him years later, told me they had by far the greatest revival the church ever experienced during that meeting.

In dealing with John Rice's early experiences, perhaps I should give a little more detail about his radio ministry. In 1926, when he gave up his pastorate in Shamrock and entered the evangelistic field full time, the radio was comparatively new. Dr. J. Frank Norris and the First Baptist Church had obtained a radio license and built station KFQB in Fort Worth. Evangelist Rice was asked to speak on that station several times, and his heart was thrilled at the response he received.

Soon he was invited to begin regular daily services over KFQB. In those days most people had little crystal sets and instead of a speaker box, such as we are accustomed to, they listened through earphones. Usually there were two sets of earphones and a whole family would gather around and each person would use one side of each earphone. In that way four people could hear at the same time. He preached the Gospel which the common people have always heard gladly, and mail came in from over most of Texas and Oklahoma.

He learned very quickly that the well is apt to run dry in daily radio broadcasting! First he preached the sermons that he had already preached in revival campaigns. He preached a sermon on the Christian home, a sermon on the Holy Spirit, a sermon on soul winning, and various sermons on other themes. But in preaching a half-hour every day, week in and week out, he discovered that it was necessary to do more studying. So he went back and preached a series of sermons on the Christian home, then a series on the Holy Spirit, then a series on soul winning, etc., and God put him on the spot to where he had to study his Bible more and more!

Then he began to preach through the Gospel of John. At first all he did was to find some text in the first chapter, preach on it, then find a text in the second chapter, and so on through the book. But by the time he had preached through John, he had begun to get the idea of expository preaching and endeavored to preach on whole passages and incidents. When he finished with John, he preached through the book of Acts.

Another thing about his radio broadcasting which drove him to the Bible in diligent study was the public answering of Bible questions. Although he was just a young preacher, he had honest intentions and promised God he would never answer a question carelessly, nor would he ever answer if he couldn't prove his response from the Bible. He said to me once when we were talking about it, "My, how I had to dig! I actually worked so hard at it, and it was so well received and appreciated by my listeners, that my answers to Bible questions became a principal feature of the broadcast. I had a beginning of heavy mail, answering questions, which has continued to this day. Now not a day goes by but there are questions about the Bible or about Christian conduct, duties and doctrines for me to answer. Multiplied thousands of Christians have come to feel that I am their pastor in this manner."

He continued the daily radio ministry over KFQB until the station burned down in 1929; then he bought time on Fort Worth's large WBAP, where he paid $25 a day just for radio time alone, and continued his daily half-hour broadcast. After he moved to Dallas he began regular half-hour broadcasts over station WRR and for the main part of the seven and one-half years in that city, he conducted a daily broadcast. During most of the remainder of the time he maintained a Sunday morning broadcast. Later in his ministry, in 1959, Dr. Rice re-entered the radio field with "The Voice of Revival," a 30-minute broadcast of sermon and song. At the time of his death it was heard on a network of 69 stations in 29 states, Puerto Rico and the Philippine Islands.

One incident which took place while broadcasting over WBAP shows how he walked by faith in those early days. In his book, *Prayer—Asking and Receiving,* he said:

> For example, for six months in 1931-32 I had a daily broadcast on WBAP at Fort Worth. The broadcast fee alone was $25 a day. Two secretaries were needed to keep up with the work, besides the expense of my family and thousands of pieces of literature given away. Day by day we went to God in prayer and God sent the money. I had no church to help on the expenses. I did not take public collections for the broadcast. And on the radio, by agreement with the station, I was never to make any special appeal for funds. I could only say, "This broadcast is maintained by the free-will offerings of God's people." Yet every week there was money in hand to pay the broadcast fee, to pay the workers, and for the necessities of life. And the way it came was by daily, believing prayer.
>
> One day, as was our custom, Mrs. Rice, one of the secretaries, and I agreed to pray for $30 to come that day. We expressly named $30 in our prayer and agreed in asking God for it.
>
> The morning mail came about 9 o'clock and contained among many letters offerings totaling $13.50 for the radio broadcast. The noon mail came with letters asking Bible questions, telling of blessings received through the broadcast, but with no money. The afternoon mail came about 3 o'clock with other letters but with no money. I had some way expected, though we had not specified, that the $30 would come in the mail that day. Most of the money for our needs came by mail, nearly all of it.
>
> However, I went into a study and began to dictate a Bible lesson. Later a secretary came to the door and said, "Brother Rice, Mrs. W_____ wants to see you." I invited her to bring the lady in, and she came to thank me for the blessings received from the radio broadcast.
>
> As she talked a bit about the blessings she had received through my Bible teaching, she opened her purse and handed me a $1 bill. She said, "I will never forget how my heart was thrilled the first time I ever heard you at an Epworth League

meeting explaining the Scriptures. And now to think of the joy I have in hearing you on the radio every day!" Tears came in her eyes and she said to me, "Give me that dollar back!" And she handed me a $5 bill instead.

"My neighbor has been listening to you, a Catholic woman," she said. "She had seemed so hard to reach and so far off from God, but now I am beginning to believe that she may get saved. It is wonderful what the broadcast is doing for people who hear it." Then suddenly she said, "Here, give me the $5 bill, and I will give you $10 instead!" So she gave me a $10 bill instead of the $5, and continued speaking about the blessings they had received. As she told how her husband had been blessed by the broadcast, she said, "I believe Frank would want me to give you everything I have in my purse except just carfare to get home!" With tears in her eyes and with trembling lips she handed me back the $5 and the $1, and then in her coin purse she found coins totaling 50¢ and handed them to me.

With happy steps she left the office and went away, and I turned again to the Bible study lesson I was dictating to a stenographer. But in the back of my mind things began to add up—$13.50 plus $10 plus $5 plus $1 plus 50¢—exactly $30. My heart ran over with joy. Thirty dollars that day was better than $50, because it was exactly what we asked for!

Solemnly, earnestly, in the fear of God I say unto you that again and again, many, many times, God has that definitely and that specifically answered my prayers for material matters and even for money. I know that God answers prayer. He has answered *my* prayers.

It was in connection with his radio ministry, this time at Dallas, that another incident took place which showed the character of the man. As my readers undoubtedly know, he had very strong Bible convictions concerning the husband's authority over the wife, believing she should submit her will to his *"in every thing"* (Eph. 5:24). One morning's mail brought a letter from a lady in Oklahoma with a six-dollar money order enclosed, to be applied on the radio expenses. But the letter said, "Please do not acknowledge this gift over the radio or by letter. I will be sure that you have received it anyway. If you should write a letter or announce it over the radio, my husband might learn of my gift. He told me never to send any money to radio preachers. I took this money from that which he gave me for household expenses, and I want the Lord to have it for the radio broadcast which has blessed so many people."

Instead of following the dear woman's instructions, he wrote her by return mail, enclosing the money order and explaining why he could not accept her gift. She wrote back to say, "I gave $50 this way on our new church building, taking the money out a little at a time from that which my husband gave me for the expenses of the household. Other preachers have taken money given in this way without protest."

But he replied again that he could not join her in rebellion to her husband when the Bible so clearly called it sin. I have often wondered how many other radio preachers would have done likewise, although some undoubtedly would. Knowing Dr. Rice as intimately as I did, I can assure my readers he would have done the same whether the amount was $6 or $6,000, because of the Bible principle involved.

Not all the lessons learned through his radio experiences were as pleasant to his memory, however, since they proved he, too, was "a man subject to like passions" (Jas. 5:17). For example, while in a big open-air revival at Dallas and carrying on his daily radio broadcast at the same time, he received a card from a man past eighty who was dying with cancer. The man begged, "I won't be here long and I'm afraid to die. Would you come and pray with me?"

Rice's burdens at that time were very heavy with preaching in the revival, advertising the campaign, leading the singing, interviewing the spiritually distressed, answering radio mail, etc. He was actually doing the work of several average men. Telling about it in one of his evangelistic sermons, he said, "Two weeks went by and I did not go to see the dying man. Then I sent a young preacher to see him, and alas, he found that his loved ones were even then gone to the funeral. How I wish now that I had gone without my food and rest and made sure that dying man had peace with God before he died! I neglected my opportunity. I can never have it again in that one case."

Another unpleasant experience, although not connected with his radio ministry, took place during those early days and ought to be mentioned in this chapter. Influenced by a host of friends whom he trusted, he agreed in the summer of 1921 to join the Masonic Lodge. Not a few preachers whom he loved and respected were members. Others told him that many Bible characters like Solomon, John the Baptist, the Apostle John, etc., were members of this ancient order. They assured him that it would help him in his ministry, especially in the matter of reaching men. What followed, however, is described in his book, *Lodges Examined by the Bible.*

But the lodge was a great disillusionment to me. A man whom I knew as a practical infidel, who laughed at the inspiration of the Bible and mocked the idea of Christ's being the divine Son of God, a rationalist who despised the churches, I found to be the most active and prominent member of the lodge! He stood at my father's elbow as the work of the degree progressed, prompting him. This was a notoriously profane man whom I had heard take God's name in vain, yet he was the lodge brother and bosom companion of my father, who before his lodge days had been an active preacher of the Gospel!

Others who made no pretense to being children of God were in the lodge room. Without loving Christ or having trusted Him for salvation, they spoke familiarly of God and were on the same basis as earnest Christians and preachers of the Gospel.

When I was asked to repeat after my father words of the Apprentice's oath, I began and then stopped. I had no idea that such an oath was a part of Masonry, and I did not want to proceed. My father and others told me that there was nothing in the oath nor in Masonry that would be offensive to God or my conscience. I continued. But I was shocked, and the more I thought of it the more shocked I was at the words I had spoken.

When I was presented with the white apron and told that I was to be buried in it and that at my funeral Masons should have charge and Masonry exalted, my heart cried out that if I should die I wanted a simple gospel sermon and I wanted sinners to hear about the blood of Christ; I wanted an invitation given!

And so, I went away that night, grieved and shocked. The Holy Spirit within me seemed offended. I never went back to the lodge. After some months' time, I came to the conclusion that I had sinned in going there and taking part in such language and ceremonies and in such company. I asked God to forgive me and promised Him never to take up the work, although good friends had volunteered to pay the cost of my first three degrees. (Later that offer was made again.)

His reaction to the lodge situation was typical of his entire life. It made no difference if father, friends, or the promise of prestige and influence were on one side; if his conviction was that Christ and the Bible were on the other side, without any hesitation he took his side with God. On the basis of Leviticus 5:4-6, he felt that God had forgiven him for taking the wicked oath of the Entered Apprentice in the Masonic fraternity and that it no longer remained binding—since he had confessed the sin and renounced the oath.

Of all his early experiences—whether in the pastorate, in revival, or in radio broadcasting—the one most thrilling, at least to me, took place shortly after his surrender to preach. Chronologically it should have been included in the early part of this chapter, but because of its personal appeal I have saved it for the last. Perhaps it would be best to give it in Dr. Rice's own inimitable style, just as he told it, word for word, in a revival at the First Baptist Church of Maywood, California. Said Dr. Rice:

I remember in one revival meeting, I went with Brother Ross. We went into Corinth community near Decatur, Texas, where there was no pastor and had not been one for a year. They had starved the previous one out. There were only two deacons in this church and one would not come to the revival.

Brother Ross did the preaching and I sang and did personal work. Brother Ross preached on Sunday and nothing happened. He preached on Monday morning and Monday night, Tuesday morning and Tuesday night, Wednesday morning and Wednesday night, and on through Friday, with not a soul saved. We did not plan to continue more than ten days.

I was discouraged. As we went down into a ravine Saturday morning to pray, I said to Brother Ross, "This has gone far enough. The Lord did not call me for this kind of business. I want to see something happen or I want to go home." Brother Ross thought so, too. So we agreed to call a day of fasting and prayer. We said, "Let's try it once more." We announced that on Sunday we would have a day of fasting and prayer.

To make a long story short, I didn't have any breakfast Sunday. I was burdened. We went before Sunday school to prayer meeting, stayed for Sunday school and preaching, and then we said, "If anybody wants to, you may stay here and pray."

Only five people stayed. One of them was the deacon. The others were an old preacher and his wife from another town, Brother Ross and I. We confessed our sins, read the Bible, prayed, and waited on God until three o'clock in the afternoon. Then others came in to hear an afternoon sermon. We prayed more, and I said, "Before we go we ought to claim some promises and say what we want to expect tonight. What do you want tonight?"

Few had anything to say. At last one said, "I would like to see one soul saved but I don't know whether there will be or not."

I asked others, but no one expected a thing. At last the dear preacher visiting from another community spoke. He said, "You young preachers ought to know that there is not going to be anybody saved. That deacon is mad at the other deacon, and they have starved out one preacher, and God is not going to bless people like that."

Then I said to Brother Ross, "Let's get out by ourselves and claim some promises and shake hands on it, expecting sinners to be saved in the service tonight."

Brother Ross said, "Why get by ourselves? Why not do it right here? What do you want God to do tonight?"

I said, "I want to see that many souls saved tonight" (holding up ten fingers).

Brother Ross said, "Do you believe it?"

I said, "Well, er. . .well, I *want* to believe it. (My, I was scared!) I will believe it if you will!"

The dear man agreed. We shook hands right there, and he said, "There will be at least ten people saved in this church tonight."

The old preacher got up and said, "Listen here, you boys, you are young and you are making a mistake. There will not be ten people saved tonight and the people will believe that God doesn't answer prayer."

I said, "But God *does* answer prayer, and we *are* going to see at least ten people saved tonight."

One man got his hat and started out the door and said, "If God saves ten people here tonight, I will never do another wrong thing as long as I live!"

The people thought, "Well, we had better go home and feed the chickens and get the cows in a little early. You never can tell what will happen. I want to see what will happen." Everybody hurried off home to do the chores and get back.

I hadn't had any breakfast, and I had stayed there all day and had not had any dinner, and I tell you frankly, I was too scared to eat any supper. I went out to the ravine and said, "Lord, it is up to You. If You don't answer in this matter, I am ruined."

And, my friends, nobody can have a revival unless God takes a hand in it. It is all foolishness trying to save people unless power from Heaven comes. So I said, "Lord, it is Your revival, not mine. I didn't save myself. I didn't call myself to preach. I didn't bring myself here. I didn't start this business. Lord, help us tonight."

I said to Brother Ross, "I am going to do everything I know to do. I will talk to everybody who comes to this place. I will do all I can, then God must save."

He agreed.

In a little while here came a buggy with a woman and a twelve-year-old boy. I talked to the boy and others. When we gathered we sang two or three songs, and the preacher preached, not very long but red-hot with earnestness. And I remember we sang as an invitation song, "Jesus Is Tenderly Calling Thee Home." Sitting in the choir was an old, drinking, gambling sinner—how many souls he was leading to ruin! His name was Jernigan. I turned to him and said, "Aren't you tired of this life?"

He held on to the bench, and I said, "Why don't you turn to God tonight?"

And he did come, out of the choir, to the preacher and the front seat. The whole crowd was moved.

I remember a little woman, Mrs. Walker. She had been grieving because her boy was following in the footsteps of this drunkard Jernigan. About the time he came this woman jumped and shouted, "My boy! My boy!" I turned around and saw her boy climbing over the benches from the back seat of the choir, coming down to the front!

And that man who got his hat that afternoon and said, "If God saves ten people tonight, I will never do another wrong thing as long as I live," went outside the church after his grown sons. Every window was a frame of faces. He grabbed one of his boys by the wrist like a child and brought him into the building and down to the front and said, "Get down on your knees!" He called for me. I got down beside him and urged the lad to trust Christ, prayed, and he was saved.

We got up. This father wiped his eyes and started elbowing his way back to the door and outside. He had another boy, so he got him and brought him in, leading him like a child. He said, "Get down on your knees!" He too was saved.

There was a boy at the back I wanted to talk to, but the aisles were so crowded with people I had to walk on the backs of the benches to get to him.

It was a little country place, and we were using kerosene lamps. One of the lamps flickered and went out. Then another back yonder flickered and went out. Finally about eleven o'clock, the last one went out. Nobody had noticed that others had gone out until we were left in darkness. Somebody went across the road and got more kerosene and filled up one of the lamps and we continued the service and people were saved. If Ross or I would stick our heads out the door, all those on the outside would run for the bushes! After awhile the thing quieted down.

Somebody said, "Let's line them up and count them and show that God answered prayer." So around the entire front of the building they stood, these new converts who found God that night.

One, two, three, four, five, six, seven, eight, nine, ten, eleven, twelve, and on—I didn't remember how many were in that line until I told this incident over the radio one time, and I got a letter from the first man who came out for Christ that night, Mr. Jernigan. He was indignant. This saved sinner said, "It is a funny thing you didn't remember how many were in that line that night. There were twenty-three grown people!"

Oh, God proved that night that He is a God who can answer by fire! We do not have any business starting a revival campaign anywhere unless we expect God to speak to hearts and make Himself real. God answers prayer! God answers by fire!

How very fortunate it was that John R. Rice learned well his lessons of faith early in his ministry and personally discovered that our great God delights in answering big prayers, beseeching His own to "open thy mouth wide, and I will fill it" (Ps. 81:10). That this man sent from God had a "wide mouth" down through the years, no one can deny!

## Chapter 8

# The Evangelist in a Pastorate

*Preach the word; be instant in season, out of season; reprove, rebuke, exhort with all longsuffering and doctrine. But watch thou in all things, endure afflictions, do the work of an evangelist, make full proof of thy ministry.*—II Timothy 4:2,5.

*And daily in the temple, and in every house, they ceased not to teach and preach Jesus Christ.*—Acts 5:42.

IN JULY, 1932, with less than $10 in his pocket, John Rice went to the Oak Cliff section of Dallas to begin an open-air revival. Since he had no money, no building, no organization or backing, he was dependent entirely upon the great omnipotence of his gracious God. *It proved more than sufficient!* He found a vacant lot at Tenth and Crawford Streets, used $5 of his money—over half of what he had—to pay for a week's rent on it, then announced over the radio that at a certain time on a certain day he would meet on that lot any who would help him build benches for the revival.

On the day they were scheduled to build the benches, enough money came in to buy a load of lumber; seats were built, and the meeting started. God's merciful blessing was upon the undertaking from the start; and three weeks later, after hundreds had been saved, a group met on July 31 to organize the Fundamentalist Baptist Church of Oak Cliff.

In the first 20 months, over 900 people united with the work. They built a huge brick tabernacle, 90 x 146 feet, the largest auditorium in Oak Cliff, and paid for it all in cash. Rice remained pastor of the church for seven and one-half years. The membership grew during the time to some 1,700, and thousands of souls professed faith in Jesus Christ as personal Saviour. In just one 6-month period there were 1,005 professions of faith.

The Fundamentalist Baptist Church was built strictly on the basis of "faith" and "cash." When the congregation, on April 15, 1934, entered the auditorium of the great new tabernacle, every brick, every piece of steel, every piece of lumber and all other materials had been paid for in cash. However, the building had a dirt floor, there were no doors or windows in the auditorium, and there were other evidences of unfinished labor. That did not trouble them during the long, hot summer months; but when the chilling winds of winter brought the famed Texas "blue northers," it became vitally necessary to shut out the air. Funds were raised without difficulty to pay cash for the 119 windows and 14 doors.

The pastor's explanation to the public was: "We had rather enter an auditorium with a dirt floor and with unceiled rafters, for which we have paid in cash, than enter a fine, cathedral-like, plush-carpeted, mahogany-pewed, pipe-organed, stained-glass-windowed church mausoleum and be haunted and harried and burdened for years by a crushing debt. We believe that our simple financial plan pleases God. He has made us happy in it and has taken care of our needs. Thus no one can reproach the pastor as one who preaches for money, nor the church as only for the rich, nor speak of the building as belonging to unpaid creditors!"

In the very first issue of *The Sword of the Lord* he offered this further explanation of why they paid cash instead of building on credit:

> There are two reasons for this cash policy. The first is that we believe it is a sin to have great and burdensome debts on church buildings, making necessary constant pressure for money and a compromise with moneyed people in the effort to pay debts. Too many churches drive away the poor people because of their constant thought of money and drives to collect money. Pastors, teachers, and officers often feel compelled to think and scheme more about raising money than they do about winning souls. Thank God, that is not true in this church!

The second reason for paying cash is that it is good business. We have gotten better prices on every item, because we bought for cash. Businessmen respect and ought to respect a church that pays cash. Debts are always a very serious problem, and sometimes they are positively wicked. Very often, probably most of the time, debts are bad business. Therefore we pay cash for all materials and for all labor that we hire.

The same issue of *The Sword of the Lord* carried a statement of faith for the Fundamentalist Baptist Church of Oak Cliff in Dallas, adopted on July 31, 1932, at its organization. That statement of faith will be found at the end of the book in Appendix B.

Remember, too, that those were dreadful depression days—the middle '30's—and the great brick tabernacle at Tenth and Storey was a tremendous testimony to the sacrificial spirit of the humble congregation, many of them the poorest people in the city. Nor was the evidence of poverty confined to church and people. The pastor and his family "lived in a ramshackle house with cracks in the uncovered floors, with secondhand furniture, with broken wallpaper." But the physical and material discomforts faded into insignificance in the light of the tremendous spiritual blessings which God showered upon pastor and people.

Perhaps if I give some of the sermon subjects announced in *The Sword of the Lord*—which saw its birth during the Dallas pastorate—it will help you get some idea as to the type of preaching which won thousands of souls and built that big church. For one thing, John Rice preached plain and hard against the sins of his day and city.

Some of his rather sensational but appealing subjects were: "Dirt at the Dallas Fair"; "The Curse of God on Beer-Drinking and Beer-Selling Dallas!" (billed as "the plainest preaching you ever heard!"); "Booze Government, Saloon-Keeping Officers, Sixteen-Year-Old Barmaids, Drugstore Bootleggers"; "Wild Oats in Dallas: How Dallas People Sow Them and How They Are Reaped"; and "The Dance! Child of the Brothel, Sister of Gambling and Drunkenness, Mother of Lust—Road to Hell!"

He preached on subjects of great prophetic interest, as the following sermon titles reveal: "The Four Horsemen of Revelation Six: Dictatorship, War, Famine, Death!"; "The November 6 Election—Another Step Toward World Dictatorship, The Antichrist, and Christ's Return"; "The Coming Inescapable World War That Will End the Present Civilization"; "A Wicked Government, A Great Tribulation, and Sudden Death to Every Sinner Not Under the Blood"; "The Death of Huey Long" or "Share the Wealth Club, the Decay of Society, and the Coming of Communism in America"; and "Is Mussolini the Antichrist?"

He preached often on the home, and the following titles are examples of how plainly he did so: "Bobbed Hair, Cigarette-Sucking, Bridge-Playing Mothers; Beer-Drinking, Horse-Racing Dads; Ruined Homes, Penitentiary Children"; "Hell in Dallas Homes"; and "Bobbed Hair, Working Wives, Birth Control, Unhappy Homes and Divorce."

He preached on subjects of vital public interest which were making headlines at the time. Some of his themes were: "The Electrocution of Ray Hamilton"; "Depression, Hard Times, Unemployment, Relief Rolls, Strikes, Dust Storms, Floods—The Curse of Almighty God on Wicked America"; "Who Murdered

Grady Self?"; "Heathen Christmas in Pagan Dallas"; and " 'Mistakes' in the Bible."

He preached on revival and also presented strong evangelistic sermons, as the following subjects indicate: "An Old-Fashioned, Fire-From-Heaven, Sin-Convicting, Soul-Saving, Home-Righting, Holy Ghost Revival—The Kind We Need and How to Have It"; "Company for Supper and Not a Bite in the House"; "How the World's Greatest Heavyweight Champion Lost His Title Because of a Woman"; "The Blood of Christ, Scorned by Southern Baptist Convention Infidels, Insulted by the Denominational Leaders, but the Only Hope for Sinners"; "Filling Stations on the Highway to Hell"; "The Blood on the Door, Sudden Death at Midnight, How to Escape the Plague"; and "The Man Who Went to Heaven Without Baptism, Without Joining a Church, Without a Mourner's Bench, Without Even Living a Good Life."

Some of the experiences of that time are mighty sweet to remember. For example, when the young church was just getting started, the sacrificial pastor's only means of transportation was a beat-up old Dodge which was getting mighty close to the end of its once useful life. After several weeks of repeatedly pushing the car downhill to start it, once almost missing his radio broadcast because it would not run—plus the continual chagrin of having wife, daughters and secretaries pushing the car down the street to get it started—it was impressed on him that he ought to ask God for a new car.

Two nights later he went to the big Fry Furniture Building for the midweek services. As soon as he stepped into the pulpit to teach the Scripture, a representative of the poverty-stricken congregation stepped up and handed him some papers and some keys. Out in front of the building a brand new, four-door Chevrolet sedan was parked; and the spokesman for the people, Mr. Bud Reeves, told him the keys, warranty and title were a gift from the men in the church. They had known nothing of his prayer, and he had known nothing of their plan.

When he went home that night he said to his wife, "If I had known God was as willing as that to give me an automobile, I would not have been pushing that old wreck up and down these hills day after day trying to get it started!"

It was during the Dallas pastorate, also, that he received one of his most thrilling answers to prayer. Although it did not have to do directly with his pastorate, but because it happened during those days, I feel it should be included in this chapter. He described the background and the incident in his book, *Prayer— Asking and Receiving.*

> How the Lord's work prospers when we go to God with big requests! One case I shall never forget when God gave a wonderful answer to my prayer, unworthy and unbelieving as I am. In 1938, I believe, I was called to a city in a midwestern state for a revival campaign. After much urging, I felt led to go and expected great things from word I had received. But lo, when I arrived, I found there had been no money to advertise the meetings, few knew about my coming, and besides, I was unknown.
>
> A crowd of not more than fifty, I judge, met me the first service. I had promised to stay about ten days, including one Sunday, away from my work in Dallas, my radio program, and my paper. Crowds grew slowly; a few were saved. Then the pastor asked me to stay over the second Sunday. "I cannot get you a good offering unless you stay through Sunday," he said. I replied that I did not come for the offering, that I was needed at home for the Sunday night evangelistic services at our church, needed for my Sunday radio broadcast, and that I must plan to return after Friday night.
>
> Sadly the pastor told how a heavy debt had stripped the people, another payment was about due, and if I did not stay over Sunday he feared the people could not give much. I told him not to worry, that I should not, and after the service that Thursday night I went to my room.
>
> There in my room I faced certain facts, and temptation assailed me. I had expected the offering that would be given me to go on a heavy printing bill. *The Sword of the Lord,* the weekly evangelistic paper which my Heavenly Father helps me publish, has never quite paid expenses. The price of $1 a year will not pay all the postage, printing and wages of workers for such a high-grade weekly paper unless the circulation runs about 10,000 copies weekly regularly. I had borrowed $450 at the urging of a good Christian lady, for six months. It was overdue, and I must renew the note or pay it. Besides, I owed the

printer $270 for printing *The Sword of the Lord* after I had borrowed the $450. Then I owed $200 to another printer for tracts which I had been giving away by thousands. At least $920 needed to be paid soon, and now I was told that for my ten days' work it seemed there would be little pay.

Satan taunted me with all the sacrifices I had made to carry on the burden of that soul-winning paper, putting into it thousands of dollars of money I could have used on my family. Satan reminded me that I had refused ever to set a price on my services, that I had no regular salary, and that now this was the way it would turn out!

With tears, that Thursday night I turned to prayer. I reminded God of a covenant I had made with Him in 1926 that He was to look after my business and I would trust Him and look after His, "seeking first the kingdom of God and His righteousness," and believing that what I needed He would supply.

I remember that I said to God, "Lord, look on the heading of that paper; it has Your name on it, *The Sword of the Lord.* Your name is in big type, mine in small type. It is Your paper, not mine. I did not save myself; I did not call myself to preach. If You want a paper, You pay the bills. If You do not want that paper, then let it die. It is not my worry; it is Yours. I am not going to stay with this little meeting trying to get a bigger offering, and I am not going to fret or worry. Lord, it is up to You to pay those bills!" And so, at last, with peace I went to sleep.

The next night we had some people saved. They took an offering for me. For the ten days' time, the check was $25. They gave me what I asked for expenses, bare railroad fare, without Pullman berth. In sweet peace I took the train that night to Dallas. Though I sleep poorly as a rule unless I can stretch out and relax in a regular bed, that night I slept in the chair car as sweetly as a child.

The next morning as my train, the Rock Island *Rocket,* left Wichita, Kansas, the porter came through the car holding a telegram, calling my name. I took the telegram, opened it and read from my secretary,

"YOU HAVE JUST RECEIVED CHECK FOR ONE THOUSAND DOLLARS FOR YOUR WORK!"

I walked up and down the aisles clutching that telegram, laughing, praising God in my soul! I could hardly refrain from telling the porter, the hostess, the passengers, how God hears prayer! I told old Satan what a liar he was. I told my Heavenly Father I would turn that blessed paper over to Him, and that I

knew now He would take care of the bills. I promised I would
love Him better than before, and oh, may He help me to do it,
always!

That thousand dollars came from a man I had never seen. I
had never appealed to him, of course, never had written to him,
nor received a letter from him, nor have I had a letter or gift
from him since, though I have since met the noble, good man.
And bless God, I have never since been in distress about the
printing bills for *The Sword of the Lord.*

However, not all the experiences of the Dallas pastorate were
so sweet. One of the many revival campaigns the church conducted was led by Rev. P. B. Chenault, then the pastor of the
Walnut Street Baptist Church at Waterloo, Iowa. After the closing Sunday night message when he had warned the people about
delaying salvation, speaking on the subject, "Today and Tomorrow," he, his wife and young baby daughter retired to the
pastor's home after light refreshments and fellowship elsewhere,
then got in his automobile to drive 900 miles to another engagement. But God intended his next stop to be Heaven, and he
never preached on this earth again.

Just a couple of hours after the happy farewells with the Rices
and other workers, a drunken driver pulled across the double line
and rammed head-on into the Chenault's Buick sedan. At 2
o'clock in the morning Dr. Rice was aroused from bed and informed by long distance telephone that P. B. Chenault was dead,
his wife was in the McKinney, Texas, hospital; but the baby was
spared any serious injury. Fortunately, God uses even tragedies
for His glory, and when Dr. Rice was invited to preach the
funeral message at Waterloo, many openly claimed Christ. The
leaders of the church asked him to remain for a series of
meetings, and real revival broke out with many, many conversions.

Not long after, another event took place which, from the
human standpoint, seemed tragic. It happened on Tuesday
afternoon, November 22, 1938. The Fundamentalist Baptist
Tabernacle was conducting an eight-day mission of the Dallas
Bible School, a forerunner of the Sword Conferences on
Evangelism. A missionary by the name of Skivington from the

South American Inland Mission was bringing a Bible message when fire was suddenly seen shooting up above the baptistry. Bedlam immediately broke out.

Dr. Rice was in his office at the time preparing copy for *The Sword of the Lord,* and he stepped out to see what was causing the confusion and to find out why folks were running down the halls. Seeing the smoke, he instructed his secretary to call the fire department, then raced downstairs to the bookstore to assist in getting out the books, records, mailing list of *The Sword of the Lord,* and other important things. After the secretary had notified the proper authorities, she discovered fire had cut off the approach to the stairs, and she was compelled to crawl out a window and hold on to the big window sill until folks below could assist in her descent.

The church building was a total loss; pianos, typewriters, dictating and mimeograph machines were destroyed, as were the books from the pastor's personal library and thousands of copies of his booklets which had been printed for sale and free distribution. Yet the Bible School did not miss a single service, and the church continued to go forward using borrowed and rented space. Since there was *no insurance whatsoever* on the property, it was a case of beginning all over again from scratch.

Once again God proved more than adequate for the situation. Dr. Rice retained the leadership of the work for more than a year after the fire until the church was well on its way to recovery. Then, on December 22, 1939, *The Sword of the Lord* announced the Fundamentalist Baptist Church had changed its name to the Galilean Baptist Church, emphasizing that no changes in doctrine, organization or position were involved in the decision.

Barely a month later, in the January 19, 1940, issue of *The Sword of the Lord,* there appeared a front-page article entitled, "And He Gave. . .Some, Evangelists." It announced the resignation of John R. Rice as pastor of the Galilean Baptist Church and told of his return to the field of full-time evangelism. He estimated that for more than half of the previous year, 1939, he had been away in revival campaigns, so the announcement did not involve much of a change!

He explained that during the year he had held two engagements of three weeks each for the Christian Businessmen's Committee of Chicago, preaching at their noonday meeting. He had
preached evangelistic messages in Bible conferences at Clear
Lake, Iowa, and at Cedar Lake, Indiana. He had preached eighteen messages at the Moody Bible Institute and had spoken for
eight days at the Pacific Garden Mission in Chicago. He had
held campaigns in the Elim Evangelical Free Church of Chicago;
the Midwest Bible Church of Chicago; the First Baptist Church
of Hastings, Minnesota; the First Baptist Church of Haywood,
California; the First Baptist Church of Kingman, Kansas; the
City-Wide Tabernacle of Lincoln, Nebraska; the Marquette
Manor Baptist Church of Chicago; the Walnut Street Baptist
Church of Waterloo, Iowa; and the Shell Presbyterian Church of
Kilgore, Texas. Even so, he had turned down twenty invitations
he did not feel he could accept.

With reluctant hearts and many tears the people of the
Galilean Baptist Church accepted his resignation. Three months
later the April 12, 1940, issue of *The Sword of the Lord*, in an announcement headlined **"Important!"** stated that the editor was
moving his family, the paper, the office, and the bookstore to
Wheaton, Illinois. The headquarters were there for 23 years;
then, in June of 1963, the large building of the Westvue Baptist
Church in Murfreesboro, Tennessee, was purchased and
remodeled, occasioning the move of the entire operation to that
location, where it has remained to the present.

After Dr. Rice resigned the Galilean pulpit, he was succeeded
by Dr. Robert J. Wells, Rev. Frederick P. Billings, Dr. Herbert
Pugmire, Rev. Robert Keyes, Rev. Thomas Bridges, Rev. Jack
Slater, and Rev. Garth Seibert. The present pastor, Rev. Robert
Wallace, was called in March of 1975 and, because the
neighborhood around the church was one of the highest crime
areas in Dallas, led the people in relocating. It is now comfor-
tably situated, with ample room for expansion, in Cedar Hill, a
suburb southwest of Dallas. The move was completed in early
fall of 1981.

*Chapter 9*

# The High Cost of Discipleship

> *Remember the word that I said unto you, The servant is not greater than his lord. If they have persecuted me, they will also persecute you; if they have kept my saying, they will keep yours also.* —John 15:20.
>
> *Yea, and all that will live godly in Christ Jesus shall suffer persecution.* —II Timothy 3:12.
>
> *. . .Neither will I offer burnt-offerings unto the Lord my God of that which doth cost me nothing.* —II Samuel 24:24.

GOD HAS not promised *or even intimated* in His Word that all-out discipleship would be a bed of roses. Quite the contrary: the above scriptural statements are simply samples of biblical teaching to the opposite. *It has never been popular to be out and out for God.*

Jeremiah was out and out for God—and the people of his day threw him into a muddy pit.

Daniel was out and out for God—and was thrown into the lions' den.

The three Hebrew children were out and out for God—and they were bound hand and foot, then tossed into a furnace of fire heated "seven times more than it was wont to be heated."

John the Baptist was out and out for God—so they chopped off his head and flaunted it on a silver charger before lustful women.

Stephen was out and out for God—and the people of his day stoned him to death and mocked while he prayed.

James was out and out for God—and they had him beheaded.

Paul was out and out for God—and the people of his day beat

him with rods, whipped him with the Roman cat-o'-nine-tails, stoned him and left him for dead, vowed to kill him, and imprisoned him repeatedly.

Do not think that you can serve God faithfully and receive the plaudits of the world. Remember, too, Jesus was out and out in His surrender to fulfill His Father's will—and the people of His day rejected Him, spit in His face, pulled out His beard, scourged Him, and nailed Him to a wooden cross between two thieves.

*Church history tells the same story!* John Huss was out and out for God—and they put him in chains, then burned him at the stake.

William Tyndale was out and out for God—and they had him tied to a stake, strangled by a hangman, then burned with fire.

John Bunyan was out and out for God—and they threw him into the Bedford prison.

John Wesley was out and out for God—and they shut him out of his own church, refused him the sacraments, slandered him, and burned him in effigy.

Adoniram Judson was out and out for God—and they threw him in prison.

Charles Haddon Spurgeon was out and out for God—and they criticized and ostracized him because of the separationist stand "the down-grade movement" caused him to take.

Charles G. Finney was out and out for God—and the preachers and churches of his day slandered him, fought him, and tried to curtail his ministry.

Dwight L. Moody was out and out for God—and they nicknamed him "Crazy" Moody.

So it has always been and so it always will be as long as the enemies of Jesus Christ are loose to foment their hatred of His cause and His truth.

John Rice found this sadly true in his ministry. He would not have cared if the opposition had come from the bootleggers, the brothels, the dance-hall and poolroom crowd, the gamblers, the atheists, or even the modernist-infidels on the inside of the church. He fought them so fiercely and openly that retaliation could be expected and even welcomed. But one of the most difficult things of his ministry was opposition from those whom he had loved, boosted and befriended.

His first major opposition came from denominational leaders within the Southern Baptist Convention. As has already been mentioned, in the fall of 1926 and spring of 1927 he was frequently a guest speaker on radio KFQB. At first, before he began his own daily broadcast, he spoke at the invitation of Dr. J. Frank Norris, the famous, controversial, and feared pastor of Fort Worth's First Baptist Church.

At that time there had arisen a very serious question about the teaching of evolution at Baylor University by Dr. Samuel Dow, the sociology professor. When his book, *Introduction to Sociology,* was examined, it was very evident the charges some of the ministerial students had been making were true and that Dr. Dow did indeed teach the ascent of man through evolution. This matter was discussed repeatedly by Dr. Norris and others on KFQB to the continual embarrassment and chagrin of the Baptist leaders in Texas.

In due time a committee of three—Professors E. L. Carnett and T. B. Masten of the Southwestern Baptist Theological Seminary and Pastor Horace Greeley Williams of the Seminary Hill Baptist Church, now the Gambrell Street Church—came to call on Evangelist Rice. They told him he should never again speak on station KFQB since that station was under the control of Dr. J. Frank Norris, a man about to be excluded from the Southern Baptist Convention and openly opposed by leaders. They charged Rice with allowing Norris to embarrass Texas Baptists by speaking on the station.

A plan had already been worked out. They informed him to the effect that if he did not cease immediately appearing on the radio station—and so allowing Dr. Norris to embarrass Baptist leaders over Baylor University—the matter would be brought to the Baptist Associational Meeting in Tarrant County, and pastors would be warned not to have him hold revival campaigns in their churches. They said the seminary students would be warned against him, and a statement would be published in the official

Baptist state paper, the *Baptist Standard,* warning churches against having him preach in revivals. They told him he would not be able to continue his work as an evangelist, could not educate his children, and would be forced out of the ministry. So they earnestly urged him to refuse to go again to preach on radio KFQB, or to associate in any way whatsoever with Dr. J. Frank Norris. It was a clear case of "cooperate. . .*or else!*"

As it so happened, he had not particularly sought the fellowship of Dr. Norris. He was in favor of Norris' fight against modernism, though he did not approve of his methods and did not favor Norris' attack on some individuals. Their association was largely a case of being necessarily thrown together by the force of circumstances. Too, the radio was a wonderfully blessed open door for preaching the Gospel of the Lord Jesus Christ.

After the impressive committee of Baptist dignitaries left and he had time to prayerfully consider the matter, he felt he did not dare, so early in his ministry especially, allow men to browbeat, coerce, or bluff him, thereby controlling his ministry. He felt that altogether too many others had bowed to denominational leaders and had thus curtailed their ministry by pleasing men instead of God. So the next Sunday he spoke again on KFQB and told the whole story to the public, vowing his independence of human leadership as long as he felt certain of God's leading and will.

He told the people that Sunday what he had already told God during the dark, long periods of the night—that if God could not open doors, could not give him places to preach, could not provide for his family apart from the approval of denominational leaders, then he would find another God to serve who could! He told them he would not preach the Gospel for a God who could not take care of His preacher.

That day—thoughtfully and prayerfully weighing the issues involved—he resolved to risk his entire ministry on the proposition that if God called a man to preach He could open the doors and provide for the man's care in that ministry. Claiming the promise, ". . .for he hath said, I will never leave thee, nor forsake thee. So that we may boldly say, The Lord is my helper, and I will not fear what man shall do unto me" (Heb. 13:5,6), he set out to prove the truth of the statement, "If God be for us, who can be against us?" (Rom. 8:31).

Following this break with the denomination in which he was raised, saved, baptized, educated, ordained and had served all his life, a surprising thing happened to his ministry. Where he had formerly preached often to rather small congregations, now he began to get great crowds of common people to hear him. Where he had before preached so often to young people that friends suggested he specialize in youth meetings, now he began to have old hardened sinners, drunkards, convicts, profane people, Catholics, and infidels to hear him preach. Where he had previously ministered primarily to those already connected with churches, now he began to reach great masses of those on the outside. Throughout the more than fifty years after the challenge and test of lordship by the denomination, he had abundant proof that Jesus Christ is the One who opens doors so no man can shut them and closes doors so no one can open them. *He has the key of David!*

Strangely and surprisingly, the next major opposition came not from some denominational leader, but from the independent brother with whom he had stood even at the cost of turning his back upon his beloved denomination, Dr. J. Frank Norris!

First, before we discuss some of the details of this unsavory incident, which was such a key event in the life and ministry of John R. Rice we cannot well ignore it, let it be said that Dr. Norris was a firm believer in the fundamentals of the Faith and that he preached them with a clearness and beauty seldom excelled. He did considerable good in the Southwest where he pastored the First Baptist Church of Fort Worth, and in the North where he pastored the Temple Baptist Church of Detroit.

These two great pastorates were held simultaneously for years as he flew back and forth between Texas and Michigan. Tens of thousands of souls were won to Christ through his preaching, and hundreds of young men surrendered to the ministry as a result of his spoken challenge. He departed to his reward several years ago, and we would not want to write anything now which would harm the independent, fundamental movement he founded or bring reproach upon those faithful, godly, zealous men who are associated with the World Baptist Fellowship, many of whom are my very dear friends.

However, even Dr. Norris' staunchest supporters admit his uncharitable and often unfair treatment of those with whom he disagreed. Some men seem to be born dictators, and Dr. Norris fell into that category. As a matter of fact, most men who accomplish amazing results—both in religious and secular fields—are predominantly dictators. But Dr. Norris not only was a dictator; also he refused to permit any who did not want his rule to go their separate ways. Instead, when they by conviction felt they must break with him, he would openly and bitterly malign them in his paper—and do anything else he could to wreck their ministry.

Previous to his attack on Dr. Rice, he had first highly praised in his weekly paper, *The Fundamentalist,* then bitterly attacked when he broke with them, such men as Rev. W. Lee Rector, Rev. Scott W. Hickey, Rev. Joe Scheumack, Rev. Jack Neville, Rev. Grover Cleveland, Rev. Mell G. Leaman, Rev. Earl Anderson, and several others. One preacher in San Antonio took him to law—which was wrong according to the clear teaching of the Bible—and sued him for slander, winning a judgment of $25,000.

It seems that Dr. Rice and Dr. Norris had entered into several disagreements about the policy which involved the latter's attacks in his paper on good men. The issue came to a head when Dr. Norris was in Detroit and had sent back an article to be published in *The Fundamentalist* which would do Sam Morris, even then a very prominent pastor and radio preacher, much harm. Clearly warning Dr. Norris that the article was wrong, Dr. Rice had it killed, apparently upsetting Dr. Norris very much. When Dr. Norris said no fundamentalist could prosper without his "love and confidence," Dr. Rice declared he depended on God, not men, for endorsement.

Obviously seeking retaliation and knowing Dr. Rice was scheduled to begin a revival campaign with the Grace Baptist Church of Binghamton, New York, on January 12, 1936, Dr. Norris secretly sent the pastor, Rev. Fred R. Hawley, a letter advising him he had better cancel the meeting because Rice had become a "Holy Roller."

On Saturday, January 4, just as Dr. Rice was preparing to leave early Monday morning for the revival at Binghamton, he received the following telegram:

REV JOHN R RICE
201 EAST TENTH STREET
DALLAS
BROTHER RICE BECAUSE A GRAVE QUESTION HAS ARISEN WE AS A BOARD ARE WIRING CANCELLING OUR ENGAGEMENT WITH YOU FOR JANUARY TWELVE LETTER OF DETAILS WILL FOLLOW PLEASE REPLY BY WESTERN UNION ON REVERSE CHARGES
                         FRED R HAWLEY

He immediately wired that in all fairness he should know what there was about him or his ministry to which objection had been made, as well as the source of the objection. A second telegram arrived from Binghamton stating his "friends" had accused him of "teaching and preaching McPhersonism and Pentecostalism."

When he learned what the objection was, Rice wrote a long letter to Brother Hawley explaining the situation, sending him various printed articles and pamphlets on speaking in tongues, sinless perfection, divine healing, women preachers, and kindred themes which made his position very clear. He told him that he had incontrovertible proof that he was not mixed up with McPhersonism or Pentecostalism and that he knew what was back of the whole accusation.

In the letter he said he was leaving immediately for Binghamton to hold a revival. If they wanted him there, that would be fine. If not, he would get some large, downtown, central location and expect God to bless in an independent campaign. He also wrote several pastors with whom he had held blessed revivals, informing them of the situation and telling them that if they wished to do so, they could write a word to the church in Binghamton.

Monday morning he loaded his family and a stenographer into the car and started out for Binghamton, two thousand miles away. He had several speaking engagements en route but did not give Brother Hawley any address where he could be reached, leaving the whole matter in God's hands.

It was not until he drove up in front of the Grace Baptist Church at 7:10 Saturday night, January 11, and saw on the large bulletin board in front the announcement that Evangelist John R. Rice of Texas was to begin a great revival on Sunday, that he knew what to expect. Pastor Hawley and his board had weighed all the evidence and decided unanimously the attack on him was unjustified. However, just to make certain, Brother Hawley took the material to one after another fundamental Baptist minister to examine, and with one accord they agreed Rice had been done an injustice and that the whole attack was an attempt of Satan to block the program of God.

Scores of pastors went to Dr. Rice's defense and wrote letters to the Grace Baptist Church, some of whom were: Rev. Sam Morris, Rev. P. T. Stanford, Rev. H. C. Ownbey, Rev. Lee Kidd, Rev. Theodore Fisher, Rev. J. E. Glenn, Rev. W. D. Herrstrom, Rev. Marion Been, Rev. Tom Masters, Rev. Garrett R. Graham, Rev. Loys Vess, Rev. Richard Ausburn, Rev. Bruce Hibbitt, Rev. Willie E. Lee, Rev. Jasper C. Massegee, and Rev. W. O. Majors.

It is not right to try to judge Dr. Norris' *motive* in the attack, but his recklessness with the truth, his wicked slander, and his unethical endeavor to wreck a revival campaign were unmistakably wrong. Perhaps, as has been suggested by many, it was a result of his seeming determination to rule fundamentalism with an iron hand, much as a pope in ecclesiastical realms or a dictator in political spheres. At any rate, in two different letters to Dr. Rice, he boasted: "No man will get anywhere in the cause of fundamentalism in the north, east, or outside of Texas if he fails to have the love and confidence of the First Baptist Church," meaning the endorsement of himself.

Nor was he satisfied to cease his attack after his initial attempt to get the revival canceled. Failing in that, he had large quantities of literature shipped to Binghamton for distribution, publicly attacking Dr. Rice. He asked all his friends who would to write malicious letters slandering Dr. Rice. He had his co-worker, Dr. Louis Entzminger, write a strong—and in many matters untrue—attack for *The Fundamentalist.* He sent repeated telegrams to Binghamton, yet ignored the invitation of Pastor Hawley, Evangelist Rice, and other interested brethren to come to Binghamton and make his charges face-to-face.

In the January 24 issue of *The Fundamentalist* he printed the following telegram over his own signature:

> DETROIT, MICHIGAN
> JANUARY 23, 1936
>
> FUNDAMENTALIST PUBLISHING COMPANY
> 408 THROCKMORTON STREET
> FORT WORTH, TEXAS
>
> IT IS WITH DEEPEST PERSONAL SORROW THAT A SENSE OF LOYALTY TO THE TRUTH COMPELS ME TO PUBLISH THE PLATFORM OF HOLY ROLLERISM AS ADVOCATED BY RICE STOP FOR MANY YEARS ORTHODOX BRETHREN HAVE PROTESTED TO ME CONCERNING HIS UNSCRIPTURAL TEACHING BUT I TRUSTED HIM IMPLICITLY AND FURTHER BECAUSE OF OVERWHELMING DUTIES I NEVER READ HIS WRITING OR HEARD HIM EXCEPT VERY LITTLE BUT NOW HAVE MADE THOROUGH REVIEW AND FOUND HE ADVOCATED THE PLATFORM OF PENTECOSTALISM OR HOLY ROLLERISM STOP NEXT WEEK'S FUNDAMENTALIST WILL GIVE REVIEW OF HIS UNSOUND TEACHING ON SO-CALLED HOLY SPIRIT BAPTISM STOP HE TAKES HUNDRED PER CENT PLATFORM OF HOLY ROLLERISM

Then, true to the promise in the telegram, the January 31 issue of *The Fundamentalist* carried a long article by Dr. Entzminger on "The Unscriptural Heresy of 'The Baptism of the Holy Ghost' and Its Evil Consequences." In the article Entzminger described the "Rice heresy" as "one of the outstanding heresies of modern times" and said "his position is typical of Pentecostals and McPhersonites." Dr. Rice immediately replied that Dr. Norris *had* known his position on these matters all along and had said in print, "I absolutely agree with him." He pointed out the fact that Dr. Norris had stated about his booklet, *Speaking With Tongues,* "I consider it the ablest answer to modern Holy Rollerism thus far published."

When attention was called to these statements, along with many quotations from Norris' published addresses showing that he believed exactly the same as Rice, instead of confessing his error and apologizing for the false accusations, Dr. Norris manufactured several statements containing doctrinal error along "holy roller" lines and attributed them to Rice. When challenged, he never was able to show where Rice had publicly stated or printed them.

However, instead of hurting the revival, it actually helped it; and it is very doubtful they would have experienced the sweet moving of the Spirit of God in Binghamton had it not been for all the prayer interest stirred up through Norris' agitation. Letters from Texas, Oklahoma, Mississippi, Kentucky, Missouri, Pennsylvania, and other states came to assure Rice of special prayer interest because of the attack.

One lady in Fort Worth read the attack in *The Fundamentalist,* and before she could finish the article became so burdened in prayer for the revival she sought her prayer closet.

A large Sunday school class in the same city had special seasons of prayer for the revival, earnestly begging God to manifest His power.

A man in Dallas wrote that there was "not a night since you have been gone but that my pillow has been wet with tears as I prayed for you."

A member of Dr. Norris' church wrote that she often woke in the night praying for the revival.

Another lady in Dallas wrote to testify she, too, woke up in the night and found herself praying for him with her face wet with tears.

Through it all Dr. Rice claimed such promises as, "Blessed are they which are persecuted for righteousness' sake: for their's is the kingdom of heaven. Blessed are ye, when men shall revile you, and persecute you, and shall say all manner of evil against you falsely, for my sake. Rejoice, and be exceeding glad: for great is your reward in heaven: for so persecuted they the prophets which were before you" (Matt. 5:10-12).

Years later his daughter Grace wrote:

> **"I saw you suffer—reproached, rebuked, reviled;**
> **Saw your good evil spoken of.**
> **Saw you remain steadfast, brave, determined,**
> > **Saw quiet victory, saw God honored in pain;**
> > **Prayed I might meet it thus."**

The experience was not easy to bear, but it fulfilled beautifully the guarantee which the psalmist had written with such positive assurance, "Surely the wrath of man shall praise thee: the remainder of wrath shalt thou restrain" (Ps. 76:10), and a gracious revival broke out in Binghamton.

God blessed mightily from the very start, and within ten days the meeting had outgrown the auditorium of the Grace Baptist Church. They invited some of the fundamental brethren of several different denominations to join them and rented the Binghamton theatre—where Gipsy Smith had held a campaign some years previous—seating 2,200 people. They had to agree to pay $1,000 rent for one month, a real step of faith for those anti-mass-evangelism depression days.

Radio station WNBF gave the crusade a half-hour daily free radio time; the newspapers gave very detailed write-ups and picture coverage, with one reporter assigned to cover every service.

In no time at all the meeting became the talk of the triple-cities area. They referred to his alleged likeness to humorist Will Rogers, to his "Texas drawl," but especially about his plain and emphatic preaching against sin. The liberal pastor of the First Congregational Church opposed the campaign publicly over the radio, complaining that some were preaching a literal Hell and that God could not save men without His Son coming to the earth to be tortured. That attack, of course, simply helped publicize the campaign and helped draw the crowds.

By the time the meeting closed on Sunday night, February 23, there had been 374 public conversions and reclamations. Out of that number, about one-fourth were backsliders coming back to Christ after losing the joy of their salvation, and the other three-fourths were first-time professions of faith in Jesus Christ as personal Saviour. The big majority of those saved were grown, mature men, heads of families. Relatively few of them were children, probably because there were few children attending the meetings those snowy, sub-zero nights.

It was an old-fashioned revival that reached old and hardened sinners. Many Catholics were converted, as were drunkards, agnostics, and others who had slipped into grievous sin.

Remember, too, that those were days when evangelists were frowned upon; mass evangelism was considered fanatical, and anything which smacked of the slightest emotionalism was almost universally opposed. In addition, the weather during the campaign averaged below zero for most of the meeting, and that winter was the worst experienced in the vicinity for years.

On one Sunday night of the campaign, Binghamton was the fourth coldest spot in the United States. Many unusual things happened, and at least two grown men got under such tremendous conviction they fainted during the invitation and had to be revived. Thank God, however, after being revived each came forward publicly to surrender to the Saviour.

One of the interesting sidelights of the Binghamton revival had to do with a message the evangelist preached, entitled, "Sodom, Gomorrah, and Binghamton—Three of a Kind!" Writing of it later, he said:

> A group of learned preachers meeting in the city took heated exception to my sermon subject. A prominent denominational official said for Binghamton, with its schools and hospitals, art and industry, its progressive and intelligent people, to be compared with ancient Sodom was unthinkable! His remarks were printed in the daily press.
>
> However, the same night in a big club within a block of the theater where I preached, was held a very Saturnalia of

debauch and sin. Fifty prostitutes were brought in from New York City. The most prominent men in the city bought tickets to the banquet and show. By midnight many of the men were drunk and many of the women naked, and by 4 o'clock in the morning, I was told, officers had to stop the breaking of furniture and had to interfere with the wild carousal. Literally hundreds took part. Many were members of the churches where these pious and complacent preachers held forth. Investigation revealed that such orgies were frequent affairs.

Many of the preachers were openly modernistic, denying the deity of Christ, the blood atonement, the new birth, and the inspiration of the Bible; yet they were shocked at the comparison of Binghamton to Sodom and Gomorrah. They were rich, increased with goods, and had need of nothing, they thought. But God knew that they were "wretched, and miserable, and poor, and blind, and naked."

I announced the same sermon subject for the following night. Still larger crowds heard me with blessings from God the second night on the same subject, and the revival continued with hundreds saved.

That incident seems to me the more remarkable in that newspaper men came to me with shocking revelations about the wickedness going on in the city, while most of the preachers either did not know or did not care.

The following morning the *Binghamton Sun* published accounts of the police raid and the evangelist's sermon side by side, giving police court records which proved his point.

After the revival was over, a prominent local woman wrote the city council and demanded an investigation. On the spot, the council appointed the city manager to investigate. Newspapers reported the findings with full-page headlines, giving Rice's sermon all the credit for the investigation. Some of the facts uncovered made the chief of police look bad because of apparent serious compromises with the underworld. As a result, he launched an attack upon the evangelist in the daily newspapers and the cooperating pastors demanded a public apology from him.

Rice did not know it until he got back to Dallas and the police showed him the wire, but the Binghamton police chief had sent a telegram to the Dallas officials asking for information. The telegram said:

BINGHAMTON N Y

C W TRAMMEL
CHIEF OF POLICE
DALLAS TEXAS

JOHN R RICE EVANGELIST SUPPOSEDLY A RESI-
DENT OF YOUR CITY CAMPAIGNED HERE
RUMORED HE HAS BEEN CHARGED WITH
HOMICIDE IN YOUR CITY CAN YOU FURNISH
ANY INFORMATION ON THIS MAN CRIMINALLY
CHARACTER OR RELIABILITY WIRE COLLECT

L C ABEL CHIEF OF POLICE

Dallas police officials wired back immediately to the effect
that the evangelist was very well known in that area, had no
criminal record, and was highly respected.

When the revival was over, the pastor of the church originally
cancelling the meeting, Rev. Fred R. Hawley, wrote the following
letters to the ministers who had shown their interest in the
meeting by writing or wiring in John Rice's defense:

Dear Brother in Christ:

Your interest in our revival meeting and also in Brother John
R. Rice is proven by your kind and helpful letter in time of
need.

Permit me to say that after six weeks together, it gives me
great pleasure to say, first of all, that he is one of the most
humble, godly men it has ever been my privilege to be associated with. At no time in his stay with us did he ever show in
any way a selfish or hateful spirit. He always was so dependent
upon God and the leading of the Holy Spirit in living and
preaching Christ. It has been my privilege to visit him in his
home, dine with him and also to have him and his family in our
home. Surely our fellowship has been very sweet and my heart
goes out to him as did Jonathan's to David.

Now as to his preaching and teaching may I say after twenty
years' experience in the pastoral work, I found him always to be
very scriptural, using the Bible continually. Brother Rice has
proven to me to be one of the most godly, scriptural preachers
and teachers. And I believe the Lord has a great place for him
in the world because he believes and preaches the Word
without fear or favor. Brother Rice has no hobby he rides, but

makes it very plain that "all have sinned," must come under the *blood* and be born again, if they are ever to be saved.

God gave to us the greatest awakening our city has seen since William A. Sunday visited this city ten years ago. We did have a great revival! Hundreds of decisions for Christ! The finances came very easy, and all our people are pleased with the results.

Again I say please accept my thanks for your kind words about our dear Brother Rice who has been a great blessing to my life, and I am sure I will be more useful because it has been my privilege to work with him.

Yours most sincerely in the work,
(Signed) FRED R. HAWLEY

Before I close this chapter I want to quote a few paragraphs from *The Sword of the Lord,* written by Dr. Rice in the issue of February 7, 1936. I think it shows most clearly the nature of the man this biography is about and how seriously he set out to follow the Saviour's explicit instruction:

*"Ye have heard that it hath been said, Thou shalt love thy neighbour, and hate thine enemy. But I say unto you, Love your enemies, bless them that curse you, do good to them that hate you, and pray for them which despitefully use you, and persecute you; That ye may be the children of your Father which is in heaven: for he maketh his sun to rise on the evil and on the good, and sendeth rain on the just and on the unjust. For if ye love them which love you, what reward have ye? do not even the publicans the same? And if ye salute your brethren only, what do ye more than others? do not even the publicans so? Be ye therefore perfect, even as your Father which is in heaven is perfect."*— Matt. 5:43-48.

The article from which I quote was written during the Binghamton crusade—right in the midst of all the slander and abuse from the tongue and pen of Dr. Norris, who was endeavoring to destroy his ministry. Similar statements appeared in repeated issues of *The Sword of the Lord* during those weeks, but I quote only this one as illustrative of them all. After discussing some other matters and quoting part of a letter to a Texas pastor clearing up some of the misrepresentations made against him, there was a subtitle, "Prayer for Dr. Norris." Then appeared the following:

I want to urge friends everywhere to love and pray for Dr. Norris. All of us have our faults. He is a great man, has won many thousands of souls, and has stood for the fundamentals of the Faith in a way that I believe has greatly honored God. He is human. The Bible plainly says, "Brethren, if a man be overtaken in a fault, ye which are spiritual, restore such an one in the spirit of meekness; considering thyself, lest thou also be tempted."

I have personally, earnestly prayed that no harm would come to the ministry of Dr. Norris or these other men who have followed his leadership in attacking me. They are good men. I have prayed that God would bring their attack to naught and God is wonderfully answering prayer. But I do not want enmity and hatred aroused, and I do not want anything to happen that would cause sinners to fail to hear these men with open hearts.

I know Dr. Norris well. He is God's good man. His pride and his feeling that the Fundamentalist cause will fare better if he can absolutely control it are very natural human temptations to which all of us are subject. If we had such great blessings as Dr. Norris has had, we might be guilty of the same thing.

I have earnestly urged my people to pray and to let no bitterness in their hearts toward this man of God who has in this matter acted so foolishly. He sometimes gets off the track, but he gets back on again; and then the next time he gets off the track, it is on the other side.

Read Dr. Norris' paper, *The Fundamentalist.* He will have some great sermons in it. Listen to him over the radio. His messages have blessed many. Write Dr. Norris a good letter and do what you can to keep the government from putting him off the radio, as he says they are trying to do. Pray for the two great churches, the Temple Baptist Church of Detroit and the First Baptist Church of Fort Worth. I know that the First Baptist Church of Fort Worth is a group of great people. Some of them are brokenhearted and praying over this latest unhappy attack. Some have written to tell me so.

Dr. Norris has great burdens, and he is not as young as he once was; and he should have our sympathy, love, and forbearance. May God bless him and his family, his churches, his paper, his radio work! I pray that no friend he has loved and been true to will forsake him, falsely accuse him, try to block his revivals and assassinate his ministry. And may the dear

Lord deal with him in just such tender mercy as all of us so sorely need.

Dr. Rice was in many controversies over truth and error—in some of which I was very closely associated with him—and I assure you from close, firsthand observation that the above was typical of his attitude during them all, and in no case of controversy was it a matter of personality; always it was a matter of principle. John R. Rice was one of God's choice men who was willing always, sometimes at great personal sacrifice, to stand for the truth and contend earnestly for the faith. In the next chapter we will show a little of how God honored him for his faithfulness.

## Chapter 10

# God's Hundredfold

*Then answered Peter and said unto him, Behold, we have for-
saken all, and followed thee; what shall we have therefore? And
Jesus said unto them, Verily I say unto you, That ye which
have followed me, in the regeneration when the Son of man
shall sit in the throne of his glory, ye also shall sit upon twelve
thrones, judging the twelve tribes of Israel. And every one that
hath forsaken houses, or brethren, or sisters, or father, or
mother, or wife, or children, or lands, for my name's sake, shall
receive an hundredfold, and shall inherit everlasting life.*—
Matthew 19:27-29.

ON HIS face before God at 2 o'clock one morning in a YMCA
room on the south side of Chicago, John Rice definitely committed himself to God to bring back mass evangelism to America—
citywide campaigns such as had been conducted by Moody, Torrey, Billy Sunday and others. He surrendered his tongue, his
pen, his paper, his entire being into the hands of God to be used
at His disposal toward this end. He did not care how it happened, just as long as it happened. If God wanted to use him to
preach to the multitudes, he was willing. If God wanted to raise
up other evangelists to do the job, he was willing for that. All he
wanted was to see great revivals return to America with their
ultimate result of the winning to Christ of hundreds of thousands
of precious souls for whom He died.

Almost immediately, seemingly, God began to open wider
doors and give him greater opportunities in his own campaigns.
Whereas he had been holding one-church meetings—and some of
them in smaller churches—now he began to have invitations

from larger churches, and groups of pastors began getting together to have him lead them in union campaigns.

As we consider the results of his campaigns, they may not compare in number with some of the large citywide crusades of the present; but let it be remembered that his union meetings were held under entirely different circumstances.

He held his meetings in a day when evangelists were either considered crooks and money-grabbers or fanatics and fools—today that stigma and reproach are largely gone.

At that time mass evangelism was scorned and often ridiculed—today it is increasingly popular.

His meetings were sponsored usually by a handful of churches and always by the smallest churches in the community—today the leading evangelists have the backing of almost every church, including the most popular and influential.

His meetings were held in a day of religious decline and disinterest—today's crusades are helped along with a "back to church" movement which has resulted in more church members and greater attendance than any other time in American history.

His meetings were handicapped by limited funds for promotion and advertising—today there seem to be unlimited resources, and union campaign budgets are often astronomical.

Just as John the Baptist was a forerunner who prepared the way for the ministry of Jesus of Nazareth, so John R. Rice was the forerunner who helped bring back large-scale mass evangelism—and almost all widely-used evangelists frankly say so, giving him the credit. Much as a big tackle opens the hole in the opposing line for his fullback to crash through, so John Rice opened the way for revival in our time. The tackle often does not receive the credit or glory of a fullback, but he is just as important to the success of the game, and the coach—whom he is trying to please—knows it! John Rice simply set out to please his Coach and was completely willing, although the thought of reward at no time was a consideration in his service, to wait for the judgment seat of Christ to receive his honor.

It would take a full-length book in itself to deal with all of the great revival campaigns he conducted, but this biography would not be complete without a brief resume of some of the highlights. Reference has already been made to the meeting at the Grace Baptist Church in Binghamton which outgrew the one-church sponsorship and ended in a victorious union crusade, while he was still in the pastorate at Dallas.

One of his first union meetings as a full-time evangelist was in Minneapolis, under the sponsorship of some sixteen churches on the north side. The chairman of the crusade, Dr. Richard V. Clearwaters—at that time pastor of the Fourth Street Baptist Church in Minneapolis, trustee of Northern Baptist Seminary in Chicago, and associated with the Northwestern Theological Seminary and Bible School in Minneapolis—reported that there were more than two hundred conversions. The meetings far surpassed the pastors' most hopeful anticipation. Large crowds were attracted, causing them to enlarge the seating capacity to one thousand early in the meeting.

In March of 1944 he went to Everett, Washington, for a city-wide campaign in the civic auditorium. J. Stratton Shufelt, who had been Minister of Music at the famous Moody Memorial Church in Chicago until he joined the Rice team, was the songleader and soloist. Rev. Forrest E. Johnson, pastor of the Calvary Baptist Church in Everett, was the chairman of the campaign. In reporting the results of the meeting, Dr. Johnson wrote:

> The record of decisions of those whose record we were able to get totaled 292. But there were many more. I personally know of four who accepted Christ who were not in the inquiry room where a record would have been obtained. How we do praise God for the great number of high-school kids that were saved. I personally received thirty-nine cards from those who gave our church as their preference. You will recall the two boys who brought so many of their buddies to Christ. It was a happy Young People's meeting that we had Monday evening at our home, hearing this high-school gang tell how they accepted Christ in the meeting.

Other reports said there were four hundred and thirty professions of faith.

In April of the same year the Rice-Shufelt team went to Buffalo, New York, for another citywide crusade. Services were held in the Kleinhans Music Hall, and crowds continued to grow until the closing service when 3,759 people, by ushers' count, jammed and crowded into the building. There were hundreds standing, and hundreds of others were turned away because of firemen's regulations. There were about seventy-five public professions of faith in that service. There were over one hundred churches cooperating in the campaign, and Rev. Seward S. Wells served as the chairman. Bill Mann was his advance man in this and many other of his union crusades.

Beginning with an Easter sunrise service, the campaign ran three weeks and closed on April 30. The total number who walked the aisles was nine hundred and ninety-seven, about seven hundred of which were first-time professions, the others backsliders who were reclaimed from a life of sin. In addition, there were thirty-four young people who publicly surrendered for full-time service, planning to take training for the ministry or mission field.

Rev. Walter W. Keeney, pastor of the Calvary Gospel Tabernacle, wrote the evangelist after the meeting had closed:

> Now that the campaign is over and we are once again engaged in our various churches, we can begin to realize something of the great results of your campaign in Buffalo.
>
> Our church received cards of forty people who made their decisions during your campaign, and this does not begin to tell the results that took place in connection with our church. Christian people have been revived, and there is a new determination among the children of God to give themselves completely to the Lord to be used in His service.
>
> Last Friday night, in our house-to-house visitation, there were ten people who accepted Christ as Saviour. The Lord was pleased to give us souls at our services Sunday, and I spoke with other pastors in the city who were also rejoicing in souls that had made decisions in their churches.
>
> I have been through a number of large campaigns in the city, one with Billy Sunday for two weeks, during which I led the song service; one with Gipsy Smith in which I arranged for the personal workers and the ushering; but never, in the twenty-five years that I have worked in the city of Buffalo, have I seen

such an evangelistic service as God was pleased to give us under your leadership.

Not only did the meetings attract the largest congregations, but there was a deep spirit of conviction wrought by the Holy Spirit that I have never seen equaled before. The after-effects proved the genuineness of the revival. People have not lapsed back into their old ways. There is a new spiritual tone and atmosphere throughout the city; and everywhere one goes, he finds Christians who are anxious to do the will of God.

One of the preachers remarked today that you are a preacher's preacher. Surely you have the Christian love of all the pastors who were privileged to labor with you for the salvation of souls. We appreciate the work which the Lord accomplished through you and Brother Shufelt while you were in our city. I cannot wish for you better than meetings such as you had in Buffalo in all of your campaigns throughout the country.

May God's richest blessing continue to rest upon you and your loved ones.

Perhaps one of his most successful union meetings was the "Christ-for-Greater-Cleveland" campaign held in the Cleveland Public Music Hall at Cleveland, Ohio. The meeting was not city-wide in organization, but it was in manifestation.

There were ninety-three cooperating churches, only one of which had a membership in excess of five hundred. The majority of the churches on its committee were so-called splinter groups and minor denominations such as Nazarene, Fundamental Baptist, Christian and Missionary Alliance, Pentecostal, Quakers, Salvation Army, mission churches and rescue missions.

The campaign ran for twenty-eight days, from February 11 through March 11, in 1945. J. Stratton Shufelt was the songleader and soloist. The entire cost of the crusade, including the renting of the big auditorium for a month, did not exceed a budget of $10,000.

Crowds continued to grow until the closing night when 3,767 people, by count of the public auditorium authorities, jammed the auditorium to hear him preach on, "Missing God's Last Train for Heaven." There were about fifty public professions of faith that night, making a total of about one thousand conversions and reclamations for the crusade. Approximately eight hundred of these were first-time decisions for Christ.

The meeting was such a tremendous success that the committee conducted a union campaign every year for some years afterward. However, the minister who was in charge of the inquiry room during the Rice-Shufelt meeting and who had been in all the subsequent campaigns told me this meeting was by far the best in manifestation of the power of God and in lasting results. Rev. George A. Bates, pastor of the Nottingham Baptist Church, was the general chairman.

Perhaps it would be fitting here to quote the testimony of one of the cooperating pastors, Dr. W. S. Ross, pastor of the Hough Avenue Baptist Church of Cleveland, now the Cedar Hill Baptist Church:

> I have been in the fire zone of revival. They want me to describe it. How can I speak of a fire I cannot describe? How can I express the tremendous sense of God's presence? How can I describe the influence of the power of the Holy Spirit playing over a crowded congregation as an eddying wind plays over the surface of a pond? You cannot describe the spontaneous impulse created by the Holy Spirit! I have witnessed a revival borne along upon the billowing waves of sacred song, but I have no language to describe it.
>
> It is comparatively easy to write of the instruments of revival. The medium through which a revival is made visible. The organization, the preacher, the songleader, the choir, the great audiences, the hundreds of seekers filing into the inquiry rooms, the personal workers, the testimonies of the born again, and the restored believers. But that is only the outward manifestation of the great work of God mysteriously wrought in the spiritual realm.
>
> Dr. John R. Rice and Mr. Stratton Shufelt did not bring the revival. It was not produced by organization and promotion. It was a divine visitation in which God demonstrated what He can do when a praying people depend wholly and absolutely on Him. It may be that God worked in spite of our careful plans, advertising and promotion schemes, rather than because of them.
>
> The spirit of the revival is manifested in the way the people sing. They sing words like men who believe them. They abandon themselves to the spirit and message of the song. Mr. Shufelt and the great chorus seem to become merged into one great choir of tremendous volume of praise.
>
> The revival is demonstrated in turning nominal Christians

into evangelists. The zeal and earnestness of Dr. Rice is reproduced in many people you never expected to see becoming definite personal workers.

At one meeting a Sunday school teacher won eight of his scholars to a public confession of Christ. The Sunday schools are reaping a bountiful harvest. The family altar is reaping a harvest, and at almost every service fathers and mothers may be seen bringing their children to Christ.

One deacon said, "I used to bring unsaved friends to my church but nothing happened. During this meeting I have been bringing them here, and God is graciously saving them one by one."

The revival is being expressed in a spirit of thanksgiving and intercession. People are being compelled to prayer in faith and deep earnestness. The Christians everywhere are singing, praying, offering praise and pleading with God for the salvation of the lost. There is a great return on the part of church members, under the inspired touch of the Holy Spirit, to exercise their priestly function of giving thanks and interceding.

The recognition of the presence of the Spirit manifesting the Lord Jesus in His atoning death, justifying resurrection, reconciling mediation, and as the one and only way to peace with God, is a sure evidence of real revival. Men with sin-blinded eyes are seeing God and the vision is being merged into virtue. Crooked ways are being made straight. Bad debts are being paid. Believers are coming out from evil doers and being separated unto God. . . .

I have been in the fire zone of a revival. I know that churches, where spiritual life is languishing, may have a revival today as surely as in the days of Wesley, Moody, Finney, and Sunday. God can still rouse men from apathy and indifference and compel them to face squarely the fateful decision upon which their whole future depends. In other words, 'He changes His angels into winds, and His ministering servants into a flame of fire.'

From January 13 through February 3, in 1946, Dr. Rice conducted a united revival campaign in Pontiac, Michigan, where forty-eight churches sponsored the services held in the two-thousand-seat Oakland Avenue Tabernacle.

In March of that year he conducted a union campaign in Miami, Florida. Services were held in the city auditorium and were sponsored officially by forty-four Baptist churches of the Miami Baptist Association. The meeting was only fifteen days in duration, but there were over six hundred public professions of

faith recorded on cards in the inquiry room, plus another estimated four hundred professions of faith in the public schools
where they were not able to have inquiry rooms or to talk privately to the students, according to the chairman of the campaign,
Rev. James H. Christie.

For five weeks in 1946, beginning April 28 and closing June 2,
over two hundred churches and organizations banded together to
sponsor a great "Life Begins" evangelistic crusade in the city of
Chicago. Speaker for the first two weeks was Dr. Bob Jones, Sr.
The third week was led by Dr. Paul Rood of Glendale, California;
and the final fifteen days by Dr. John R. Rice. J. Stratton
Shufelt led the music throughout the campaign.

The meeting was held in the Chicago Arena seating over seven
thousand people, in the same neighborhood where the big Billy
Sunday tabernacle had been built twenty-eight years previously.
The Jones-Rood-Rice Crusade was the first effort at a united
campaign in Chicago since Sunday's meeting of 1918.

Frank W. Sheriff of the Christian Businessmen's Committee
was chairman of the general committee, and W. G. Haymaker
was executive director. Chairman Sheriff reported of the
meeting:

> The united 'Life Begins' campaign in the Chicago Arena was
> brought to a glorious conclusion. . .when a great crowd heard
> Dr. John R. Rice's final message, "When God's Patience Wears
> Out." It was a stirring address that gripped hearts of all who
> heard and made the redeemed glad they were saved and
> burdened and anxious to win the unsaved to Christ. Over thirty
> decisions, clean-cut and definite, were made, bringing the total
> for the campaign in all services to over two thousand.
>
> In addition, there doubtless were four hundred young lives
> fully dedicated to the service of Christ, wherever led of the
> Holy Spirit; and it would be safe to say that hundreds of Chris-
> tians made secret decisions to serve Christ better and to walk
> more closely with God. Homes were re-established, family
> altars started, separated husbands and wives reunited, and
> many of the Lord's people given a new vision of their respon-
> sibility to witness and win others to Christ.

One leading Chicago minister, a man who had been on Billy
Sunday's committee in 1918 and a veteran evangelist himself,

said that although the crowds did not equal those of the Sunday meetings in 1918, the results were greater and far better.

In September of 1946, Rice went to Dayton, Ohio, for a union meeting with about one hundred sponsoring churches. Originally invited by the Christian Businessmen's Committee, he refused to go unless Bible-believing pastors and churches came in and officially sponsored the campaign. These pastors and churches were invited separately to unite; and the crusade was limited, as all of the Rice crusades have been, to the fundamental, evangelical churches. Dr. Daniel C. Campbell, pastor of the First United Presbyterian Church, was general chairman.

Services were held in the Memorial Hall with a seating capacity of about twenty-seven or twenty-eight hundred. Harry D. Clarke, for eight years Billy Sunday's songleader, had charge of the music. There were more than five hundred public decisions for Christ in the Memorial Hall, including both conversions and backsliders reclaimed. In additon, there were approximately four hundred and fifty others who claimed Christ in the four high schools where the evangelist spoke. Others were saved in other services apart from the night meetings in the Memorial Hall.

In January of 1947, Dr. Rice, again with Harry Clarke as songleader, conducted a campaign sponsored by about twenty churches in Lima, Ohio. Services were held in the South High School auditorium, and three hundred and fifty-three public professions of faith were recorded in the inquiry room. An estimated additional two hundred claimed Christ when the team spoke in high schools over the county. Dr. Harman J. Dutton was chairman of the campaign.

On February 18 through March 5, the Rice-Clarke team conducted a union campaign in Marion, Ohio. Rev. R. W. Faulkner, pastor of the Calvary Evangelical United Brethren Church, was general chairman. There were over two hundred first-time professions of faith in this campaign.

In March and April of the same year the Rice-Clarke evangelistic team held a big united tent revival in San Pedro, California, sponsored by about twenty-five different churches and religious groups. The tent had a seating capacity of about fif-

**A typical pose of a compassionate-hearted evangelist pleading for sinners. (Dr. Rice, taken in 1945.)**

teen hundred and was located just two blocks from Sixth and Beacon streets, a spot which was written up in Bob Ripley's "Believe It or Not" column as the toughest corner in the world. Rev. Fred H. Ross, pastor of the First Methodist Church, was general chairman. There were over six hundred registered decisions for Christ in the inquiry room.

Space does not permit listing details of other campaigns, but some of the outstanding crusades were conducted in Moncton, New Brunswick, Canada (two tremendous ones); Presque Isle, Maine; and Springfield, Missouri. Actually, it was about this time that Dr. Rice was forced to make a decision as to whether he wanted to hold great citywide campaigns or help mold and influence the Christian public through the pages of *The Sword of the Lord*—which was growing by leaps and bounds.

He was always on the go in those days. In fact, when United Air Lines inaugurated its "100,000 Mile Club" (now called the Executive Air Travel Program) and invited him to join in 1956, the United representative who came to Wheaton and went through his flight records immediately placed him in its most prestigious category, giving him the "Million Miler" plaque, showing he had already flown more than one million miles. Later, in 1973, the Rome-based Alitalia Air Line made him a member of its exclusive *Freccia Alata* (Winged Arrow) Club, presenting him with a beautiful silver plaque. Membership in the latter is limited to 2,000 at any one time and consists of "an elite of leading personalities in the world of business and politics, in the arts, in society, all having a common, vital interest: communication, fundamental to human progress and prosperity."

Dr. Rice naturally concluded that more permanent good could be done for Christ and evangelism through the paper, so he was compelled to turn down more and more opportunities for citywide crusades. As his son-in-law Walt Handford expressed it in a letter to me: "One of the keen human disappointments in Dr. Rice's life has been that after his pioneer labor bringing back citywide evangelism to America, his crushing load of editorial responsibility made it impossible for him to maintain full-time an evangelistic party or to do the ground work necessary to open other large meetings." I do not think he ever regretted his choice.

The thrilling story of his ministry through *The Sword of the Lord* will be told in the next chapter.

*Chapter 11*

# "The Sword of the Lord and of John R. Rice"

*The Lord gave the word: great was the company of those that published it.*—Psalm 68:11.

*. . .and they cried, The sword of the Lord, and of Gideon.*—Judges 7:20.

THE SWORD OF THE LORD was born on September 28, 1934, when Dr. Rice was pastor of the Fundamentalist Baptist Church at Dallas. There were 5,000 copies of the first issue printed. The main heading, which advertised the sermon for the next Sunday night at the church, was "Divorce, Remarriage and Adultery."

One front-page article entitled, "We Want to Help Poor People Get Work," contained an offer to "publish free any advertisement for those who want work." Interested parties were instructed, "Write out your ad; make it brief, not over fifty words; give exact information of what you can do and what work you want and where you may be reached by mail or by phone." The editor said, "I would like to help worthy people find work, and those who can use help will do me a favor if they let me know what kind of help they need and when. This free service is designed for sincere people who would honestly do good, reliable work." Remember that this was at the peak of the bitter depression which plagued all of America and especially the Southwest.

Most of the front page was taken up with a box notice entitled, "The New Paper and Its Policies." This article is so interesting and shows so clearly how *The Sword of the Lord* has maintained its original position right to the present hour, that I quote it here in its entirety:

> Here is the first issue of *The Sword of the Lord and of John R. Rice.* Readers and advertisers have a right to know the what and why of this paper. Here is a very frank and personal word about the paper.
>
> The paper is not a denominational organ. It does not represent the Baptist denomination or any other. Nor is it a church bulletin. It is simply the voice of Evangelist John R. Rice in print, preaching the Gospel, rebuking sin, defending the faith, teaching the Bible and winning sinners to the Lord Jesus Christ. It will be simply an extension of my ministry in the pulpit and over the radio.
>
> For several years I have had many calls by letter and telephone and in person for printed copies of sermons which I delivered. Every time I announce on the radio that I will preach on "The Sin of Adultery," or "The Unpardonable Sin," or "Baptist Infidels," or any other sermons that arouse great interest, I am besieged with inquiries as to whether I can furnish that sermon in printed form. I have usually had to state regretfully that I could not do it.
>
> For years I have prayed that God would give me a paper in which to print my sermons and Bible teachings on great matters about which people need to know the will of God. Now God is answering my prayer, I believe, and I will be able to print my sermons and Bible studies which have been so greatly in demand all over the country by people who have heard me preach in person or on the radio. *The Sword of the Lord* will be a weekly paper, carrying Bible messages, red-hot condemnation of sin and tender appeals to the sinner.
>
> Subscribe to the paper today. Put a one dollar bill in an envelope and mail it to John R. Rice, 201 E. Tenth St., Dallas, Texas; and *The Sword of the Lord* will be mailed to your home for one year. Already subscriptions are coming in, and I anticipate that hundreds of earnest Christians will want to regularly read this paper.
>
> You will read sermons by John R. Rice and keep up with the wonderful growth and work of the Fundamentalist Baptist Church, our fight against modernism and unbelief, and our great revivals. Also you will greatly help us to make this paper possible during the strenuous days of beginning publication. Send your subscription today, $1.00 a year.
>
> If you have friends you want to know what it means to be a fundamentalist, you could do them no greater favor for a dollar

than to send them *The Sword of the Lord.* Help spread the good word. Six months' subscription, $.50.

I have no idea of financial profit from the publication of this paper. The time and labor necessary I will gladly give to spread the Gospel and help people. The financial responsibility will be very heavy; and oftentimes, I have no doubt, I will need to meet expenses out of my own pocket. The Fundamentalist Baptist Church in Oak Cliff, of which I am pastor, is greatly interested in this paper; but I alone am responsible, financially and otherwise, humanly speaking.

It is my earnest prayer that the dear Lord, who has blessed and has so marvelously provided for my ministry, will take this venture also under His powerful care, and provide all needs to His own glory. I believe that He put it in my heart to begin the publication of *The Sword of the Lord.* I want the paper to please Him, even though it should sometimes please no one else.

This paper will maintain a constant war on booze, on horse-race gambling, on modernism and unbelief in the churches, and on sin of every kind, in the church as well as out. We owe no allegiance to any denominational headquarters. We have no board of directors to consider about the policy of this paper. The paper will contain straight-out Bible teaching and plain preaching. The editor is an out-and-out fundamentalist and premillennialist, who believes every word of the Bible without apology or compromise.

## ADVERTISERS—TAKE NOTICE

The advertising policy of this paper will be controlled by the same principles that affect the reading matter. We will not take advertisements from picture shows. We will not accept an advertisement from any drugstore, cafe or grocery that has a beer license. It might be easier to get advertising enough to pay the expenses of the paper if we were not so strict, but I do not want a single ad in this paper that would displease the Lord Jesus Christ.

The paper will be vigorous, sometimes startling; always, I trust, read with great interest by those who agree with it and by those who do not.

We solicit advertising only on the basis of merit. Our church does not have personal solicitation for donations for any purpose. We do not even canvass our own membership for the support of the pastor, building fund or anything else. Certainly then the advertising manager, Mr. Ray Rucker, does not solicit ads on a donation basis.

Advertising space will sell at a very reasonable rate. This issue of the paper is five thousand copies. In a few weeks we will have ten thousand copies scattered every week through Oak Cliff.

The paper will be more eagerly read, we believe, than any weekly publication in Dallas. We believe to advertise in *The Sword of the Lord* will be good business, and on that basis alone we solicit ads.

The paper will be distributed free from house to house not later than Friday morning of each week. The paper will be delivered by mail to subscribers at the rate of $1.00 a year. Send subscriptions to John R. Rice, 201 E. Tenth St., Dallas, Texas.

Mr. Ray Rucker is advertising and circulation manager of *The Sword of the Lord.* Leave calls for him at the church office at 201 E. Tenth St. or phone 6-6888. We believe you will find Mr. Rucker a Christian gentleman, an experienced advertising man, reliable, courteous and helpful in every way. He will be glad to help you work out a profitable ad.

Earnestly coveting the prayers and support of Christian friends everywhere in this new effort to bless Dallas, arouse Christians and get the Gospel to sinners.

Sincerely Yours,
JOHN R. RICE

You will note from the above that the policy of the paper changed very little from its inception until Dr. Rice's death, almost a half of a century later. It still highlighted the sermons of the editor; still fought sin, modernism and unbelief; still promoted revival; the editor still received no profit from the publication—not even a penny from his long hours of labor—and he had to fulfill the prophecy of meeting the expenses out of his own pocket on many an occasion. In like manner, no advertising was accepted which "would displease the Lord Jesus Christ." At a sacrifice of hundreds of thousands of dollars, he repeatedly refused questionable advertising—such as ads for the Revised Standard Version, appeals for money from questionable organizations, books promoting unsound doctrine, and many other types of advertising happily accepted by other evangelical publications, apparently without any qualms of conscience whatsoever.

The original issue, under the title, *The Sword of the Lord and of John R. Rice,* stated the paper's policies:

**"An independent religious weekly to preach the Gospel, expose sin, spread premillennial, fundamental Bible teaching, and foster the work of the Fundamentalist Baptist Church, 201 East Tenth Street, Dallas, Texas."**

Within a year it had been changed to read as follows:

**"An Independent Religious Weekly, Standing for the Verbal Inspiration of the Bible, the Deity of Christ, His Blood Atonement, Salvation by Faith, New Testament Soul Winning and the Premillennial Return of Christ. Opposes Sin, Modernism and Denominational Overlordship."**

You will note this to be exactly what appears on the heading of every issue today, with the exception of the second sentence. That now reads, "Opposes Modernism, Worldliness and Formalism," and is essentially the same as the former in meaning.

From the very first this paper has been a soul-winning instrument God has used in the salvation of many hundreds. The initial issue, as a prophetic forerunner of things to come, resulted in the salvation of a man who thought he had gone too far for God to forgive. This man had not been inside a church for sixteen years, but when he saw the paper and read about the Sunday night message, "Divorce, Remarriage and Adultery," he determined, as a result of his own unhappy home, to hear the message. He came and was happily saved that night. When the editor made note of it in a subsequent issue, he said, "I pray that God will make this paper the instrument in turning many prodigal men, many wayward women to the house of God, where they may hear the Gospel and be saved as were this man and boy (his fourteen-year-old son was also saved that night)." How wonderfully the editor's prayer has been answered!

The third issue of *The Sword of the Lord,* October 12, 1934, told of the editor's plans to preach in a south Dallas church the following Sunday afternoon. He wrote: "When Brother Mangum came to invite me to the services, he brought good news. A man in south Dallas last week was reading *The Sword of the Lord,* and as he read the article on 'Race Track Gambling, Drunkenness and Lewdness at the Dallas Fair,' he was happily converted. Brother Mangum promises he will be present Sunday afternoon, the Lord willing. Praise the Lord for evidence of His favor upon this paper."

So you see, someone was converted from both of the first two issues of this paper. By the time of Dr. Rice's death, the office had records of nearly twenty-six thousand others who had written in to say they had trusted Christ through some sermon in it. How many thousands of others trusted Him through the clear evangelistic messages in this publication who did not write to tell us! Our Heavenly Father keeps the books, and one glad morning editor and converts will rejoice together around the Throne of Grace in Glory.

This paper, from its humble beginning, grew to where it became the largest independent, fundamental religious weekly in the world. Approximately one year after its inception it had reached a circulation which included subscribers in forty-one of the forty-eight states, Canada, Mexico, Brazil and Norway. At the time of his death, weekly circulation was in excess of 130,000 copies and was going into every state of the Union, plus one hundred and one foreign countries. To give you some idea of its growth, I am reproducing the average print order from the first year through 1980, the time of Dr. Rice's death, including the yearly totals and the grand total.

| Year | Average circulation weekly | Total printed including samples | Grand total |
|------|---------------------------|--------------------------------|-------------|
| 1934 | 7,200 | 100,800 | 100,800 |
| 1935 | 6,100 | 317,200 | 418,000 |
| 1936 | 8,000 | 416,000 | 834,000 |
| 1937 | 9,100 | 473,200 | 1,307,200 |
| 1938 | 6,200 | 322,400 | 1,629,600 |
| 1939 | 5,900 | 306,800 | 1,936,400 |
| 1940 | 5,600 | 291,200 | 2,227,600 |
| 1941 | 9,100 | 473,200 | 2,700,800 |
| 1942 | 12,100 | 629,200 | 3,330,000 |
| 1943 | 20,800 | 1,081,600 | 4,411,600 |

| | | |
|---|---|---|
| 1944 | 30,800 | 1,601,600 | 6,013,200 |
| 1945 | 44,600 | 2,319,200 | 8,332,400 |
| 1946 | 43,388 | 2,275,176 | 10,607,576 |
| 1947 | 36,800 | 1,913,600 | 12,521,176 |
| 1948 | 35,400 | 1,840,800 | 14,361,976 |
| 1949 | 50,345 | 2,617,978 | 16,979,954 |
| 1950 | 66,654 | 3,466,001 | 20,445,955 |
| 1951 | 70,629 | 3,672,690 | 24,118,645 |
| 1952 | 91,122 | 4,738,344 | 28,856,989 |
| 1953 | 89,812 | 4,764,500 | 33,621,489 |
| 1954 | 98,313 | 5,294,818 | 38,916,307 |
| 1955 | 104,944 | 5,663,475 | 44,579,782 |
| 1956 | 106,592 | 5,553,212 | 50,132,994 |
| 1957 | 67,656 | 3,518,112 | 53,651,106 |
| 1958 | 78,028 | 4,057,474 | 57,708,580 |
| 1959 | 69,445 | 3,611,157 | 61,319,737 |
| 1960 | 61,479 | 3,258,400 | 64,578,137 |
| 1961 | 57,162 | 2,972,426 | 67,550,563 |
| 1962 | 66,222 | 3,443,530 | 70,994,093 |
| 1963 | 68,551 | 3,564,638 | 74,558,731 |
| 1964 | 70,769 | 3,680,003 | 78,238,734 |
| 1965 | 78,674 | 4,169,702 | 82,408,436 |
| 1966 | 88,740 | 4,614,471 | 87,022,907 |
| 1967 | 67,087 | 3,592,561 | 90,615,468 |
| 1968 | 83,616 | 4,348,019 | 94,963,487 |
| 1969 | 95,658 | 4,974,190 | 99,937,677 |
| 1970 | 130,975 | 6,810,715 | 106,748,392 |
| 1971 | 143,727 | 7,617,543 | 114,365,935 |
| 1972 | 203,424 | 10,578,035 | 124,943,970 |
| 1973 | 220,375 | 11,679,869 | 136,623,839 |
| 1974 | 288,184 | 14,985,593 | 151,609,432 |
| 1975 | 269,088 | 13,992,582 | 165,602,014 |
| 1976 | 218,157 | 11,344,155 | 176,946,169 |
| 1977 | 273,616 | 14,228,017 | 191,174,186 |
| 1978 | 244,519 | 12,714,969 | 203,889,155 |
| 1979 | 172,929 | 8,992,314 | 212,881,469 |
| 1980 | 131,383 | 6,831,868 | 219,713,337 |

Incidentally, it was on the tenth anniversary that *The Sword of the Lord* doubled its space from four to eight pages and made plans for great expansion. At Dr. Rice's death it was sixteen full pages in size and contained three or four full-length gospel messages every week. Some issues were twenty-four and even thirty-two pages.

Each week there was at least one sermon by one of the greatest preachers of the past, such as Charles Haddon Spurgeon, R. A. Torrey, D. L. Moody, Billy Sunday, J. Wilbur Chapman, F. B. Meyer, A. T. Pierson, George W. Truett, Sam Jones, H. A. Ironside, W. B. Riley, Bob Jones, Sr., or some other greatly used evangelist, pastor or missionary. In every issue was a full-length gospel sermon by one of the greatest preachers of the present, such as Jack Hyles, Tom Malone, Tom Wallace, Curtis Hutson, Bill Rice, Robert G. Lee, Lee Roberson, W. A. Criswell, and many others.

Every issue contained at least one sermon addressed to the unconverted. Always there was at least one strong Bible message. The vital public issues of the day were forcibly and scripturally dealt with, and many ministers learned to look to *The Sword of the Lord* when questions of controversy arose. Reports of outstanding revivals were presented regularly; missionary stories and Christian fiction were often featured, plus my own column of illustrations and incidents, the editor's notes, teen talks, and many timely answers to Bible questions of general interest. There were articles for children, for women, book reviews, soul-winning helps, and Viola Walden's scrapbook clippings for everyone.

In one of the old issues of the paper, November 10, 1939, I noted with interest a two-paragraph apology which I think is indicative of the humility of this man of God. The item was simply headlined, "An Apology," and said:

> Last week *The Sword of the Lord* mentioned the name of the editor on the front page too many times. No one else has mentioned it, but the editor felt conscience-stricken that his name should be put in headlines so often, and begs the forbearance of the readers.
>
> Many, many letters indicate that you who read *The Sword of the Lord* are concerned about the engagements and the ministry of the editor. Many letters ask me where I am going and about results of revivals. Such interest seems to justify announcements and brief reports about such services.

I looked up the previous issue and counted carefully, noting his name ten times. Once was on the masthead where he was listed as the editor of the paper; once it was to announce a new tract he had written; and another time his name was given in the address where folks could write to receive the tract. The fourth reference simply stated that one of his sermons was "a radio message of John R. Rice." Three other places his name was mentioned only in letters reporting conversions. Two other times his name was mentioned to announce services at the church for the next Sunday, and the other time was simply to advertise his engagement in Chicago. Nothing about it was of a boastful nature whatsoever; yet he felt his name had been used too many times, and he must apologize in print the following week.

From the time of its very humble beginning, publication of *The Sword of the Lord* was a faith proposition, entirely dependent upon the mercy and goodness of God. Elsewhere we have related the story of how he received, in answer to prayer, the check for $1,000 from millionaire industrialist R. G. LeTourneau, which helped save the paper.

On another occasion he felt led to ask God for five thousand four-month trial subscriptions. Workers put big posters up on the wall in the office as a continual reminder of the goal, then prayed earnestly and daily for the subscriptions. Dr. Rice stated publicly in the paper that they were seeking five thousand subscriptions. A definite time was set for the campaign to close; and when that time rolled around, it was discovered they had *exactly* the five thousand subscriptions. But some of the workers complained that since his secretary had given thirty subscriptions herself, it was sort of helping God out. They prayed again, and the next day's mail brought in subscriptions from stragglers making the total five thousand and thirty! Just as God first made the fleece wet for Gideon, then the next morning made it dry, so God gave them five thousand subscriptions with the secretary's thirty, then five thousand without them.

*The Sword of the Lord* has always been *entirely* dependent upon God for its existence, and I say from experience as the former Associate Editor, then a Contributing Editor and member of the board of The Sword of the Lord Foundation all that time—the paper would fold up tomorrow if God took His hand off it! And I speak with just as much authority and just as emphatically when I say that Dr. Rice would have wanted it to fail if and when God took His hand off. *The Sword of the Lord* continues today, under the leadership of Dr. Curtis Hutson, as a miracle of God's grace. May it ever remain so until Jesus comes again!

When Dr. Rice moved *The Sword of the Lord* headquarters from Dallas to Wheaton in 1940, the office work was done in his home. Libby, in a Father's Day letter to him, reminisced:

> "How many thousands of dollars you have put into printing the books and *The Sword,* economizing on your personal needs, stretching the meager balance to cover music lessons and textbooks and yards of cotton for little girls' dresses. And Mother, bless her heart, cheerfully cooperating—enduring all the office equipment for addressing and mailing *The Sword* set up in the dining room, so she couldn't serve supper on Fridays until the mail bags were at the post office. And Mother, who loves pretty things, putting up with the front room as a bookstore, and the back room a Sword office, and the attic storage for all the Sword books. You made *The Sword* a family enterprise, and the methods I learned in those days I have used a thousand times since. Remember how we threw the packages of *Bible Facts About Heaven* from the printer's truck, bucket-brigade style, up to the third floor attic? That's once you were grateful for the girls' boyfriends!"

In 1945 a basement office was rented in the business section of Wheaton. In 1946 a large, two-story brick warehouse was purchased and remodeled. In 1952 another two-story brick building, just a block from the warehouse and in the business section of the town, was purchased to take care of the growing work. Then, in 1955, the First Presbyterian Church property was purchased to provide location for a proposed future building. Finally, in 1963, God led in a move to Murfreesboro, Tennessee, where the paper is now printed and where a staff of approximately 90 workers had its headquarters at the time of his death.

Perhaps I should say here that in 1947 the Sword of the Lord Foundation was incorporated under the laws of the State of Illinois as a non-profit organization. At that time Dr. Rice relinquished, without any remuneration whatsoever, the property, paper, office equipment, book copyrights, etc. He did not own, nor does any member of his family today, any part of the Sword Foundation.

This chapter would not be complete, I feel, without quoting some of the glowing letters received from all over the world, giving grateful appreciation for the ministry of *The Sword* in lives. First, let me give some testimonials of those who have been saved through its pages.

An army sergeant stationed in Virginia wrote:

> I thank God for true Christians who publish such a great paper. *The Sword of the Lord* is fourfold dear to me, for it was through it that I turned to God and was gloriously saved. It means much to me to be able to read such true Gospel explained so simply that anyone can understand.
>
> Since accepting Christ as my Saviour, I have dedicated my life to Him and plan to enter a religious school this year to prepare for His service.

A lady in North Carolina wrote to tell what results the paper, along with the *What Must I Do to Be Saved?* booklet, accomplished in her family. She said:

> Your *Sword of the Lord* has been a special blessing this year. When I first began taking it, only my mother and I read it much. Then my three sisters took to reading it, too. My youngest sister, then unsaved, read your booklet, *What Must I Do to Be Saved?* and was saved a short time later.
>
> I started to tell you about this year's blessing. My father, now 73, who says he was converted when a young man but became a backslider and has lived a long time out of fellowship with the Lord, has returned to the Lord and greatly enjoys your sermons now. At first he almost thought there was no hope for his restoration to the joys of salvation; but after reading your sermons and studying the Scripture references given, has been greatly comforted. He now reads his Bible every day and enjoys talking about the things of the Lord, which he didn't before. Please pray with me that my father may continue to grow in grace.

A man who is now a minister in Arkansas wrote:

Twelve years after returning from the army my heart was filled with hate, my mind with infidel doubts and arguments, such as "How do you know Jesus is the Son of God?" "How do you know there is a God?" "How do you know that we are not the descendants of an ape?" which had come from one of Roy Chapman Andrews' books.

As a career I planned on getting rich writing murder fiction, which I had hoped would be taken over by some movie company. My infidelity brought no happiness, no assurance; and I was driven to thoughts of taking my own life. But if there was life beyond the grave, I would be in Hell; so I was afraid to take the chance of going to Hell.

An aunt had loaned me a lot of old issues of *The Sword.* I had read a lot of them. With nothing to do one night I decided to look over the book advertisement. While lying in the bed about ten, my eye caught a catchy sermon entitled, "Why Half of the Preachers and Church Members I Know Should Go to Hell for Twenty-Four Hours," by Joe Hankins.

I started reading it. I thought I was tough and hard boiled, but was soon weeping like a baby as it seemed I was falling straight into Hell. I cried, "Jesus, save me!". . . He did. . . . A few months later I surrendered to the ministry while helping my grandfather, went to church Sunday, told the pastor, and made it public.

My doubts had vanished. After becoming a member of your book club, my faith was strengthened by Dr. Rimmer's book, *The Theory of Evolution.* Your book, *Is Jesus God?* helped me understand more about the deity of Christ.

My whole life has been radically changed from infidelity, immorality and debauchery, by this one issue of *The Sword,* to hope, life and faith.

Some time ago a friend in a small upstate New York community had *The Sword of the Lord* sent to eighteen different homes where there were thirty-three people, not including children. Of that number she had classified them: one soldier who was a Christian, four carnal Christians, one recent convert of two months, and twenty-seven "just plain sinners!" Out of these eighteen subscriptions, she later was able to report with rejoicing that seven had been saved, including her eighty-year-old grandmother; five had been restored into fellowship with the Lord; two were very interested in God's plan of salvation and had been asking many questions; six had no recent contact with her so she did not know the result; and seven were needing much prayer from the problem of the unequal yoke.

A lady in Michigan wrote:

> One of my brothers to whom I had *The Sword* sent has turned to Christ; he and his wife have already been baptized.

From Newark, New Jersey, a lady wrote, saying in part:

> Someone sent me a subscription about two years ago and since then I have been saved. Your paper had a great deal to do with the greatest event in my life. Since that day, and every day now, I find blessings from it. . . .

From Michigan a lady testified:

> I think it is the best Christian periodical that one can get. I choose *The Sword of the Lord* above all other magazines; it has such a soul-winning ministry and lots of good reading for Christians. I get such a blessing out of reading any of those sermons.
>
> My daughter was saved through reading *The Sword of the Lord,* so I can't say and praise enough your wonderful paper . . .but I feel so indebted to you for the rich blessings that I have received.

A man in South Carolina wrote:

> I accepted Christ October 9, 1953, soon after a friend gave me a *Sword* to read. I found it so inspiring to my hungry soul that I subscribed for it. I couldn't express in words the strength I have received from the *Sword.*

On one occasion *The Sword of the Lord* published a long list of those who had recently been converted through Sword literature. One brother wrote, rejoicing over the report, saying:

> We are praising God today for a special reason. In *The Sword of the Lord* you published a list of names of those who were saved through reading Sword of the Lord literature. My mother's name was in that list. . . . I subscribed for *The Sword* to be sent to my mother and also sent her a copy of the little booklet, *What Must I Do to Be Saved?* and have been praying to that end for some time. Thank God, my prayer has been answered! Thanks to *The Sword of the Lord* and the little booklet. . .please pray that my father will also be saved.

A man in Canada declared:

I have never read a paper which preached against sin like *The Sword;* that is the kind of preaching we need. I sent the paper to my uncle a little over a year ago; he was eighty-two years old, and he accepted Christ as his Saviour. He was a railroad engineer and drank and cursed; now he is so thankful that he is a Christian. He told me that he sent ten subscriptions to some of his friends. He doesn't get out much as he is not too well, but getting *The Sword. . .* strengthens him spiritually. So his conversion was a real joy to me.

From Mississippi a young man wrote to tell how much he appreciated *The Sword of the Lord* with its sermons by great men of the past. After saying many kind words about the paper, he added:

About three or four years ago, while I was still unsaved, my uncle sent me a one-year subscription to your paper. Of course, I didn't care anything about spiritual things then. But seeing this paper come in week after week, I began to get curious to know what kind of a paper it was. So I read a few articles— I don't recall the articles I read now— but a little while after that I began to feel burdened over my sin, and after a while I read more of your paper. Finally my burden got so heavy I accepted Christ as my Saviour, and now I can hardly wait each week to receive your wonderful Christian paper.

A lady in Kansas addressed her letter to the office, saluting workers as "Dear Friends," then added:

For "friends" you are. First it is a "joy" (yes, and my duty) to write you, for I was saved through a sermon in *The Sword.* That sermon was called "History's Horror Picture."

And since I have been saved *The Sword* keeps me fed on God's Word. I'm so happy to be able to go to *The Sword* and find out what is right and wrong—what will please Christ and what will not!

A lady in Canada wrote to say:

Along with my money for subscription to *The Sword of the Lord,* I just want to say how I've enjoyed your Christian paper. I've been getting it now for four years or more, and I would not want to be without it. It was the means of my finding Christ, and I have never regretted a day of it since I let Him come into my heart. My desire is just to live for Him from day to day. May God bless you and yours in your wonderful work.

A man in California testified:

> I do praise God and thank Him for the ministry of Dr. Rice and *The Sword of the Lord,* for it was through this paper that I found Christ as my Saviour five years ago, while stationed in the army in Southampton, England. . . . Now I have the assurance of my eternal destiny and at present am attending the Bible Institute of Los Angeles preparing for full-time service for my Lord.

In November, 1935, a lady living at Electra, Texas, paid twenty-five cents for a year's subscription tor a man in Alabama. When he got his first copy, he read it and commented, "There is nothing to it. John R. Rice is nothing but a Holy Roller." The second, third, fourth, fifth, and sixth copies came to him; and he concluded that perhaps John R. Rice was a good man. The paper kept coming; he became more interested; finally, conviction came so heavy upon him that he repented of his sins, trusted Christ, and was saved. The minister who became his pastor wrote the editor telling how he baptized him into the church and how the man grew so rapidly in spiritual things that within a year he had been made a deacon. The pastor described him as "now a devout Christian, a booster of *The Sword of the Lord,* and firm as a rock."

Another lady wrote to tell of a godless neighbor who lived on a farm near her for whom she felt led of the Holy Spirit to subscribe. Each week as she went by her friend's house to take the eggs to town, she saw the beloved *Sword of the Lord* lying in the gutter by the mailbox where the indignant lady had thrown it. She felt surely her money had been wasted on that subscription, yet she remained instant in prayer about it.

One day the lost woman became sick, and those who came in to care for her did not know they were supposed to throw *The Sword of the Lord* in the gutter when they brought in the mail. One day, when the woman was on the road to recovery, she happened to notice the paper on the stand beside her with the other mail. She picked up the paper, and one of the sermon titles caught her eye; she read it, and God began to stir her heart. She read the entire paper through, then began looking forward eagerly for each succeeding issue, eventually coming to know Christ because of it.

These are just illustrative accounts of how God uses the paper in winning the lost to Himself.

Because of the type of paper it is, it is not surprising that pastors are among *The Sword's* strongest boosters. A pastor in New York, who had been given a few copies of the paper by a friend, wrote to tell what a "great spiritual blessing to my soul and such a boon to my personal spiritual life" those copies had been. He went on to say:

> I am just a young man in the ministry, having been in the ministry only about seven years; but during that time I have had the privilege of reading a good many religious magazines and papers. I can truthfully say without exaggeration that your little paper is the most spiritual and uplifting I have ever had, and even though the copies I have are back issues, I am constantly reading them over and over and receiving fresh blessings for my soul.

From Georgia a pastor wrote to say:

> *The Sword of the Lord* is without a question the greatest evangelistic paper in America. . . .

A minister of a Reformed church in Ohio wrote:

> After having read *The Sword of the Lord* regularly for several months, I must say that its testimony is second to no publication that reaches my desk, and there are seventeen in all—that is, weekly, bi-weekly, and monthly periodicals. . . .

From Texas a pastor commented:

> Without reserve I can say that I enjoy your paper, *The Sword of the Lord,* very much, holding it in greater esteem than any similar paper with which I am familiar.

A pastor in Pennsylvania said:

> As a pastor, I find this paper the most practical, inexpensive and worthwhile paper that comes to my desk.

The minister of a Brethren church in Indiana wrote:

> . . .I am convinced that such a paper is a blessing to any and every home and should be in every Christian home in America.

From Oklahoma a pastor enthused:

> The paper has been a real inspiration to me. I often read it through at one sitting. I hardly ever miss reading a single article. It often encourages me when I am discouraged about the hardness of people's hearts and often about the coldness of Christians. I believe that it gives me greater boldness in preaching against sin. I would not want to be without it at all.

The pastor of a large Methodist church in Philadelphia wrote the editor:

> I want to send you this letter of sincere appreciation for your very fine publication, *The Sword of the Lord.* I appreciate its fine Christian testimony, your true stand for the old-fashioned Gospel presentation.
>
> One of the young men in my church, who was converted while in the Armed Services under the influence of reading one of your books, and who has had *The Sword of the Lord* sent to several young Christians in my church, stays here at the parsonage with me. I am glad to be identified with your testimony through *The Sword of the Lord* and have my people receive it.
>
> I am ashamed of the fact that many Methodist ministers have compromised in their tradition as Methodists in having revivals in their churches, but not all of them have bowed their knee to the whims of modernists. I happen to be one who hasn't.

A Presbyterian preacher in Arkansas wrote:

> I am enjoying *The Sword of the Lord.* My only regret is that I never discovered it until last year. Although I subscribe to, and read, many other religious journals, *The Sword* is the one I prize most highly. You are sounding the note of evangelism as no other publisher that I am acquainted with. Keep sounding it. Effective evangelism makes Heaven ring with shouts of triumph and the Devil tremble with fear. Keep the emphasis right where you have it.

From New York City came a letter from an Episcopal priest, a man with an earned Doctor of Philosophy degree. He said, after commenting about another matter:

> I also believe, however, that the section of the Faith which you hold—the necessity of repentance, faith in our Lord's death on the cross to atone, and forgiveness of others—is

taught more effectively by your people and by your paper than by us. I find it to be so much more effective, at this point and under your presentation, that your paper fascinates me and helps me more than I can say.

From Florida a minister wrote:

My dad gave me a gift subscription to *The Sword* in 1949, and I have not been without it since; and, the Lord willing, I don't intend to be without it. I have bought subscriptions for others from time to time, and when I go out in revivals I try to make people acquainted with it. . . . I recommend it without fear or reservation.

From Texas a former army chaplain wrote to tell of the blessing a Sword Conference on Evangelism had been to him, then added:

Upon leaving the conference and going into evangelistic meetings for the remainder of the summer, I held in each meeting special veterans' services—and my present to each veteran was a subscription to *The Sword*. And I know of definite conversions from these subscriptions!

So, Dr. Rice, keep plugging on. You have little idea of the reach or influence of your paper. God grant that it may continue to convict, convert, and to bring revival!

From Utah the pastor of a Community church enthused:

I would not be without *The Sword* for anything in this world. . . . As long as I can read print, I will be reading it, talking it up, doing all within my power to increase its circulation. *The Sword* ought to be in every home in America.

From Kansas a preacher wrote:

I think I may accurately say that your *Sword of the Lord* and other literature have been among the great stabilizing forces which have come to bear on my ministry. In an age of doubt, confusion and skepticism, a young minister very often needs what he does not get in college or seminary—positive assertion of truth without apology or hesitation. And such I have found in *The Sword of the Lord* and in Dr. Rice's writings.

A Baptist preacher in Pennsylvania wrote to tell how he had been blessed, saying:

Seven years ago my wife and I started taking *The Sword of the Lord* and have not missed an issue since. The influence of the articles contained in this paper has been great. During the days when God was dealing with me to go into the full-time ministry, this paper brought much enlightenment. My plans and efforts were to be a dance instructor; but, of course, I could not continue in that channel after seeing plainly what God's Word has to say about that matter.

Many other spiritual helps have been ours through *The Sword of the Lord* which are far too numerous to relate in a letter.

## From North Carolina a preacher explained:

This is the sixth year I have been taking *The Sword of the Lord,* and it is still the greatest religious paper in America to me. I keep all the copies and go back over them years later. The sermons and illustrations have been a great blessing to my ministry.

## From Tennessee a minister wrote:

I have been a reader of *The Sword of the Lord* since May, 1938, and have on file in my study copies of your paper from that date. If I were able to subscribe to only one religious publication, it would be *The Sword of the Lord.* I look forward to its coming every week. . . . I think it is indispensable for the man who is a preacher of God's Word.

## From Kentucky a preacher testified:

While I was a student in the Southern Baptist Seminary in Louisville, yours was the one paper that I read to keep my evangelistic fires kindled. That habit has been continued now in my pastorate. I have been telling others about *The Sword.*

## From New York a Baptist minister wrote:

As I have now seen ample evidence of the spiritual value of the reading of *The Sword* by the saved and unsaved, I would rather have every person in my area receive the paper than have an assistant or associate pastor.

## A pastor in Georgia wrote to say:

Dr. Rice, I say this with all earnestness—*The Sword,* next to the Bible, has meant more to me and to my ministry than any other literature printed. Our prayers are always for you, the staff, the contributors who go to make up such a wonderful paper that is rich with the Word of God, true to the Bible with the spirit of evangelism that is unexcelled by any paper in the world.

From Tennessee a preacher wrote to describe how revival broke out through the influence of *The Sword of the Lord* in his church:

> I sent *The Sword* to several young men in our church and some older ones, too. I also gave copies to the members of our church. It was not long until the Holy Spirit began to work. Our church began to get burdened for the lost; cottage prayer meetings were organized by the young people, the young men conducting these services.
>
> In a short while four of these young men were called of God to preach the Word; the prayer meetings grew until there was no home large enough to take care of the people, and we moved the prayer meetings to the church. A real Holy Spirit revival was the result. Many souls were saved both in the cottage prayer meetings and the church. The church was almost trebled in membership. The revival fires are still burning warmly; prayer meetings are still being held; souls are still being blessed and saved.
>
> It would be impossible to tell in one letter how the Lord has blessed and used *The Sword* in starting revival fires in our own hearts and many others.

From Michigan a Methodist minister wrote:

> Some months ago *The Sword of the Lord* began arriving in our home. Being a pastor my first thought was, "Just another periodical which I will not have time to read," but upon closer inspection I discovered that here at last was a real soul-stirring evangelical paper. I immediately sat down and mentally devoured every article written in your paper. And, praise God, not only was I mentally refreshed but my soul was spiritually fed.
>
> Being a new pastor of a Methodist church which was living in an apostate condition has been a drain upon my very soul, but I find in your paper "showers of blessing" which encourage me to go on fighting the battle of faith. Oh, that all Methodism would see the vision and have the burden for lost souls that is expressed by you, Dr. Bob Jones, and other writers in your paper.

Several churches have tried sending *The Sword of the Lord* to every home in their membership with great blessing. When the author of this book was pastoring the Morningside Baptist Church at Graham, Texas, we did so with much profit and blessing. Below are printed the testimonials of four other pastors who tried the same thing. They said:

> It helps to build an evangelistic church. . .builds family altars. . .backs the pastor's stand against worldliness and modernism. . .makes people hungry for. . .soul-winning power.
>
> It is the true friend of the pastor who has an earnest, evangelistic heart. . . .
>
> . . .we have had 125 conversions, the Sunday school and church have tripled. . . .
>
> A real Holy Spirit revival was the result. . . . Many souls were saved. . .the church has almost trebled in membership. The revival fires are still burning warmly. . .impossible to tell in one letter how the Lord has blessed. . . .

Preachers in other lands are just as enthusiastic with its praises. For example, from far-off Australia a Baptist preacher wrote:

> Three of our Tasmanian Baptist ministers have been receiving *The Sword of the Lord* from some source in America, and they have found it to be a source of inspiring help. I may add that they are three of the keenest evangelical men in our state. At our recent minister's retreat, I had the privilege of seeing your paper; and I was so taken with it that I was able to borrow the loan of a few copies, which I have thoroughly enjoyed. I feel that your paper would do a great job if it were in the hands of more of the ministers and preachers of our churches. . . .

From Egypt a minister wrote:

> (The) Young People's Society of our church is a subscriber of your most valuable weekly. Really, words cannot express our appreciation of your sermons and the sermons of the outstanding pulpit masters which appear in your weekly. I get great help from these sermons in preparing my messages. Four years ago you sent me your book, *Home: Courtship, Marriage and Children.* I intended then to translate it into the Armenian language, but, owing to the lack of financial means, could not do it. But I studied it well, gave several lectures about the contents to our young people.

And you will be amused, in a tender fashion, of course, with the testimonial from a native pastor in South India:

> I am not receiving now *The Sword.* Since it stopped I am weeping before the Lord to make it possible to get this precious weekly again. I have filed each issue away for reference. . . .

Laymen are just as enthusiastic in praising the paper as preachers. A man in Jacksboro, Texas, wrote rather humorously:

> Now for a testimony of *The Sword of the Lord.* We certainly can say a loud amen! My wife burns her dinner reading *The Sword of the Lord,* and I almost run into light posts coming from the office with it. Our prayer is that it will always be full of the Gospel as it is now.

And another Texan wrote:

> I want to tell you how wonderful I think *The Sword of the Lord* is. I haven't been taking it but a few months. Mrs. Q      , my neighbor, took it, and she would let me read it. She begged me to send for it. So I borrowed the money to get it, but I thank God I did. It helped save my mother (Mrs. R      ). When it is out I can't see how I can do without it.

A man in the Eastern State Penitentiary at Philadelphia wrote, and his letter is typical of the attitude of many behind bars who have access to the paper:

> Since we have been receiving *The Sword of the Lord,* I have been a faithful reader. . . .
>
> Christian men in this institution, especially those born again intramurally and those whose seeking is one of the most heartwarmingly desperate needs of God—all of these are reaching edification and illumination through *The Sword.* From their conversations, no Christian publication is so avidly read and so often quoted. They count on it—they *read* it through—they *study* its great messages—they *rely* on what they learn.
>
> The forthright, undeviating stand of the editors of *The Sword* is compared with the unseemly compromising of the truth that we find in too many publications of today. In short, *The Sword* is making news, godly news, in this institution.

A life-termer at the Huntsville State Prison in Texas wrote to tell how friends sent him *The Sword of the Lord:*

This paper has done me much good, and I have read every issue for the past three years. Many others here have been brought nearer to our Saviour through your many fine articles and also those of Dr. Appelman. A large amount of good work is done, and prison work would reap a huge reward of saved souls if a stronger effort were made in that direction. So from experience, I would recommend *The Sword of the Lord* as the best way in which to reach prison inmates.

From Georgia a man wrote:

Dr. Rice, I was under the influence of alcohol for four or five years. I thought I couldn't quit drinking; but when the power of God takes hold of you, all things are possible. I want you to know that *The Sword of the Lord* supplied the spiritual strength through the Holy Spirit for me to overcome this awful habit. I am now vice-president of my Sunday school class, Bible quiz reader of my B.T. U., and I enjoy any part of the Lord's work.

During World War II a pastor felt impressed to send copies of *The Sword of the Lord* to men from his church in the service. One of the men's reaction is described as follows:

I can't express in words how much I have enjoyed these papers. I have received many a blessing by reading them. The readings were so interesting, and I could hardly quit reading until I was through. I read them word for word all through. I want to thank you for sending them. I have been enlightened on several things I wasn't sure of by reading these papers.

These sermons by those evangelists and ministers are certainly soul stirring. . . . I am sure I will be living a better life from now on. You may be several hundred miles away from here, but you are doing a work of the Lord right here in our camp. I have let my buddies read them, and I am sure they are thinking more about their souls also.

A young woman whose husband was preparing for the ministry thrillingly reported:

I would like to tell you what *The Sword of the Lord* has meant to me. I was saved three years ago last January 1. I had only been to church once in the previous twelve years when out of curiosity I began to read my Bible, became alarmed about my condition, knelt beside my divan one night and accepted the Lord.

A friend of mine lent me a *Sword of the Lord* she had received from one of her neighbors. It was like manna from Heaven to a three-week-old "babe in Christ." How I did eat it up! It was so simple to read, easy to understand. I subscribed right away for it; and I can truthfully say that, next to my Bible, no literature has helped me to grow in grace so.

We have many Christian papers in our home now, but no other can near measure up. By the way, through your paper I was led to a deeper consecrated life and a desire for soul winning. My husband has been called to preach. . . .

May the Lord bless you in your work. I have the paper now in several Catholic homes. I am praying for the Holy Spirit to make them read it.

A Christian in Canada wrote to say:

I was not interested in saving souls until I was receiving your paper about six months. *Now I can scarcely think of anything else,* for I feel so much of my time has been wasted. . . .

I talk about Jesus so naturally now; no one takes offense; they seem to love it.

*The Sword of the Lord* has made friends in some unusual ways! For example, a friend in Tennessee wrote to say:

I would like for you to know what I think of *The Sword of the Lord.* I was a half-hearted Christian several years ago, not too much concerned about God. But *I found one of your papers in a trash can and read it.* There was a sermon in it about lukewarm Christians. It did me much good.

Today I'm a whole-time worker for my Lord. I'm poor, but have a wonderful Saviour. I don't know how much your paper is but I want to send it to my dad who is not a Christian. I am going to do without my meals one day as he reads lots. I want you to pray that he'll be saved. Please send it to him.

As an illustration of the value of this paper to shut-ins, a lady from South Carolina wrote:

But when *The Sword* comes into my home, it feels just like a visit from Heaven. I can read awhile, then pick it up and read again. There is always something to bless my soul. *I had rather be without food awhile than this paper.* May God bless you . . . .

A Methodist layman in California wrote to tell how his son-in-law, a Bob Jones University student, sent him the paper as a Christmas gift. He added:

> I am now indebted to both of you. I was born and raised a Methodist and have taught in a Sunday school class for 15 years. Methodism lost its evangelism years ago, I think; and your *Sword of the Lord* paper has been one of the most helpful means of my getting my name on the saved list. I am sure my future teaching will show a marked improvement.

A young mother of three children in California wrote to tell how the paper had saved her from modernism and error:

> It came into my life at a time when I needed a clear light on the right path. For many years I have attended a modernistic Methodist church. As you can imagine, this did nothing to put my soul at peace.
>
> About two years ago I became anxious that as a Christian my life did nothing to prove it. At the time I was taking my son to a Seventh-Day Adventist clinic for treatment for an ear condition. Their literature was available free and before I realized it, I was caught in the web of fear. I was afraid to let go of the Adventists as they said that only the people who kept the seventh day were to be saved. My parents, relatives and husband all tried to dissuade me, but I was so caught I couldn't see my way out.
>
> Little by little I began to understand that not by works but by faith alone I would be saved. Then I saw your ad in the *Moody Monthly* and I sent for a copy of your paper. How glad I am that God led me to read your paper and show me that He wants all of us to abide with Him through eternity, not just those who keep the seventh day. Truly, I feel sorry for these people as they are bound by so many laws that serving God is done in fear of Him, not because of love for Him. . . .

A number of ministers and ministerial students have written to tell how *The Sword of the Lord* has saved them from modernism. As an example, a ministerial student in Canada wrote:

> First of all, I want to explain my position. I am a student preparing for the Christian ministry and believe in the statement of faith at the top of your paper. I was saved and grew in grace and felt the call to the ministry sometime later. But how innocent and ignorant I was! I believed everyone believed in the Bible—exactly what it teaches and what I believe. I had

never heard of modernism, but I have now. I am here at one of the leading colleges in Canada which is modern right to the core. They teach religion here all right, but it is not the Christian religion.

It at first got me down and I was going to give up the ministry. I could have become an atheist. Well, I became cold and hardened. I had subscribed to your paper for six months, and I hated it because—well, anything like that was too emotional. I believe you know what modernism can do with a young fellow.

But one day I believe the Lord led me to read a copy of your paper. At once the Holy Spirit told me: "This is what you have always known; this is really the Christian teaching," and immediately the dense and Hell-deceiving fog lifted; I was free from my prison. I read all the back copies, as somehow I saved them, and how the Holy Spirit did marvelously warm my cold heart and at the same time gave me the burden for souls which every real Christian should have.

I read your sermons and have been wondrously built up in the most holy faith; the sermons by the other great men of God have also been a real source of blessing.

Your paper has saved me from this curse of modernism; it has made me useful for the Lord instead of useless. It has increased my faith, boldness and courage and has told me to be a soul winner instead of a soul damner. God has richly blessed me through your paper. I heartily stand beside you in your fight for complete separation from the show, dance, cards and other things of the world. . . .

Before I close this chapter with its testimonials about *The Sword of the Lord,* perhaps I should let you know what some of the greatest preachers in America, past and present, have said about this paper. The late Dr. Walter L. Wilson, long pastor of the Central Bible Church in Kansas City, founder and president of the Kansas City Bible College, and noted Bible conference speaker, declared:

*The Sword of the Lord* is one of the most widely read papers in Christian circles. I find it everywhere I go, and always the comments are favorable.

Personally, I am happy to see it come to my desk. It stirs the heart, refreshes the soul, and increases the zeal for better service to our King.

Dr. Harold L. Lundquist said:

> *The Sword of the Lord* is especially appreciated for its con-
> sistent, faithful and fearless witness for the truth in a world
> where there is endless confusion and compromise.
> The sermons both old and new are excellent.
> I enjoy the paper. I read it regularly with real blessing.

The widely used and greatly blessed Jewish evangelist, Dr.
Hyman J. Appelman, enthused:

> *The Sword of the Lord* is utterly, entirely, scripturally,
> spiritually, evangelistically, sermonically, inspiringly different
> from other periodicals of the same or any other kind, not only
> in the U.S.A., but anywhere in the world. Those who are in
> charge of it, beginning with its matchless editor, Dr. John R.
> Rice, and all of its staff, as well as its contributors, are men and
> women who have been, and still are, at the very forefront of the
> battle for Jesus Christ and the souls of men.
>
> The paper breathes devotion to Jesus Christ, compassion to
> the souls of men. Every issue is a blazing torch of fire, enough
> to set aflame the heart of the coldest, the most backslidden
> Christian, and the farthest-away-from-God sinner. There are
> just no words in my vocabulary to express the depths of my ap-
> preciation and the heights of my commendation for *The Sword
> of the Lord.*

The late C. O. Baptista, long head of the C. O. Baptista Films,
wrote to tell how the paper blessed him when his office was in
Chicago and he read it mornings on the train from Wheaton.
Then he added:

> Since moving our work to Wheaton, I have continued to read
> *The Sword.* I think the good it has done me is tremendous. The
> material is like the best books; but because it comes in news-
> paper form, one is more apt to read more of the good things. I
> find there is hardly a column that the Lord is not exalted and
> the Word of God made more clear.

Evangelist E. J. Daniels, director of "Christ for the World,"
wrote to say:

> I am writing to tell you what a blessing *The Sword of the
> Lord* is to me. I consider it by far the greatest religious weekly
> in America today. Each issue is packed with spiritual manna
> for hungry souls. You give a balanced diet for the soul in almost
> every issue. I sometimes marvel at the way you can find so

much great reading matter to give your subscribers week after week. God is evidently leading you, else you could not do it.

It has been a pleasure for me to get subscribers for you in my meetings. Some have wondered why I boost your paper in my revivals when I have a paper of my own. *But I feel that I cannot do otherwise when I know that your paper will be such a blessing to all who receive it.*

The late Evangelist Joe Henry Hankins commented publicly:

It gives me real joy to commend *The Sword of the Lord* to all Christians everywhere, especially to preachers and evangelists. I consider it the best evangelistic weekly published today. Dr. Rice's sermons and articles are always of the highest caliber and feed one's soul.

The selection of full-length sermons, many times mechanically recorded with illustrations and all, by the leading evangelists and evangelistic pastors of the world, is superb. I know of no other religious periodical which gives its readers such a wealth and variety of fresh, rich and inspiring evangelistic matter.

Dr. W. Herschel Ford, once pastor of the large First Baptist Church at El Paso, Texas, and author of the many *Simple Sermons* books, before his death wrote:

*The Sword of the Lord* is certainly one of the finest Christian publications in America. Everything about it breathes the atmosphere of Bible Christianity and New Testament evangelism. . . .

*The Sword of the Lord* has a world-wide ministry.

I have received letters from many countries around the world commenting on my messages in this paper. I wish that *The Sword of the Lord* could be placed in the hands of every ministerial student in our country. I commend it without reservation.

Dr. Robert G. Lee, late pastor of the Bellevue Baptist Church in Memphis, Tennessee, and three times president of the Southern Baptist Convention, declared:

*The Sword of the Lord* deserves a great increase in the number of subscriptions. When a weekly magazine of such evangelistic fervor and faithfulness to the Word of God is published it should be read by millions.

The bright fire of this ably-edited paper that stands for "the faith once delivered to the saints"—that makes prayerful efforts to win the lost and to build them up in a most holy faith—will be made the brighter and the more far-reaching by a great increase in the number of subscriptions.

Dr. Oswald J. Smith, retired pastor of the largest church in Canada and noted missionary leader, wrote:

> I know of no paper that is reaching the unsaved for Christ like *The Sword of the Lord*. Its messages on salvation are clear and explicit.
>
> I am glad to speak very highly of it because it is the one publication that carries full-length gospel sermons. I know it is eagerly read by ministers everywhere and that God is using it to the salvation of souls.

Dr. William Pennell, pastor of one of the largest churches in Georgia, the Forrest Hills Baptist at Decatur, spoke at a birthday banquet for Sword workers one year and gave ten reasons why he loved *The Sword of the Lord*. Among other things, he said:

> It is not an organization that is self-seeking. It is seeking to glorify and edify the body of Christ. It is seeking to build up churches, not tear them down. It is seeking to aid, not to hinder. It is seeking to reach, not to slap. It is seeking to love and not hate the work of God in churches.

And he testified:

> I would not be on fire for God had it not been for the promotion of *The Sword of the Lord*.

In his quaint and unique way, Dr. Jack Hyles, pastor of one of the world's largest and most influential churches—the First Baptist Church of Hammond, Indiana—described it like this:

> *The Sword of the Lord* is: Daddy being at home during a storm; a hometown paper telling us the happenings of the Fundamentalist family; and a tool through which we may walk with the giants. If one does not subscribe to *The Sword*, there is nothing like it to substitute for it.

Dr. Tom Wallace, pastor of the Beth Haven Baptist Church in Louisville and president of Baptist International Missions, Inc., spoke of his firsthand observation regarding the blessing the magazine has been to missionaries and servicemen in many parts of the world. And about his own church, he declared:

> *The Sword* is a clear voice for fundamentalists and separatists and has been a tremendous personal help to me in pastoring my people over the years. I've found it to be a very effective tool in unifying people. It has been a preacher and teacher to my congregation and many times has guided our church through the issues of the day.
>
> Again and again we have held subscription campaigns. I have personally subscribed for loved ones and friends and have encouraged my people to do the same. I have not been disappointed with the effect of these subscriptions.

Dr. Verle Ackerman, pastor of the huge First Baptist Church of West Hollywood, Florida, spoke of four things that impressed him about *The Sword of the Lord:* the *sermons,* the *stand,* the *separation,* and the *soul winning.* Encouraging others to subscribe, he said:

> We must have this tool at our fingertips at all times to give us courage, strength and vision to fight the battle that is in front of us.

Dr. Parker Dailey, pastor of the Blue Ridge Baptist Temple in Kansas City and vice-president of the Baptist Bible College at Springfield, Missouri, wrote:

> I began pastoring at the tender age of twenty with only one semester of Bible college training, plus a year of secular college work. Dr. Rice's books and his paper, *The Sword of the Lord,* provided me with ideas, encouragement, and instruction. His many quotations from other preachers and his allusions to their work served to help me build a library based upon sound, fundamental writings. His *Soul Winner's Fire* and *Prayer—Asking and Receiving* were especially meaningful to me. Thank God for his ministry.

Dr. John Rawlings, pastor of one of the largest churches in America, the Landmark Baptist Temple in Cincinnati, called *The Sword of the Lord* "the jugular vein of worldwide evangelism," and added:

> *The Sword* was born in the heart of one man; however, that birth did not stop there, but has reached out to touch mul-

titudes of lives as perhaps no other weekly paper has been able to do in the 20th Century.

It is mobile in its ministry, flowing freely like a mighty, life-giving current of cold, sparkling water. It is good for the missionary, the busy pastor, also for the housewife and the young people, for the busy executive, and the laboring man. *The Sword of the Lord* is a life-giving stream giving out, blessing, restoring and encouraging, giving the family of God purpose and direction for their lives. It has every right in the world to claim for itself the motto, "America's Foremost Revival Weekly."

The former pastor of the big Central Baptist Church at Pomona, California, Dr. Ray Batema was introduced to *The Sword of the Lord* while a student at Tennessee Temple University. He explained:

I believe *The Sword* has, next to the Bible, had more influence on my life than any other Christian literature, past or present. . . . I have always appreciated the firm stand for the fundamentals of the Faith taken by *The Sword of the Lord*. Its constant emphasis on soul winning has been a reminder and challenge to keep soul winning first in my ministry. . . . *The Sword* has also been responsible in my life for the constant encouragement and challenge to stand without compromise against worldliness and formalism.

Dr. Truman Dollar, who is pastor of the Kansas City Baptist Temple and vice-president of the Baptist Bible College East in Shrub Oak, New York, testified:

*The Sword of the Lord* is one of the most important fundamentalist publications in America today. Every family that believes in revival, righteous living and soul winning should subscribe.

*The Sword of the Lord* is important to pastors. Each week I delight to read great sermons from leading contemporary pastors and evangelists, as well as the sermons from leaders of the past.

Important news of fundamentalism is always involved. The issues of the day are explored in a rational and biblical way.

*The Sword of the Lord* is important to families. The poetry, inspiration, columns for children, women, pastors' wives, and family devotions are of great importance. Christian literature

for the family is needed. I find that *The Sword* fulfills that
need.

*The Sword of the Lord* is even vital to consumers. The advertising makes available to Christian readers products of interest.

One of the best known preachers in America today is Dr. Jerry
Falwell, pastor of the Thomas Road Baptist Church, founder and
chancellor of Liberty Baptist College, and director of the largest
syndicated telecast of its kind in the world, The Old-Time
Gospel Hour. He glowingly testified as follows:

When I became a Christian in January of 1952, someone
almost immediately gave me a copy of *The Sword of the Lord*. I
was also given one of Dr. John R. Rice's books to read. So, my
spiritual teeth were cut on *The Sword of the Lord* and the
publications of Dr. John R. Rice. I learned fundamentalism
and separatism at his feet.

Through the years, *The Sword of the Lord* has helped me to
develop a correct perspective on many controversial issues.
When I was a very young Christian, I learned the rationale for
my separatist position. I learned why the Hollywood movies are
not acceptable for a believer. I learned why the dance is scripturally wrong. I learned why a child of God should separate
himself from the world. I was already against the things of the
world because my pastor had taught me accordingly. The Holy
Spirit living in me convicted me not to do many of the things I
had done as an unconverted person. However, *The Sword* gave
me, as a young believer, the scriptural premise for all these
positions I have been led to take.

When I finished my work at Baptist Bible College in
Springfield, Missouri, I moved to Lynchburg, Virginia, to
found the Thomas Road Baptist Church. *The Sword of the
Lord* was a great help to this young pastor in those early days
when I found myself preaching four to ten sermons weekly. I
had preached my first sermon two weeks before graduating
from Baptist Bible College. *The Sword of the Lord* became a
source document for good, sound doctrinal teaching and
preaching to my young congregation. . . .

I have been a pastor for nearly a quarter of a century now. I
preach twenty times each week, on the average, and travel
6,000 miles every seven days. My schedule, like that of many
pastors, is very hectic. *The Sword* therefore continues to serve a
great function in my life.

At a glance, I can see what God is doing through other pastors, evangelists, and missionaries worldwide. I can be helped by reading the sermons and the various excellent columns in *The Sword.* The very relevant issues facing Fundamentalism from time to time are fairly and objectively presented in *The Sword.* In other words, I am able to stay current on our world of "fundamentalism and separatism."

Another outstanding pulpiteer, Dr. Tom Malone, chancellor of Midwestern Baptist College and pastor of the Emmanuel Baptist Church in Pontiac, Michigan, gave a glowing testimony, declaring:

I think it was almost forty years ago when my mother, living in Chicago, Illinois, handed me a small package of papers. It was eight or ten of the early issues of *The Sword of the Lord.* I had been in the ministry only six or seven years, and I was searching for every good thing I could find to read to help me in preaching. I literally absorbed those early issues of *The Sword* and have received it weekly ever since. . . .

I am somewhat familiar with the fundamental publications of the past seventy-five years in America. Many of them are no longer extant. I think *The Sword* is the greatest publication in the history of Christianity in America.

*The Sword* is the greatest compilation of Biblical sermons there is in existence. A significant part of the literature of the great Elizabethan period in England was the homilies or sermons which were delivered and published during a period of approximately one hundred years. Surely the most influential Christian literature published in America in the past half century is that of *The Sword of the Lord.* Through *The Sword* you read the sermons of the spiritual giants of the past and feel their heartbeat. Where does one find more of the sermons of Spurgeon, Moody, Sunday, Truett, Bob Jones, Sr., and others? It is staggering to think of the multiplied thousands of preachers who have read these sermons and have been blessed and have used the sermons to preach and win multitudes. The sermons of contemporary giants of the faith also appear every week in *The Sword.*

*The Sword of the Lord* has let us into the heart and soul of the greatest Christian I ever knew, John R. Rice. His position as a Fundamentalist in the middle of the right road has been constantly pictured in the periodical. His sermons, answers to questions, dealing with issues, soul winning, revival, and the promotion of Fundamentalism and Fundamental churches is an insight into the soul of a man who had a spiritual impact on the world.

I recently made *The Sword* subscriptions available to Emmanuel Baptist Church families and Midwestern Baptist College students. I would like to see it go into every home of our large church family and into the hands of every Midwestern student.

Undoubtedly Evangelist Jesse M. Hendley spoke for the majority of evangelists all over America when he testified:

I do commend *The Sword of the Lord* everywhere, without limitation.

It is impossible to read *The Sword of the Lord* without being tremendously stirred to complete surrender and earnest endeavor to win souls to Christ. Without question, this great periodical has been responsible for much of the present-day evangelistic and revival spirit which is sweeping over our nation.

When there were practically no voices crying out, "we can have revival now," the editor, Dr. John R. Rice, was given by the Lord a vision of the resurgence of mass evangelism; and with soul on fire, with bull-dog tenacity, backed by the Word of God, this modern Gideon forced thinking, Bible-taught Christians to seek the Lord for soul-winning power and blessing. This resulted in revivals, first in the hearts of individuals and laymen, then in the churches where these people attended, and finally in great citywide campaigns; and the influence has grown with a spiritual tide until today this paper is found wherever people have an evangelistic spirit.

I find it nearly everywhere I go in the studies of pastors who love the Lord, the Word, and lost souls. I want to commend it heartily to every person who names the name of Christ. It will stir, and keep on stirring, wherever it is read.

When he came to Murfreesboro in 1975 to preach the dedicatory sermon for a new Sword building, Dr. Jack Hyles, pastor of one of the world's largest churches—the year Dr. Rice died they averaged over 26,000 in Sunday school and baptized 6,446—told of the tremendous influence of *The Sword of the Lord,* calling his message, "A Paper That Saved a Nation." When the records are opened in Heaven, this evaluation may prove to be far more truth than poetry.

In closing this chapter with its glowing testimonials, I want to say that *The Sword of the Lord* was a tremendous help in molding my ministry when I was just a young preacher. I believe, under God, it did more to help kindle a holy fire in my bones than any other human instrument. With all my heart and soul I thank God for leading John R. Rice to launch *The Sword of the Lord* on September 28, 1934, and for the fact that it stayed true to the Faith throughout the succeeding years.

*Tens of thousands of preachers across the land and around the world echo a hearty "Amen!" to my sentiments.*

*Chapter 12*

# "What Must I Do to Be Saved?"

*They that sow in tears shall reap in joy. He that goeth forth and weepeth, bearing precious seed, shall doubtless come again with rejoicing, bringing his sheaves with him.*—Psalm 126:5,6.

*But these are written, that ye might believe that Jesus is the Christ, the Son of God; and that believing ye might have life through his name.*—John 20:31.

THE GOSPEL tract which has won more people to Christ than any other in modern times, perhaps, had a very humble beginning. It was written in San Antonio, Texas—dictated to a public stenographer in the midst of the busy press of a revival campaign—and first published in *The Fundamentalist,* the paper edited by Dr. J. Frank Norris. Later the author corrected it, rewrote it, and mimeographed it on sheets of typewriter paper.

Although not nearly as attractive in the mimeographed form as most gospel tracts, God used it to touch many hearts, and scores were saved through its message before it ever enjoyed a regular printing. As a matter of fact, about the time I was writing this book, a man signed a decision slip from one of those mimeographed copies and sent it in. His wife had been a Christian, and after her death he had found the mimeographed sheets among her personal effects. He read it when grieving over the dear wife who had gone to Glory, and was saved. So fifteen or twenty years after it was mimeographed, it did the blessed soul-saving work in the heart of a sinner for which it was prepared.

The mimeographed sheets were so well received and so mightily blessed by God that with a good deal of timidity the author finally raised $75 to have ten thousand copies printed in booklet form. The pamphlet was sixteen pages, had small eight-point type, and was three and a half inches by six inches in size. The first ten thousand copies were soon exhausted, and he began to print more, making minor corrections from time to time. Since the very first edition had the decision form, many thousands of people have written to the author stating that they found Christ through its message. By the time of Dr. Rice's death there had been over 48 million copies of the tract printed—32.9 million in English—and a total of 10,340 conversions reported from the English editions alone.

It had been printed in nearly two score foreign languages, to the author's knowledge, and undoubtedly in several others by missionaries who did not let him know how they were using it. These languages included Spanish (both an American edition as well as an Old World Spanish edition), Indonesian, Portuguese, Italian, German, Syriac, Dutch, Armenian, Danish, French, Japanese (over 8 million copies), Korean, Samoan, Chinese, in Tagalog and Ilongo in the Philippine Islands, and in eight languages in India: Tamil, Telugu, Malayalam, Hindi, Angami, Kanarese, Marathi, and Gujarati. It had also been printed in the Hausa, Kamba and Bangala languages in Africa and the Sinhalese language of Ceylon.

Dr. Rice said to me, "I think the pamphlet is effective for several reasons. First, it uses many, many Scriptures. Second, it is long enough to deal with problems and answer them. Third, the language is very simple, so simple that children read and understand it. This is one reason it translates easily, missionaries tell me. Fourth, the decision form calls for immediate action and often secures that decision."

Since this message, *What Must I Do to Be Saved?* is the most famous of all Dr. Rice's writings, we are including it, complete, under Appendix A at the back of the biography, as indicative of his preaching.

It would be impossible, of course, to print even a good representative portion of the letters received from those who

have been saved through reading *What Must I Do to Be Saved?*
However, it would be unfair to this biography if I did not include
some.

A Congregational minister from Ohio wrote:

> . . .I think *What Must I Do to Be Saved?* is the best printed
> soul winner in existence, for I was saved through reading it in
> 1947. Praise His name!

A pastor in Arkansas wrote requesting one hundred and fifty
copies, then went on to say:

> Some of our men have been using this tract with blessed
> results. I have a Sunday school teacher, a man of forty-five,
> who fifteen months ago was a wicked cross-country truck
> driver. He was handed one of your *What. . . ?* and a Pocket
> Testament League Gospel of John with our church name
> stamped on it. His testimony is that he kept these in his truck
> and would read them as he had time, and he says that the mes-
> sages of these two booklets were used of the Lord to show him
> his condition and need. He is now an ardent, fervent Christian
> and soul winner. Five of his fellow truck drivers have been won
> to Christ and baptized into a fervent soul-winning Baptist
> church as a result of this man's conversion and through the use
> of these tracts.
>
> I just wanted you to share this blessing with us because it
> was your message that the Holy Spirit used to bring conviction
> and repentance to these men.

The secretary-treasurer of Whosoever Heareth, Inc., wrote the
following letter of genuine interest:

> I believe you will be interested to know the wonderful way
> the Lord has used the little pamphlet, *What Must I Do To Be
> Saved?*
>
> Howell H. Smith of Harlingen, Texas, former millionaire
> cowboy who threw away a quarter of a million dollars in 1949-
> 50 in riotous living, was won to the Lord from acute alcoholism
> by Evangelist Clifton W. Brannon of Longview, Texas. Mr.
> Smith had come to hear Evangelist Brannon preach; they were
> later introduced. Mr. Brannon talked with him personally
> without a decision, then he handed him one of Dr. Rice's
> pamphlets on *What Must I Do to Be Saved?* Howell promised
> to read it before retiring. He did and the next day confessed
> Christ.

Before his death, Mr. Smith was witnessing for the Lord all over the Southwest. Everywhere he told publicly how Dr. Rice's *What Must I Do to Be Saved?* explained clearly what Evangelist Brannon had said to him. He praised Dr. Rice wherever he went as did Mr. Brannon, who was an ardent admirer of Dr. Rice.

From North Nigeria, West Africa, a native wrote in his very broken English:

I received your letter and your pamphlet on 1-13-51 with many surprise. As I have gone through it I found myself a lost sinner. Your book has taken up my heart, and I have claimed Jesus as my Saviour.

Some times of rejoicing over the conversions won through this tract are increased because of the circumstances surrounding them. For example, on one occasion a letter was received from a man in Wilmington, Delaware, who had signed and returned the decision blank. Four days after Dr. Rice had written a letter of encouragement and instruction to him, the letter was returned stamped "Deceased." How grateful to God the editor was that this soul had been reached in time through the tract!

Dr. Rice received a letter from David H. Johnson, the general director of The Evangelical Alliance Mission, more popularly known as TEAM. He enclosed a circular prayer letter from two of their missionaries, Rev. and Mrs. John Reid, then added the following personal postscript: "I do not know the exact count of the number of copies the translations of your book gotten out by our Word of Life Press in Japan. However, I do know that they have done a splendid work, and we are all very grateful for what you have done to help us get the Gospel out to the people in Japan."

The prayer letter from the Reids had to do primarily with the account of the conversion of a criminal named Furukoshi-San. The criminal's testimony is quoted as follows:

I was born in a cold village which is Nagano Ken. I had been brought up under the law of my parents; but while I was unaware of it at first, I gradually turned against the love of my parents and sought the companionship of bad friends. I finally turned out to be a man who liked to live in sin.

In the twenty-fourth year of Shoowa (1949), I was put in jail in Saitama Ken, with three accomplices, under the court sentence of robbery. Thus my freedom was deprived both spiritually and bodily. My life in that prison became just like a living-dead carcass. But in that life I recognized my crime which I committed and realized for the first time my sin, and I repented of myself severely. How I desired to escape from that life that nailed my body and soul unmoveable! One day I asked the convict next to me to lend me something to read, if he had it. The booklet which he lent me was entitled: *What Must I Do to Be Saved?* by John R. Rice, who is an evangelist of America. I could not understand the meaning at first. In that booklet was written a verse from the Bible: "All have sinned and come short of the glory of God."

Certainly I am a sinner. I am here owing to the crime which I committed, and I am paying the full price for it. Moreover, where the sinners are destined to go is called *Hell*; how pitiful a stray sinner I am! What must I do? What must I do to be saved?

The Reids' prayer letter did not tell how he found peace and joy through Christ, but stated that he was released from the prison in March, 1952. They commented that they have been working with him for six months and had seen no one in their experience any more "sold out" to the claims of Christ than he. Thank God for this conversion half way around the world through the little tract which had such a humble beginning!

Some friends in a midwestern state wrote:

I want you to know that a young lady, 19 years of age, who is an inmate of the Industrial School at Beloit, Kansas, was gloriously saved two weeks ago. She was a very lovely young girl and graduated from. . .high school a year ago but fell into the hands of a wicked gambler and car dealer. She was apprehended at a house of prostitution. . . .

God laid her heavily on my heart so I wrote her several times and sent her your booklet, *What Must I Do to Be Saved?* . . . She wasn't allowed to answer at that time, but the day she was saved she was allowed to write to me.

She testified so greatly to God's wonderful saving power and how he had lifted her. She begged me to go to her older sister which I had already done and who accepted Jesus, too. She said how clearly the tract made things to her, so I surely wanted you to know. I have sent her more to give to other inmates. Also I gave her sister one and her parents, whose home was broken and relationship still very bad. . . .

A Youth for Christ director in Kansas wrote:

Your booklet, *What Must I Do to Be Saved?* played an important part in the conversion of an airman from Forbes Air Base. His wife was leaving him because of drink; I had been requested to see him. I dealt with him over an hour. . .when I got ready to leave he commented that he had not asked me to come and was not going to be pushed into anything. . .after praying with him I left your booklet with him.

The next day I had to go to Eldorado to speak. He tried to call me after reading your booklet, being under deep conviction. As he read the booklet he wept and remarked to his wife, "Did you know a Man died for me?" The next day he went to a good Bible-preaching church. The preacher asked him if he were saved. He said, "No, but I want to be." That night he was wondrously saved and has been walking with the Lord ever since. He is literally devouring the Word in a manner I have never seen in a new convert before.

From Indianapolis a man wrote:

In the past month I have been attending church services. I have always believed in a Higher Power, but never did I before accept Jesus Christ as my personal Saviour. I just finished reading the little book entitled, *What Must I Do to Be Saved?* After a few moments of meditation I gladly confessed Him as my Saviour. So may I ask that you remember me and pray for me. . . .I am sincere and will try to do whatever God the Father wants me to do. Thank you.

Down in Texas a Baptist preacher wrote to thank the editor for *The Sword of the Lord* and tell what a blessing it had been to him. He added:

I think your little tract, *What Must I Do to Be Saved?* is one of the most effective I have ever seen. My uncle was converted as a result of reading one and now I have sent one to my sister. Please pray for her.

A missionary from Portugal wrote to tell what a blessing two of the articles in *The Sword of the Lord* had been to him. He went on to say:

The day before yesterday I went to a Lisbon church to pick

up tracts. Mr. Fereire, who was in charge, told me that there is a great deal more response to Dr. Rice's booklet, *What Must I Do to Be Saved?* than from any other tract. He is constantly getting letters from people who have signed the page or have copied the page and written in claiming to accept Christ.

From India came a letter from a man saved through an edition of the tract in the Tamil language. His letter, translated, said in part:

> I was born in a Hindu family, and I worshiped Hindu gods till now. But I had no satisfaction. Three months ago I joined the Indian army. After a little wound I was sent to a hospital. A Christian worker visited the hospital and gave me two booklets: *Way to Life* and *What Must I Do to Be Saved?* Being convinced that I am a sinner, I yielded myself to the Lord Jesus and I have changed my name from Raja Ram to Raja. Please pray for me, as my family will certainly persecute me for this new faith.

In Idaho, a man under conviction but not able to grasp in his thinking the simplicity of salvation, saw another man throw the booklet, *What Must I Do to Be Saved?* on the ground. He picked it up, read it, understood the plan of salvation for the first time, then immediately put his faith and trust in Jesus Christ. Another poor lost sinner, a woman in Long Beach, California, was sitting on a sidewalk bench waiting for her bus when she moved her hand and felt something on the bench. She looked down and saw a copy of *What Must I Do to Be Saved?* picked it up and read it, then trusted Christ as her personal Saviour and wrote to say so.

From the Corentyne Coast of British Guiana a man wrote:

> I have read one of your booklets, *What Must I Do to Be Saved?* It enlightened me very much. I was worshiping a goddess by the name of Kalie. I used to offer up goat's blood as a sacrifice to this goddess yearly. In our mother country, India, they (Madres) used to offer up human sacrifice. I was deep in idolatry. I am the only one out of my family who has come out from this heathen worship. I was the most wicked man that Rose Hall Village ever produced, and everybody in the village was afraid of me because I was a notorious drunkard, a gambler; and there were worse acts I used to do.

Praise God, I have accepted Jesus Christ as my personal Saviour; I am saved through His precious blood. Most of the people in this village are Madres and Hindu idol worshipers. British Guiana is a dense country.

I am confessing Christ to others and begging you to please send me a few copies and other Christian literature.

A pastor who wrote to order five hundred copies of the tract said in his letter:

I should also like to report that Mr. I____ C____, formerly owner of the C____ lumber company of D____, Indiana, was saved as a result of reading a copy of the booklet. He united with our church in Owensboro, Kentucky, and was baptized by me. He passed away suddenly a few months ago and I had his funeral. Just thought it might encourage you to know that *What Must I Do to Be Saved?* was responsible for his conversion.

A young airman stationed in Louisiana wrote ordering five thousand copies and said:

We have seen several souls saved here in the A.F. and the *What. . . ?* had a vital part as an instrument through which God spoke. It was a little over four years ago when I read a *What. . . ?* and God set me straight then concerning salvation. Soon after that I made a decision to trust Jesus as my own personal Saviour.

It is extremely difficult to stop quoting from the thousands of glowing testimonials of reported conversions through this popular booklet, *What Must I Do to Be Saved?* However, space absolutely forbids it. Oh, the joy, as my readers can well imagine, which will be Dr. Rice's when he meets all the fruit of his labors "over in the Gloryland."

*Chapter 13*

# The Twentieth Century's
# Mightiest Pen

*And further, by these, my son, be admonished: of making many books there is no end; and much study is a weariness of the flesh.* —Ecclesiastes 12:12.

*In scattering divine literature, we liberate thistledown ladened with precious seed, which, blown by the wind through the Spirit, floats over the world. The printed page never flinches, never shows cowardice; it is never tempted to compromise; it never tires, never grows disheartened; it travels cheaply, and requires no hired hall; it works while we sleep; it never loses its temper, and it works long after we are dead. The printed page is a visitor which gets inside the home and stays there; it always catches a man in the right mood, for it speaks to him only when he is reading it; it always sticks to what it has said and never answers back; and it is bait left permanently in the pool.*

*The printed page is deathless; you can destroy one, but the printers can produce millions more; as often as it is martyred, it is raised again; the ripple started by a given tract and widened down the centuries until it reaches the Great White Throne.* —THE INDIAN CHRISTIAN.

IT IS ONLY after careful research and earnest inquiry that I title this chapter, "The Twentieth Century's Mightiest Pen." At the time of his death, Dr. Rice had more than 200 different titles in print with a combined circulation in excess of 60 million copies, about a third of which were big, clothbound volumes. He wrote a few other booklets, plus one volume of sermons, no longer in print. About a dozen of his books had been translated into at least 37 foreign languages.

It should be added that even these fantastic totals are not complete. No records are available for all the decisions that have been made from Dr. Rice's books which were printed in foreign languages. Too, translation permissions were granted to anyone and everyone who requested them, often with no further reports from the requestee as to how many were printed. And many who did acknowledge the results of a first edition failed to report the reprints.

Before making the claim that Dr. Rice was the leading author of the twentieth century, I wrote to such prominent publishing houses as Moody Press, Broadman Press, Fleming H. Revell Company, Zondervan Publishing House, Baker Book House and others, asking them to give me the combined circulation of their leading authors. Those mentioned by name very graciously replied, giving accurate statistics as far as possible. Some few others did not reply. However, of those replying, none had an author whose writings had reached a combined circulation anywhere at all comparable to that of Dr. Rice.

As an illustration of how his writings compare with other popular authors, permit me to quote from Dr. E. Schuyler English's excellent biography of Dr. H. A. Ironside. Dr. Ironside's writings were voluminous and, I suppose, blessed the hearts of hundreds of thousands just as they have my own. Again and again I have been thrilled with the richness and sweetness of the gems of grace his pen has produced. In my own mind I thought him to be perhaps the leading writer of our age. Yet when I checked in the book, *Ordained of the Lord,* I read:

> The sale of Ironside's books has been remarkable. About one quarter of a million copies of his expository writings have been distributed, and more than one hundred fifty thousand volumes on miscellaneous subjects. Of the smaller works, the sales of booklets and pamphlets approach three hundred fifty thousand, and one hundred fifty thousand of his various tracts have been sent forth. . . . Sales number more than nine hundred thousand, and this does not take into consideration foreign publications, as by Pickering and Inglis, Ltd., London and Glasgow.*

Just as with his work as editor of *The Sword of the Lord*—for which he never received a penny in salary—so Dr. Rice's writings were a labor of love for his Lord, and one hundred per cent of all the royalties and profits went directly into the Lord's work. Not only so, but he contributed many thousands of dollars of his own money to help get out this literature.

By way of example, during World War II his booklets were very popular with the servicemen and servicewomen. Chaplains in both European and Pacific theaters wrote asking for thousands of dollars' worth of them free. No honest request was refused. Just one of those many requests came from the Chaplain General of the American forces in Europe, after the surrender, requesting over $5,000 worth of booklets. The request far exceeded available money, so he and Mrs. Rice prayerfully sought the will of God. Finally, agreeing together that they had the mind of the Lord, they mortgaged their home in Wheaton for $6,000 and put the money into free literature. Then, month by month as the payments were due, they paid the money out of their own pocket until years later the mortgage had been liquidated.

Commenting about it in his book, *All About Christian Giving,* he said:

> But hundreds of men in our armed services wrote to say how they found Christ as Saviour through these booklets. A chaplain on one transport, the *Marine Devil,* told how more than one hundred boys found Christ on the crowded ship in one crossing. Later word came that missionaries DeShazer and Glenn Wagner had won to Christ the Japanese Naval Commander who had led the attack of three hundred and sixty planes on the American fleet at Pearl Harbor, December 7, 1941. They went over my little booklet, *What Must I Do to Be Saved?* with him. Then this man took that message in the little booklet we have spread by the millions and gave it on his lecture tour to one group of eleven hundred men!
>
> I have sweet assurance that in the long, beautiful eternity of blessing in Heaven I will have sweet fellowship with many souls who were kept out of Hell because of money that we gave to get out the Gospel, which resulted, from the human viewpoint, in their coming to Christ for salvation.

Several years ago Dr. Rice told me he learned early in his ministry the secret of getting through giving. As Proverbs

11:24,25 says: "There is that scattereth, and yet increaseth; and there is that withholdeth more than is meet, but it tendeth to poverty. The liberal soul shall be made fat: and he that watereth shall be watered also himself." So he discovered that the more he gave his literature away, the more God blessed the sale of them to others.

He told me how, when his sixty-four-page booklet, *Bible Facts About Heaven*, first came from the press, he was speaking over WMBI, the Moody Bible Institute station in Chicago. Feeling the clear leading of God about it, he obtained permission from the program director to offer it free to any who would write in and request it. So many requests began pouring into the radio department that they had to ask another department of the Institute to take over the mail and the job of sending out the booklet. He had only printed five thousand copies of the booklet and was compelled to order another five thousand from the printers immediately. During the two weeks a total of seven thousand copies were mailed out free at a cost to him of hundreds of dollars.

"But," he smilingly told me with that characteristic twinkle in his eye, "then the cash orders began to come in. Hundreds of people have found Christ through its message. It has had an amazing circulation—there have been over four hundred and fifty thousand copies printed—and it is a book we have not needed to especially advertise."

One of the outstanding characteristics of Dr. Rice's writings, aside from the heart-warming plainness and simplicity of speech, has been the remarkable number of conversions from them. There had been 22,923 people write to say they trusted Christ as a result of one of his books, booklets, or messages in *The Sword of the Lord* by the time of his death. This does not include the thousands reported saved through foreign translations—or the tens of thousands saved in his crusades and through his radio and television ministries.

Not at all unusual was the incident in Oklahoma, as he stood by the book table in one of his meetings, when a woman walked up and pointed to the tract, *What Must I Do to Be Saved?* saying, "That booklet won my brother to Christ!" Immediately a man nearby spoke up, pointing to the booklet, *Rebellious Wives and Slacker Husbands,* saying, "My brother and his wife were separated, had been separated two weeks, and were applying for a divorce. I got this booklet for them and both of them read it. They went back together, confessed their sins to each other, and now their home is wonderfully happy."

At the close of this book, in Appendix C, you will find a list of his writings and their total circulation at the time of his death. I would like, of course, to give many testimonials of the blessing resulting from each of his books and booklets, but because of the number of titles involved it would be impossible.

Instead, permit me to quote from an early issue of *The Sword of the Lord,* written by Dr. Rice, telling how he got into the book business. Remember that he was still in a pastorate in Dallas at this time and his writings were very limited compared to the present, but I think it will show the heart attitude of the man and thereby serve the purpose of this biography. The title of that article in the July 10, 1936, issue of *The Sword of the Lord* was, "The Blessings of a Gospel Book, Bible House." He said:

> Paul used every means possible in getting out the Gospel. He held revivals; he trained young preachers; he wrote letters that are now books of the New Testament, and probably many others. He organized churches, taught the converts, raised money for the poor saints, and was the most successful of all foreign missionaries. He preached to Jews and Gentiles, to the rich and poor, in jail chained to a soldier, and to kings on their thrones.
>
> In I Corinthians 9:19-22 Paul said about this matter:
>
> *"For though I be free from all men, yet have I made myself servant unto all, that I might gain the more.*
>
> *"And unto the Jews I became as a Jew, that I might gain the Jews; to them that are under the law, as under the law, that I might gain them that are under the law;*
>
> *"To them that are without law, as without law, (being not without law to God, but under the law to Christ,) that I might gain them that are without law.*
>
> *"To the weak became I as weak, that I might gain the weak: I am made all things to all men, that I might by all means save some."*

Paul was a marvelous soul winner, and the reason was that he took every possible opportunity to get out the Gospel. He said, "I am made all things to all men, that I might *by all means save some.*" Paul used all the means at his command to spread the Gospel, and so should we.

For some years this pastor has felt the need to use every means possible to spread the Gospel to every creature as Jesus commanded. For that reason, I have held revivals, taught in Bible conferences, preached in jails and on the street, and at an enormous expense preached the Gospel to unnumbered thousands, likely millions, of radio listeners on a dozen different stations in Fort Worth, Dallas, Chicago, Wichita Falls, Abilene, Beaumont, Akron, Oklahoma City, San Antonio and Binghamton.

Several years ago some pastors were greatly impressed with my sermon, *Can a Saved Person Ever Be Lost?* and urged me to put it in print. With a great deal of hesitation I wrote the sermon out and first scattered several thousand copies in mimeograph form. The demand was greater than I had expected. Then I found that the great mass of Christians knew nearly nothing of the Bible promises concerning the return of Christ and His reign on earth. So I wrote down *Christ's Literal Reign on Earth from David's Throne at Jerusalem.* These two mimeographed sermons seemed to be greatly used of God; and when I got $150, I had them printed in booklet form! My fears and trembling were turned to joy when the booklets proved helpful to many and they were ordered from far and near.

A young man in Fort Worth, a Seventh-Day Adventist, wrote me saying he had heard my Bible teaching over the radio and was impressed with the simple clearness and sincerity of it. He was greatly troubled, he said, over the Sabbath question and asked if I would make a study of the question and write a sermon or Bible study on this subject. I felt led to follow his suggestion, and the little booklet, *Sunday or Sabbath, Which Should Christians Observe?* was the result. It has helped many understand the Sabbath question, has released a number of Seventh-Day Adventists from the bondage of the law, and I am told by a number of preachers that it has greatly helped to clarify the typical meaning of the Sabbath and the Lord's Day and to show that our Sunday is not a Sabbath at all and that Christians are not under bondage to keep a Sabbath since we have a far better day, the Lord's Day, to observe voluntarily. Dr. H. A. Ironside has printed this booklet in *The Moody Church News,* and it has blessed many in the pamphlet form.

Next came the most popular of all my booklets, *What Must I*

*Do to Be Saved?* which has been translated and printed in 3 languages, and of which some 200,000 copies, we estimate, have been distributed. We have the names of over 500 people who have trusted Christ as Saviour through reading this booklet, and decision slips have been returned by readers who claimed Christ as Saviour from the English, Armenian and Spanish editions. Multiplied thousands of copies of this booklet have been distributed free. Fourteen thousand copies were given away, for instance, in ten days at the fat stock show at Fort Worth.

After *What Must I Do to Be Saved?* came *Speaking With Tongues, Is It the Bible Evidence of the Baptism of the Holy Ghost?* It was the answer to the Pentecostal doctrine of speaking in tongues and has done great good. Friends in Chicago had an extra edition of several thousand copies printed for distribution there. It has helped many Christians see that what they need is not tongues or any other fanatical manifestation, but the real power of the Holy Spirit in life and witnessing to win souls; that Christians should seek not to speak with tongues, but should covet rather to prophesy, and that soul-winning power is the Bible evidence of the baptism or filling of the Holy Spirit.

*Bible Baptism* with sixty-four pages was completed after long Bible study and included material found in Chicago University library and Moody Bible Institute library that was invaluable. I remember that the first printing cost me $364. But word has come from many who were baptized because of it. A Canadian preacher wrote, "I have just baptized nine who read your booklet on baptism. Send me another $1 worth for I know a number of others who will be baptized just as soon as I can get them to read your book."

In the midst of my first revival in Dallas, which lasted fourteen weeks and ended with a newborn church of 300 members, I wrote *Rebellious Wives and Slacker Husbands*—on the Christian home. My booklet on *Hell, What the Bible Says About It* grew out of a series of sermons on Hell in which my own heart was stirred and broken over sinners.

Next came the booklet, *The Second Coming of Christ in Daniel,* then *Bible Lessons on Revelation,* concluding the study of my five years' course of correspondence lessons through the Bible (the other books had all been put in mimeograph form). Later the *Bible Lessons in I Corinthians* were put in print. Then *The Church That God Blesses and Why,* telling the story of God's blessings on our church in Dallas. *Be Ye Not Unequally Yoked Together With Unbelievers* was the outgrowth of my study of the lodge question and modernism and what Christians should do about them. Then *Unchristian Christian Science* is a reprint of some articles in *The Sword of the Lord* on the unscriptural heresy of Christian Science.

When Raymond Hamilton was electrocuted, I preached the following Sunday night on the subject, "Crime, Capital Punishment, the Wages of Sin and Deathbed Repentance." God so blessed the sermon that many were saved. The next day I dictated it in full at one sitting, and the booklet has gone into the hands of every sheriff in Texas, to two hundred members of the Dallas police force and to thousands of others—everybody else who would write for it. Taken down stenographically as preached is *The Dance—Child of the Brothel, Sister of Drunkenness, Lewdness, and Divorce, the Mother of Lust—A Road to Hell!* The language is colloquial, the sentences sometimes broken, sometimes awkward but always positive. The language is not that of the quiet study but of the preacher under white heat before a great congregation.

A large book, *The Coming Kingdom of Christ,* has just been printed.

That is part of the story of how I got into the book business!

## HOW GOD HAS BLESSED THESE BOOKLETS

There can be no doubt of the blessings of God upon these booklets of mine. Two of them particularly, *What Must I Do to Be Saved?* and *Hell, What the Bible Says About It,* have resulted in people being saved, altogether several thousand. That is proof enough. But each booklet was written for a particular purpose and has abundantly proven itself pleasing to God.

Rev. L. O. Engelmann translated *What Must I Do to Be Saved?* into Spanish, and it has been broadcast in Mexico by him and other missionaries. He also rewrote the book on *Hell* in Spanish and tells me that from these and other like books he has received reports of some 600 professions of faith.

A Baptist minister in Sweden wrote asking permission to print and publish in the Swedish language part of my book, *Bible Baptism.* Sunday school teachers, mothers and jailors particularly have written for my book on *The Electrocution of Raymond Hamilton.* On the other hand, preachers seem to be more interested in *The Church That God Blesses and Why,* and numerous congregations have been founded on the simple plans which God has so greatly blessed in Dallas and which are discussed in this book. . . .

## IS IT RIGHT TO SELL BOOKS IN A CHURCH HOUSE?

For many years I have been selling booklets (and giving away many more) in revival services. Only God knows the labor and expense I have had, and likewise only He knows the joy it gives to get out the Gospel. There cannot be a shadow of a doubt of the results.

"Is it right to have a book store in a church house?" you ask. That depends entirely on the kind of a bookstore and the way it is carried on. If a preacher preaches only for money, then he is wrong. Likewise, if a bookstore is run only for money, then that is wrong. But if the preacher preaches to get out the Gospel, then the laborer is worthy of his hire and should be paid for his preaching; and there is no wrong in that. So if a bookstore is run to get out the Gospel and people buy the books, then there is no wrong in that.

When Jesus drove the money changers and merchants out of the temple He said, "My house is the house of prayer: but ye have made it a den of thieves" (Luke 19:46). He made a whip and drove out those who sold doves and oxen in the temple and said, "Make not my Father's house an house of merchandise." (John 2:16).

Certainly the house of God should not be a den of thieves, but a house of prayer. If a bookstore is to be run by thieves or crooked principles, then of course it ought not to be in the church house. Incidentally, it ought not to be anywhere else. Nobody ought to have a den of thieves anywhere, in the church or out.

The man who lives to make money ought not to carry on his business in the church house. But it is equally true that he ought not to carry it on anywhere else, for the love of money is the root of all evil; and when one's heart is set primarily on moneymaking, he is an idolater. Idolaters ought to be driven out of the house of God, but their idolatry does not please God anywhere else. Actually, the temple is no more.

The New Testament says nothing about church houses, and New Testament churches had none. They met in the open air, or in private homes, or in the street, or wherever they could. Jesus explained to the woman of Samaria that true worship of God never is to be carried on in any particular temple, but in the spirit, in the heart. The human body of every Christian is now the temple of God on earth. Jesus said,

*"Woman, believe me, the hour cometh, when ye shall neither in this mountain, nor yet at Jerusalem, worship the Father.*

*"Ye worship ye know not what: we know what we worship: for salvation is of the Jews.*

*"But the hour cometh, and now is, when the true worshippers shall worship the Father in spirit and in truth: for the Father seeketh such to worship him.*

*"God is a Spirit: and they that worship him must worship him in spirit and in truth."*—John 4:21-24.

The important matter is not now any house but the heart. A home, a warehouse, a theater building, a street corner, a tent or a brush arbor—all these are just as truly the house of God, when used for real worship by spiritually-minded Christians, as the finest temple in the land. God is not now concerned primarily with houses; He is concerned with men's hearts.

In Acts 17:24 Paul declared to the superstitious Athenians, "God that made the world and all things therein, seeing that he is Lord of heaven and earth, dwelleth not in temples made with hands."

A plasterer finishes the walls of a church house and is paid for his honest labor. That is not making the house of God a house of merchandise. A preacher preaches the Gospel, and the people in their offerings provide for his needs. The money is brought, bills are changed, and yet that does not make it a house of money changers nor a den of thieves. So when a Scofield Bible or one of Moody's sermons is sold in a bookstore or in a church house, it is not desecrating the house of God.

Sunday morning, June 28th, the Fundamentalist Baptist Church voted unanimously to provide room for The Sword Book Room under Mrs. Ridgway's direction. As soon as possible, a prominent store building should be secured on Jefferson Street. More Bibles and good Christian books could be sold there over the counter in a retail shopping district; but a church house is a mighty good place to get out the Gospel, and we ought to get it out like Paul. So I sell books along with revivals, radio preaching, religious papers and personal work that, like Paul, "I might by all means save some."

It would be hard to say which book was Dr. Rice's personal favorite. Like most authors, if you had asked him his preference, he probably would have given the title of the latest from his pen. Yet if I were to hazard a guess, I would say he was the most excited about the huge 416-page doctrinal study, *Our God-breathed Book—THE BIBLE*. He believed explicitly and implicitly in a verbally inspired, eternal, infallible, inerrant

Scripture, and much of his fight for the Faith over the years related to this, either directly or indirectly. Since he believed in word-for-word inspiration, some falsely and unfairly accused him of holding to "mechanical dictation," a term he considered slander. Dr. Rice had high hopes for the usefulness of this excellent study on the Word of God, and it has, indeed, benefited a great host of people.

Other best sellers from his pen, noting the number of copies in circulation at the time of his death, included *Prayer—Asking and Receiving* (362,413); *THE HOME: Courtship, Marriage and Children* (254,196); *Hell! What the Bible Says About It* (352,744); *Can a Saved Person Ever Be Lost?* (371,822); *The Power of Pentecost* (47,172); *Bible Facts About Heaven* (451,493); *Lodges Examined by the Bible* (164,233); *The Backslider* (232,763); and *The Soul-Winner's Fire* (141,287). These totals are for editions in English only and do not include translations in other languages.

The story of Dr. Rice's printed ministry would not be complete without at least a brief reference to the work released posthumously, the John R. Rice Reference Bible. Mr. Sam Moore, president of Thomas Nelson, the world's largest publisher of Bibles, contacted Dr. Rice in mid-1977 about the feasibility of preparing a completely new reference Bible. Talking about it in his "Editor's Notes" in the September 16, 1977, issue of *The Sword of the Lord*, Dr. Rice wrote:

> Mr. Sam Moore, President of Thomas Nelson (Bible) Publishers, came to see us more than a month ago and asked me to undertake writing notes for a new reference Bible, somewhat after the pattern of the Scofield Reference Bible. The Scofield Bible was the best reference Bible in the world and has been enormously useful. However, in some places it is too dispensational. It left the historic position of Spurgeon, Chapman, Moody, Torrey, and Bill Sunday, etc., for the Plymouth Brethren position about the Holy Spirit.
>
> I feel inadequate for the task, and it is an enormous task. And yet it may be that God wants the long years of study, all the digging, memorizing, all the writing on doctrinal answers to Bible questions, deeply preserved in simple form in a reference Bible for the use of multitudes hereafter. So I am undertaking

> it prayerfully. . . . We pray that God may breathe upon us from
> Heaven as we try to do a permanent work to bless thousands.

Dr. Rice was preeminently qualified for a work of this nature. About a half-century before undertaking this project he had been asked to prepare lessons covering the entire Bible, Genesis to Revelation, for Sunday school teachers. From this evolved a series of correspondence courses used in conjunction with his pastorate and his wide radio ministry. Added to this was the immense amount of research and study involved in a lifetime of counseling and answering questions posed by radio listeners, magazine readers and individuals in his congregations. Too, Dr. Rice had written major commentaries on Genesis and seven major New Testament books. His insight into the Word of God, both from devotional and theological viewpoints, was unsurpassed. And then there was his divinely-given knack of "putting the cookies on the lower shelf," a unique ability to express truth in the language of the common people.

Dr. Rice spent about two and one-half years working on this project, and it was nearly four years before it became available to the public. In his "Editor's Notes" for November 23, 1979, he expressed gratitude for the completion of his part, saying,

> I thank God He let me live long enough to prepare a reference
> Bible, putting in this permanent form help on Scriptures all
> through the Bible, the result of many, many years of study,
> preaching and answering questions, in prayerful mediation
> with the Spirit's leadership.

If the original planned publication date had been met, Dr. Rice would have seen the fruit of his labor in its finished form. However, numerous delays, so common in the printing business, pushed it back repeatedly; and it was about two months after his death before it was finally released. The initial printing was 60,000 copies, which sold out in less than 6 months, and the publisher expects this unique reference Bible to do much good. Indeed, it was a fitting "crowning work" from one who had made the Word of God his very life.

Let me close this chapter by quoting from *The Autobiography of Charles H. Spurgeon,* compiled from his diary, letters and records by his wife and private secretary. Dr. Rice's ministry, like Spurgeon's, if Jesus tarries, will live on for centuries. Mrs. Spurgeon wrote about the mightiest pen of the nineteenth century:

> It is impossible to estimate the total number of volumes of Mr. Spurgeon's works that have been issued in this country, in the United States, and in many other lands in which they have

**This ancient Crusader's Sword was presented to Editor John R. Rice by his brother Dr. Bill Rice, on the 25th anniversary of THE SWORD OF THE LORD in 1959**

been translated into foreign languages. Many millions of copies must already have been sold; and, although it is now eight years since he was "called home," there is, apparently, no diminution in the demand for them. Indeed, the many new works from his lips and pen published since his promotion to higher service, the still larger number of reprints or extracts from his writings, and the ever-increasing circulation of his sermons, make it almost certain that his publications are distributed even more widely now than they were during his lifetime on earth, while testimony to their usefulness is constantly being received from all quarters of the globe.

It may, therefore, be concluded that, great as was his influence in the pulpit, his power through the press is not a whit less; and there seems to be no valid reason why his testimony to the truth should not be continued by means of the printed page, until the Lord Himself returns.

## Chapter 14

# Sword Conferences on Evangelism

*And he gave some. . .evangelists. . . .*—Ephesians 4:11.

*And Moses said unto him, Enviest thou for my sake? would
God that all the Lord's people were prophets, and that the Lord
would put his spirit upon them!*—Numbers 11:29.

JOHN R. RICE was not only an evangelist himself, but in the
spirit of a Moses he would have been willing to make all of the
Lord's people evangelists, if possible, to bring about real revival
in his generation. The greater portion of his life was dedicated to
raising up evangelists and bringing back revival.

As previously related, he remained as pastor of the Fundamentalist Baptist Church, later the Galilean Baptist Church, until
early 1940 when he entered again into a full-time revival
ministry. In April of that year he moved to Wheaton, Illinois, in
order to be near Chicago, the train and plane center for
nationwide travel. Wheaton was selected principally because it
had a good Christian academy and college which would help in
his daughters' education. Then, too, downtown Chicago was only
25 miles away and readily accessible from Wheaton.

More and more his heart became burdened about the lack of
evangelism, the coldness and deadness of the churches, the indifference of both pastors and people, and the trend toward modernism in schools and denominations. One night in a Y.M.C.A. on
the south side of Chicago, the burden became so heavy he stayed
on his face before the Lord until two o'clock in the morning,
definitely committing himself to God to bring back mass
evangelism and citywide campaigns to America. To help in that

matter, he set up special Sword Conferences on Evangelism in various strategic centers.

As far as I can tell, the first of these conferences was held at the Bethany Reformed Church in Chicago, where Dr. Harry J. Hager was pastor. The conference was sponsored by *The Sword of the Lord,* and speakers included Dr. Oswald J. Smith, Dr. Joe Henry Hankins, Dr. H. A. Ironside, Dr. P. W. Philpott, Dr. Robert J. Wells, Professor Talmage Bittekofer, Evangelist George Stephens, Dr. John R. Rice, and the host pastor, Dr. Hager.

Professor Elbert Thurwalden Tindley, the famous Negro singer, and his wife helped in the music. People came to the conference from Illinois, Indiana, Wisconsin, Michigan, Iowa, Missouri, Kansas, Texas, and other places; and much good was done. A vision of what could result from conferences such as these was seen by Dr. Rice, and he began making plans for others.

In 1945 a large conference on revival and soul winning was sponsored by *The Sword of the Lord* at Winona Lake, Indiana. Speakers included Evangelists Hyman J. Appelman, Jesse M. Hendley, Joe Henry Hankins, Rolfe Barnard, Robert J. Wells, Sam Morris, Bob Jones, Sr., G. P. Comer, B. R. Lakin and others. Music was led by J. Stratton Shufelt and Professor and Mrs. Tindley. Tremendous good was done and much enthusiasm kindled. I remember how challenged I was at this conference—a young evangelist just two years out of seminary—when my wife and I attended. Six of the evangelists, Drs. Rice, Jones, Appelman, Hendley, Wells and Hankins, pledged themselves to work together to bring back nationwide revival crusades. They settled on a code of ethics and agreed to try to unite Bible-believing churches in such campaigns.

Other conferences were held at Winona Lake in 1946 and 1947. The attendance at these conferences was the largest of any meetings at Winona Lake, with the possible exception of the Bible conference itself. Yet, following 1947, Dr. Rice was notified that he and his team were not welcome back for other conferences on those grounds, established and made famous by the same Billy Sunday-type evangelism they were seeking to restore to America. Years later, deciding they wanted the crowds Sword conferences attracted, Winona begged him to return. Dr. Rice declined.

By this time Youth for Christ was beginning to make its impact upon the nation. Since the work of this organization was interdenominational and evangelistic, there was quite naturally a real connection between them and the interdenominational work of mass evangelism in citywide campaigns. Sometimes they worked together and sometimes separately, but each made its own impact on evangelism.

From two principal sources—first, from Bob Jones University where there was great emphasis on soul winning and revival, and second, from among Youth for Christ workers—God began to raise up many evangelists. Among these were Jack Shuler, Merv Rosell, Billy Graham, T. W. Wilson, Bill and Elmer Piper, Torrey Johnson, Eddie Martin, and many, many more. Although the leadership did not encourage full-time evangelists, the Southern Baptist Convention, because of its emphasis on revival and soul winning, also turned out many remarkable evangelists, such as Hyman Appelman, Joe Henry Hankins and Jesse Hendley.

During the latter part of Dr Rice's ministry, his main concern, apart from the editorship of *The Sword of the Lord,* was these conferences on evangelism. Dr. Jack Hyles, Dr. Lee Roberson, Dr. Beauchamp Vick, Dr. Tom Malone, Dr. Jerry Falwell, Dr. Bill Rice, Dr. Curtis Hutson, and many others were active with him in conferences which reached thousands of preachers and did much good in stirring revival fires. If you could visualize one hundred preachers, for example, coming from one hundred scattered areas to a Sword Conference on revival and soul winning, hearing the Word preached with power and anointing, getting their own hearts ablaze, then returning to those one hundred scattered areas and starting revivals in each of them, perhaps you will see why Dr. Rice considered this type of ministry so important and worthy.

One colleague suggested to me that perhaps it was the price Dr. Rice paid in his stand against the compromise of Billy Graham, detailed later in our book, that caused God to so bountifully bless his later conferences on evangelism. There is no doubt that his stand *did* hurt tremendously. The circulation of *The Sword of the Lord* dropped at least one-third almost immediately after the break with Graham, and the climb back to its original position—and beyond—was a long, hard, difficult haul. Yet through it all Dr. Rice remained cheerful, confident and enthusiastic.

God, once again, gave him His hundredfold—this time in the form of highly successful conferences on evangelism that changed the ministries of hundreds of preachers and, in turn, put the Fundamentalist movement back on the map to stay.

A struggling young minister came to a Sword Conference from his little church in California and got a vision of what could be done. He made holy vows, then returned to Pomona and built the Central Baptist Church of that city into one of the leading soul-winning centers on the West Coast. One year Ray Batema baptized 65, the next 213, the next over 400, the next over 800, then over 1,600 the following year!

Then there was the full-time mailman and part-time hardshell Baptist preacher who mothered a handful of twenty people in an Atlanta suburb. In his postal deliveries one day he noted a copy of *The Sword of the Lord* and an announcement about a Sword Conference right there in Atlanta. Unable to believe the fantastic claims being made for the ministries of the speakers, he determined, like the queen of Sheba regarding Solomon's temple, to go and see for himself if these things were so. That conference revolutionized the life of young Curtis Hutson, starting a flame that has never been extinguished. He returned to his "little flock" a new preacher; and when he resigned in 1977 to enter full-time evangelism, the Forrest Hills Baptist Church was one of the largest churches in the State of Georgia! Dr. Hutson later became the president of the Sword of the Lord Foundation and Dr. Rice's successor as editor of *The Sword of the Lord.*

A young Southern Baptist pastor in Florida, a graduate of liberal Stetson University, so discouraged in the ministry he was ready to quit, went to a Sword Conference and had his heart touched. He spent one night on a raft, having a prayer meeting and making holy vows to God, then returned to Florida to build one of the largest churches in that State, baptizing thousands and later launching Trinity Baptist College. The ministry of Dr. Bob Gray and his Trinity Baptist Church in Jacksonville is a tribute to what Dr. Rice's Sword Conferences accomplished.

Admittedly, these are outstanding examples, but they are illustrative of what has been accomplished many-fold on a smaller scale. And in the cases cited, perhaps it is only that greater time has elapsed, enabling us to see the picture more accurately.

Who can tell what will result from the tremendous conferences Dr. Rice led in the 1970s? When an effort to jointly sponsor a great conference with other groups fell through, colleagues convinced Dr. Rice to do it alone; and the National Conference on Soul Winning and Revival at the Indianapolis Convention Center in August of 1974 resulted. Over 6,400 packed the auditorium for the opening service on Monday night to hear Dr. Rice and Dr. Jack Hyles. The crowd was even larger the following night when Dr. Tom Wallace and Dr. Jerry Falwell preached—and the same tempo continued for a solid week, with over 6,000 in attendance on Sunday night to hear the final message by Dr. Hyles. Only once, on Saturday, did the attendance drop below 5,000 for an evening service.

Even the daytime sessions were well attended. As many as 3,200 assembled in the morning, and over 4,000 were present one afternoon to hear Dr. Hyles deliver his famous two-hour lecture on soul winning; then they fanned out over the area to witness for Christ to the lost.

The following year the National Conference was conducted at the Dallas Convention Center in Texas, and over 6,100 jammed the auditorium for the first evening session. Unlike the Indiana conference which covered seven days, this one started on Sunday afternoon with a message by Dr. Jerry Falwell and closed on Wednesday night with messages by the late Dr. G. Beauchamp Vick and Dr. Rice.

A Sunday afternoon through Friday night format was decided upon in 1976 when the National Conference convened in the Atlanta Civic Center. The opening night session saw over 5,400 present, and no evening service had less than 3,100 in attendance, with nearly 4,000 there for the final service on Friday night.

In 1977 the National Conference went to Michigan for a Sunday afternoon through Friday night affair at the huge Cobo Arena. There were over 5,000 present on the opening Sunday night and in excess of 4,100 on the closing Friday night. One feature of this Detroit conference was the televising of Dr. Rice's Wednesday night message, "You Must Be Born Again!" for later national prime time showing. At the close of the message, as people were streaming down the aisles of the huge arena to claim Christ, Dr. Rice turned to Dr. Ron English and said, weeping, "This is the way it used to be in great citywide campaigns." And Ron said later, "For a moment I felt like I was with the young evangelist who blazed revival trails all over America." The one-hour program was aired on 160 stations, and over 19,000 people wrote or phoned (14,353 wrote; 4,729 called) the Sword offices for the free book offered at the time, *Born Again, A Know-So Salvation;* and there were 871 known professions of faith in Jesus Christ through this effort. That telecast was later made into a film for viewing in churches and is still available.

In the final three years before Dr. Rice's death, five more National Conferences were conducted. In 1978, some months after Dr. Rice's first heart attack, the conference assembled in the huge Murphy Center Arena on the campus of Middle Tennessee State University at Murfreesboro. In 1979, conferences were held in both Columbus, Ohio, and Birmingham, Alabama. Two were held the last year of his life: the first in Wichita, Kansas, and the final one—when Dr. Rice was in a wheelchair most of the time—consisted of a return visit to the Civic Center in Atlanta.

In addition to these major conferences, Dr. Rice and others continued to hold many two-day mini-conferences which carried the same impact but reached smaller numbers, of course.

Perhaps an indication of the value these conferences of the '70s played in American fundamentalism can be seen in baptismal statistics. In mid-1966 Dr. Rice set out to discover how many churches had baptized as many as 200 people the previous year. He could only find 20, twelve of which were Southern Baptist in denominational affiliation. A decade later, in the mid-1970s, *The Sword* published a list of pastors and churches baptizing 200 or more. Most, but not all, were Baptist churches; and this time there were 36 Southern Baptists and 80 independent Baptists. Three churches had baptized over 2,000, and Dr. Jack Hyles had baptized 7,273. The 123 churches combined had baptized 54,435 precious souls!

In mentioning Dr. Rice's ministry through Sword Conferences, possibly note should be made also of the Women's Jubilees he inaugurated. Feeling a burden for the failure of American homes, even in Christian circles, Dr. Rice set up meetings for ladies only in different sections of the country. Speakers included his wife and his six daughters, plus other influential and greatly-used women such as Mrs. Lee Roberson and Mrs. Jack Hyles. Dr. Rice also spoke to the women on timely themes of special interest to them, and a "princess" was crowned (along with her court). Only eternity can properly evaluate what it did in the lives of women who attended. Some six or eight of these conferences were conducted every year, drawing literally thousands of women, and attendance was well over 1,000 at several of the rallies.

We think it is safe to evaluate the conferences—both those on evangelism geared especially for preachers and the Jubilees for ladies—as doing more permanent good than even his great citywide crusades of the earlier days. Oh, that the breath of Heaven in kindred endeavors might be upon others today to bring *real revival* back to America once again!

## Chapter 15

# "... And My House"

*...but as for me and my house, we will serve the Lord.—*
Joshua 24:15.

*In the house of the righteous is much treasure. ...—*Proverbs
15:6.

*Blessed is every one that feareth the Lord; that walketh in his*
*ways. For thou shalt eat the labour of thine hands: happy shalt*
*thou be, and it shall be well with thee. Thy wife shall be as a*
*fruitful vine by the sides of thine house: thy children like olive*
*plants round about thy table. Behold, that thus shall the man*
*be blessed that feareth the Lord.—*Psalm 128:1-4.

JOHN RICE always preached much about the home and insisted that children could be raised, even in our sin-crazed twentieth century, in such a way that they would never go wrong but
would always live for God. From the very start skeptics came to
him and said, "Your children are small now. Wait till they
become teenagers. Or wait until they are grown and leave your
home and authority. You will see it is not so easy."

As I write these lines his children are grown and long ago all
left his house and authority. Yet a sweeter family of daughters
could not be found anywhere, all of them in full-time service for
the Lord Jesus Christ or married to a man in full-time Christian
work of some kind.

All of his boys were girls, as he was so fond of saying, and the
first of his six daughters, Grace Jean, was born October 22, 1922.
Then came Mary Lloys, Elizabeth, Jessie Ruth and Joanna, born
in a series of about two years apart. Six years later another baby
arrived whom the Rices prophetically named Joy. Describing it

in his book, *The Home—Courtship, Marriage and Children,* when discussing birth control, Dr. Rice said:

> I remember when my wife and I first learned that our sixth daughter was on the way to our home. I was so busy that I thought, with a little vexation, that another child would be a burden. The mother was active in church work, taught a large class of young women in Sunday school, and had much visitation to do, besides her mothering of five daughters God had previously given. I thought that another child would be a burden, and I feared that there would be many problems in connection with rearing a sixth one coming six years after the fifth one. But how groundless were my fears!
>
> When the little one came, we named her Sarah Joy—Sarah for my beloved mother who has long been in Heaven and Joy because that is exactly what she was. Oh, how she lightened my burdens! I was carrying a load of work almost insupportable, yet I found myself growing young again playing with my baby! I have had more joy in teaching her, more delight in watching her grow, more fellowship with her, perhaps, than with any of the other five beloved daughters. The others I love as much but this one I seemed to need more! How foolish I would have been if I had taken any means to prevent this gift which God so graciously gave to our home!
>
> There has never been a moment since she was born that I could have imagined it anything but a calamity if we did not have her. You see, little children have a way of proving to the fathers and mothers that God knew what He was doing when He gave them.

Joanna had been a baby so long she was a little fearful when Joy was born that she would lose her place of honor in the family. So Dr. Rice jokingly told her, "That little old thing can be Mother's baby and you can be Daddy's baby!" Even as a married woman, with several children of her own, she still signed her letters to him, "Daddy's Baby."

The seriousness with which he set out to face the God-given responsibility of training his daughters for Christ is seen in a paragraph from his pen right after Joy's birth:

> Just a few months ago God gave us our baby, Sarah Joy. The other five children had all been converted. We had rejoiced more than once that now all of our little ones had found peace in Christ, and we would be a united family in Heaven. And

now, with the joy that comes with our five-month-old baby,
there comes also a heavy responsibility that we cannot shake
off. I have just been thinking, "What if we should all get to
Heaven but this little one, and she be left outside!"

I have gotten accustomed now, with some difficulty, to
speaking of "my six little girls" where I used to speak of "my
five girls." Wouldn't it be a sad and terrible tragedy if, when we
get to Heaven, Mrs. Rice and I would have to speak again of
"our five little girls" and never mention the other because we
failed to win her to Christ? I thank God that He helped us with
the other five, and that they each one  when they were five or
six years old, were taught to trust in Christ and did. With
prayer, with tears, with deep anxiety, the other children were
won to Christ.

I will never forget how happy we were when the first one,
Grace, found the Saviour. What a load lifted! Then with Mary
Lloys, the second girl, who in 1930, while her mother was
reading to her the story of the crucifixion from Matthew, suddenly burst into tears and said, "Mother! Mother, I want to be
saved!" And when little Joanna found Christ not long ago, we
were so happy. Now, what if the new one should grow up
without any faith in her father's God, without loving Christ or
trusting Him? What if she should wander away in sin and
break our hearts? Home could not be happy as it ought to be
with one prodigal. So, father and mother, I beg you, win your
children to Christ.

Thank God, those fears were groundless! Mrs. Rice and Joy,
then a little less than five years old, spent a week with him in a
revival campaign in an Illinois town. Joy was greatly impressed
at a Sunday afternoon baptismal service and later, resting before
the evening service, she questioned, "Daddy, was that little boy
old enough to be saved?" The boy she spoke of was about eight
years old and had been baptized that afternoon. He told her that
he thought he was; and then, noting the concern on her face,
asked if she were wondering if she were old enough to be saved,
too. When she replied in the affirmative, they went over the
Scriptures carefully together, sitting on the bed; and when he
had finished explaining the simplicity of salvation as taught in
John 3:16, little Joy asked Jesus Christ to come into her heart.

It is not surprising that the daughters turned out right. For one
thing, God always had first place in the home. There was never

any doubt or discussion as to whether other things would come ahead of God or not. Each girl knew He had priority *in everything*. They always were present at the house of God for all of the services. Describing it later, Dr. Rice said:

> My wife and I, both university graduates, naturally were taught that little babies must never be taken into crowds and that little ones must be at home asleep by eight. We did not heed such talk, but all of our six daughters were taken to church in a basket when they were four or five weeks old. Usually there was no money to pay a maid to stay at home and keep the children. And if there had been money to hire a maid, we would not have wanted the kind of maid who was willing to stay away from church. And we would not be guilty of keeping someone else from the house of God that we might worship with more freedom.
>
> So the little ones were to lie quietly or to sit up and play with a rubber toy or nibble a Graham cracker. There was no crying, no jabbering, no confusion to disturb the public service. Others were forbidden to disturb the baby. The mother heard the sermon, took part in the song service, and otherwise lived a normal life.

Second, there was always very strict discipline, strong punishment for sin and an early education in the philosophy, "You can't do wrong and get by." The Bible says, "Foolishness is bound in the heart of a child; but the rod of correction shall drive it far from him" (Prov. 22:15) and, "Withhold not correction from the child: for if thou beatest him with the rod, he shall not die. Thou shalt beat him with the rod, and shalt deliver his soul from hell" (Prov. 23:13,14).

Third, there was a strong spiritual atmosphere in all their homelife. Family devotions were conducted regularly, morning after morning, without fail. As soon as they could read, even with halting words and some help with pronunciation, they read the Bible with their mother and father at the breakfast table. Spiritual talk was common and answers to prayers many. The girls remember from early experiences—as far back as consciousness can record the memory—of being aware of the reality of God. When children hear no songs but gospel songs, when they hear preaching of the Word of God regularly along with grown people, when they are punished for disobedience consistently, when they are taught to pray and read the Bible as little children, they soon come to realize their need for a Saviour and eagerly, willingly put their trust in Him.

As a Father's Day surprise when Dr. Rice was in his seventy-fifth year, Miss Viola Walden asked Mrs. Rice and the six daughters to write tributes or reminiscences for publication in *The Sword*. Mrs. Rice titled her remarks, "To the World's Best Father"; and because what she wrote sums up so beautifully what family life was like in the Rice household, I am quoting most of it here:

> I suppose the first item on my list is that he is a loving dad. I have often seen fathers who liked their children after they were big enough to walk and talk, but my children's father liked them when they were tiny. I remember how tenderly and efficiently he bathed the first one when she was only a week old and I was too scared to attempt it. He liked to feed the small ones before they had learned to handle a spoon. And the first thing he taught them to say was, "I love Daddy."
>
> Being a loving father, he liked to be with them—he romped with them and played games with them. I have seen them all lined up, he leading the gang as they ran in a circle through the front room, the kitchen, the dining room and the living room, and all somersaulting over the big overstuffed chair in the living room. As they grew older he played tennis with them and tried to teach them to play golf and bowl. In skating they were the teachers and tried to support and help him.
>
> He entertained our small ones on car trips by making his windshield wipers obey him. When he wanted to make them stop he would say to the children, "Now watch." Pointing to the wiper he would say, *"Stop,"* and the wiper would stop. He would do it again and again and they looked with wonder. They never did catch him putting his foot on the accelerator, then lifting it to cause the wiper to stop and start.
>
> He liked to give them thrills in driving. Once he drove a little too far out into the Gulf of Mexico and the waves went over the spark plugs and killed the engine. He had a little trouble getting out that time, but he thought the fun was worth it.
>
> He sang with them for hours on long car trips. Many a roundelay they had—"Old MacDonald had a farm. . ." and

Away down yonder, not so very far off,

**A bluejay died of the whooping cough.**
**He coughed so hard with the whooping cough**
**That he coughed his head and his tail right off!**

He especially liked "The Beatitudes" in a beautiful round they had learned at school. Each Christmas they sang together many, many carols, and as they grew older they began to sing *The Messiah* at Christmastime. They had the help of boyfriends, some of whom later became husbands and stayed on to sing every Christmas large sections of the great oratorio. Strangely enough, the fellows the girls liked all liked music, and since they are married each couple has its own duet. Once a friend asked, "Do all the boys who marry Rice girls have to be singers?" I suppose they would have to like to sing. A singing dad set an example they could not ignore.

In a household where six girls each practiced on a musical instrument—violin, piano, accordion, and clarinet—or practiced vocal exercises, the father never complained about the noise. He might be reading or playing a game in the room next to the music practice room, and with only an open archway between, but he did not mind the screeching of the violin or sour notes made on the instruments.

Along with all the fun went work and responsibility. Our dad insisted that "anyone who did not work was not worth his salt." Their beds were to be made as soon as they were up, and other duties were to be performed religiously. Duty and work were spiritual matters.

Besides the work at home they were expected to join their dad in his effort to get out the Gospel. Before they could operate a typewriter or addressing machine in the office, they could help give out circulars about revivals, run errands, or clean the office. By the time they were in junior high school they were regularly helping in the office, and in high school they took courses in typing and shorthand, getting ready to be better helpers.

Dr. Rice was a good disciplinarian, firm and consistent. He knew how to apply the rod when the rod was needed. Our dad set the standards for our house. He decided when the children should get up and when they should go to bed. He set the hours for them to be home when they went out evenings. They were never confused about what was expected of them and were convinced that Dad's standards were right, no matter what the rest of the world did or thought. The family ate together and thoroughly enjoyed being together. There was never a problem of the children wanting to be out somewhere else for fun—they had more fun at home; a good dad saw to that. They still like one another, still prefer one another's company. There was no generation gap in our family, and there still isn't. Our girls thought their dad was the smartest man in the world and the best man. And they still think so.

They felt perfectly free to go to him with any problem. They knew they would have a sympathetic ear. They talked of anything and everything with their dad. Their boyfriends came under his scrutiny, and the girls listened when he gave them advice. If he said, "That one has very poor manners—he is very impolite," or made other observations, they took them to heart.

They had great delight in the times of family devotions, when we sat at the table after breakfast and read the Bible and prayed. We read the Bible completely through, again and again. Our girls now say that they learned the important lessons of life during this time. It was during the Bible reading they received their sex education, their lessons in good manners, their social graces, their standards for living, and their comfort for the pressures of the very busy and demanding life in an evangelist's home. They knew they would be watched and that their daddy would be judged by their actions. They were concerned that their daddy's reputation and his straight preaching would not be jeopardized by the way they lived.

Though Dr. Rice has been away from home more than half the time on missions for the Lord, he never left the matter of his children's discipline in the hands of others. He set the rules when he left. He checked up when he got back. If things had begun to slide a bit in his absence, he took things in hand and set them on the right road again. He was determined that in the home of one evangelist he would see that the children turned out right; he was determined under God to turn them out right.

Thank God for a faithful father who took time for his children. He always had time to answer their questions, to know their problems, to teach them the things they needed to know, to pray with them and comfort and guide them as they had need.

I could wish for every child a father like my children's father. While he was winning other children to the Lord, he did not neglect to win his children and train them for the Lord.

All six daughters wrote glowing, exciting tributes. Grace wrote hers in verse and the other five penned in prose, but each was of the type any father would love to have said, in truth, of him.

While they are too lengthy to include in this chapter in their entirety, believe me when I say no dad anywhere ever received any
warmer accolades, written lovingly and sincerely. Perhaps their
best testimonials, however, are in the form of how they turned
out—the living affirmation of their personal character and labors
for the Lord Jesus Christ.

Each of the girls was given to God when she was born and is active now in His service. All the girls helped work their own way
through college. All of them learned to work at their father's office under careful, strict supervision. I know from firsthand
observation that it was harder on them when they made mistakes than on others. They always had a very clear understanding about the time they must be in bed, and if they went
out at night they were to be back at a certain time, usually
earlier than anyone else! When they had dates there were always
chaperones. But that old-fashioned way of raising girls paid big
dividends in the Rice family, and they are lovely Christian
women today.

Grace Jean, the eldest and the only one of the six who did not
meet her husband during student days at Wheaton College, until
her death was married to Allan MacMullen, a Baptist minister
who has pastored in Idaho, Missouri and Texas. She authored *A
Reward for Jerry,* a fiction for boys and girls, and served as the
first editor of *The Joyful Woman,* a Christian magazine for
ladies. She also assisted her dad with the musical score on
several of his songs. The MacMullens adopted two children,
David Allan and Allana Jean.

Mary Lloys married Charles Himes and together they planned
to go to Tibet as missionaries, but ill health prevented the fulfill-
ing of that desire. Charles is also a Baptist pastor, having served
churches in Kansas, Wisconsin, Colorado, Tennessee and
Nebraska. At one time Mary Lloys wrote the "Kid's Korner"
column in *The Sword.* Five children were born of this union,
three girls and two boys: Lloys Jean, Faith Elizabeth, Charles
Andrew, Jr., John Rice, and Joanna Ruth. The Himeses
presented the Rices with their first four grandchildren.

Jimmie Elizabeth married Walter Handford, and he labored

for a time in evangelism, then pastored churches in Illinois and South Carolina. Since 1965 he has served the Southside Baptist Church in Greenville, building it into one of the largest churches in the area. Libby, as she is popularly called, formerly wrote "Kid's Korner" in *The Sword* and has penned a number of books: *Romance at Red pines* (fiction); *Your Clothes Say It for You; The Exiled Prince* (the story of Daniel for children); *The Fugitive King* (the story of David for children); *Those Kids in Proverbsville; The Smudged Postmark; How to Win Your Unsaved Husband; Me? Obey Him?* plus numerous Christian crossword puzzle books. She succeeded Grace as editor of *The Joyful Woman.* The Handfords also adopted children: John Walter, Paul Stephen, William Lee, Judith Ann, Deborah Sue, Ruth Elizabeth, and Margaret Jean.

Jessie Ruth, a gifted artist, married Don Sandberg, a gifted musician. After serving for a time as church youth and music leaders, the Sandbergs entered the teaching field on the college level. Since 1972 they have been teaching music and art at Tennessee Temple University in Chattanooga. Jessie has written *The Sword's* weekly women's column since its inception and has authored three books: *With Love...and a Pinch of Salt; From My Kitchen Window;* and, *Fill My Cup, Lord!* Four children were born to the Sandbergs: James Scot, Mark Ray, Carol Joy and Don Robert.

Joanna, the fifth daughter, married a young man from Kentucky, Bill Rice—no relation to her Uncle Bill Rice—and he, after serving several churches as an associate, has pastored churches in Virginia and Georgia. He was one of my assistants at Portsmouth, Ohio, and won hundreds of people to Christ through personal evangelism. He is an outstanding soul winner. They have four children: Linda Jo, Laurel Ann, John Robert, and William Carl.

Joy graduated with highest honors from Wheaton College and she, too, married a Baptist preacher, Dr. Roger Martin, who has pastored churches in Kentucky, Oklahoma, Colorado, Missouri and Tennessee. Since 1969, both have been teaching at Tennessee Temple University, she in the college of Fine Arts division and he as professor of New Testament in the seminary. They have six children: Bruce William, Roger Edward, Jr., David George, Marilou Joanna, Melody Joy, and Holly Renee.

At the time of his death, Dr. Rice also had eight great-grandchildren.

An insight into the seriousness with which Dr. Rice took his responsibilities as a father, plus the love and compassion he felt towards his daughters, is seen in Joanna's testimony, when she was talking about how lonely Dr. Rice often was on the road without his family. She related:

> One such time he called long distance and made arrangements for me to be excused from school for a week and to take a long train trip alone in order to spend some time with him in a meeting. It was a tremendous week for a 13-year-old girl—hearing my dad preach several times every day, eating every meal together, taking walks along the Ohio River bank at night, sharing hot tamales (when mine fell through a grating in the sidewalk he said, "Here, finish mine; I was just eating it to keep you company"), and sharing our hopes and dreams. I thought I was helping my dad and didn't realize until my husband suggested it, 25 years later, that Daddy planned it, not because he needed me but because he felt I needed some special time with him!

Joy said:

> I have memories of moments of delight and laughter in song—batting a tennis ball with him, watching him on roller skates for the first time when he was over fifty, riding a Ferris wheel with him, singing duets in the car on long trips, riding horses with him. In our home, meal times with Daddy were a special delight—never a dull moment, or an eager pushing away from the table to escape to more desirable companions. Daddy seemed to know about everything and took an interest in all our questions.
>
> Daddy and Mother together made home a spiritual center, a school specializing in character training and great Christian truth; we learned by precept and example the values of loyalty, convictions and high standards, and hard work.

Libby emphasized the same, saying in her Father's Day letter:

> You taught us that since we didn't know how we would be

serving the Lord when we grew up, we should learn everything we could about everything. Then, when we saw a job that needed to be done, we'd be ready to do it. You gave us a liberal education—the kind you can't get at school. Think of all those trips! New York, by way of Arkansas, with its bald-knee cyprus in the swamps; Virginia, and Mount Vernon; Liberty Hall in Philadelphia; the Statue of Liberty in the New York harbor, viewed from a small ferry; Niagara Falls; Chicago and Moody Church. . . .

Thank you for those trips—not just for the sense of history and love of country we soaked up, not just for the basic competence we learned in meeting new situations; but also for the feeling that there was a whole world of wonder and delight, a curiosity about ideas, and things, and functions, that enrich everyday living.

You taught us that God had a perfect will for us, that we could know what He wanted us to do, and that the only thing left to do was to follow His will. I often did not understand all that was involved, but I was always sure that when Daddy said, "This is what God wants us to do," it really was God's will. How I long to give my children the same certainty: you can know God's will; you can do that will.

You taught us there were no double standards. What was right for the children was right for the grownups. Remember when Mother went to Texas and left me in charge of the cooking? I spent the week's grocery money on a bargain case of canned peas—10¢ a can! You valiantly ate peas for entree, vegetable, salad and dessert, without complaint. And it wasn't until last summer that I discovered you don't really care for peas! (Suppose that's why?) You were as demanding on yourself in the large things as in the small, and I thank you with all my heart for this.

You taught us to put the Lord first, even if it meant going to revival meetings every night, weeks on end, and groggily studying in the early morning hours. How else could we have learned so much Scripture, and heard so many great preachers? How else could we have learned the compassion and burden for unsaved people? How else could we have stored the precious memories of being "family" in the car, going to and from the services? I remember being awakened from a sound slumber to the words, "Jimmy, would you like a tutti-frutti ice cream cone?" *Tutti-frutti?* Even today words are mystic and tantalizing. I can't remember the flavor, but I can remember wondering how Daddy knew I would love a tutti-frutti cone!

You taught us that families were for loving and caring. You gave us more personal attention, even when you were away in revivals much of the time, than my friends got from their fathers. You kept track of our studies, our boyfriends, our new enthusiasms, and your letters answered our mixed-up adolescent needs with a tenderness that spilled over the strictness of your decisions and made them bearable. Were the rules hard? Yes. Did it hurt to be different? Yes. Did I always understand your decisions? No. But I never doubted that you really cared how I felt—your tears proved that—or that you knew what was the right thing to do.

You taught us that life had many "oughts," but that there was a time for fun and joy, too. Remember when you drove down the steep embankment so we could picnic by the river, and then couldn't get the car back up the grade? You drove down the creek bed, to our fearful delight, until you found an easier grade. Remember the tennis games down at Northside Park? Remember jumping to meet the huge waves in the Gulf of Mexico? Remember the hours that we spent listening to phonograph records of Caruso and Galli-Curci and "The Stars and Stripes Forever"? My very earliest memories of you, in the Fort Worth days, are watching you play with the children—blowing up a long balloon; your trying out Grace's new roller skates and landing in an undignified sprawl at the bottom of the hill; playing a game of "London Bridge" by the fragrant honeysuckle at the back door.

There's another memory from those days. I remember hearing you preach over the radio, and being so convicted of my sins that I couldn't wait for you to get home so I could get saved. (Grace wasn't sure I really got saved, because I smiled so much. She just didn't know how deep the conviction had been, and how sweet was the relief!) You couldn't have given me a greater gift—the assurance of salvation based upon the Word of God, and the means for steady spiritual growth.

You taught so many things, consciously, systematically, as if you had an itemized list of Things Every Child Has a Right to Know. But you taught us even more when you were not consciously teaching. I watched and learned when you spoke gently and reasonably to an angry employee; I watched when you slept but clasped your Bible tight; I heard you praying far into the dark hours in the night; I saw you weep when you took a stand for the fundamentals of the faith, and so lost a lifelong friend. I watched and learned, and even today measure many an action by "What would my daddy do about this?"

In her tribute, Mary Lloys wrote:

As a tiny girl, I remember Daddy peeling an orange or an apple for me, cutting my meat at the table. Daddy was the surgeon who with the point of his handy pocketknife removed the little splinters from my finger and comforted me with a kiss. Daddy was the fiery preacher whose sermon on the second coming of the Lord was so moving that his five-year-old little daughter, me, couldn't sleep in her bed until she had finally trusted the Lord Jesus as Saviour.

Flying kites, or shooting fireworks, or rowing a boat were all great adventures with Daddy. And the night after night of attending revival meetings were a joy. No one ever thought of asking if she had to go!

Later on, softball, tennis and volleyball were great fun with Daddy. He insisted that we help with housework, learn to cook and sew and clean, but we also must work in the office, running machinery, rolling *The Sword of the Lord* copies for mailing, learning the most efficient way to do a job. During those adolescent years I remember Daddy singing with us often, challenging us to memorize chapters of the Bible, always learning with us and encouraging us. Daddy coached our girls' trio, encouraged us to practice piano and singing, and paid for innumerable lessons.

When he was away from home in revival meetings, his frequent letters and phone calls reminded us that Daddy loved us. His leading of family devotions taught us to love the Bible, and we each heard him pray for our individual needs.

Daddy was the first to make me aware of my responsibility to win souls. He has constantly been inspiration and example through the years. I still read everything he writes over and over. When I have a special need I want my father to know so he can pray for me.

In her tribute to her father, Jessie wrote:

Perhaps it will seem strange that the first thing which comes to my mind and therefore the first thing I want to thank you for is *memories*—memories of the special pair of stilts you built for me on my seventh birthday, memories of the times you prayed for me in my childish fears, memories of the sweet, solemn kiss you gave me on my wedding day, memories of the special poems you wrote for me on my birthday and on Valentine's day, memories of your eager participation in family games and song fests.

The second thing I want to thank you for is your determination to give me as much equipment as possible for a rich and full life. Thank you for insisting on the piano lessons which I sometimes failed to appreciate but have used since almost every day of my life. Thank you for encouraging me to write and draw and sew. Thank you for teaching me to swim and play softball. Thank you for your patience in showing me how to serve a tennis ball, how to drive a car, and how to find the square root of a number.

The third and most important thing I want to thank you for is your part in developing in me a deep faith in the Lord Jesus Christ. Thank you for your emphasis on early salvation, for your insistence on the importance of Christian fellowship and the habit of faithful attendance at church. Thank you for the constant exposure to the Bible in family devotions and in the everyday events of life. Thank you for teaching by precept and example that God really does answer prayer. Thank you for proving that "he that winneth souls is wise."

Last of all, thank you for your confidence in me, for your constant reminder that I could be anything and do anything God wanted me to be and do. Thank you for providing for me the best example of Christian womanhood a girl could want by marrying the girl who became my mother! Thank you for your constant love and concern and prayers for me in the years since I have left the home nest.

God bless you, dearest Daddy!

Perhaps in closing this chapter about Dr. Rice's family it would be well to give an illustration indicative of his wife's character, a woman who stood by her husband in every move he made. Undoubtedly she was his strongest defender and greatest encouragement. Unlike many another wife of a famous husband, she is very humble, friendly and willing to do anything at all to serve her Lord. A gifted, trained musician, she served as his pianist during his early ministry. She also learned to fill in at any of the places in the big Sword of the Lord organization when an emergency arose with need for a helper.

Best of all, she is a very earnest, successful soul winner who loves to talk about the Lord and His goodness. Once when a lady in Lexington, Kentucky, had read *Prayer—Asking and Receiving* and had gotten under deep conviction, she called long distance to talk to Dr. Rice. Told that he was not in the office and would not return for at least three weeks, the distraught lady inquired if

Mrs. Rice were there. When the operator completed the connection, the weeping woman begged, "Mrs. Rice, will you please tell me how to be saved? For nine months the words, 'You are lost,' have been ringing in my soul. I do so want to be saved."

Mrs. Rice read to her over the phone a few Scriptures such as John 6:37, ". . .him that cometh to me I will in no wise cast out," and John 5:24, "Verily, verily, I say unto you, He that heareth my word, and believeth on him that sent me, hath everlasting life, and shall not come into condemnation; but is passed from death unto life."

When the woman protested that she did not have faith enough to claim those promises, Mrs. Rice took her to Matthew 10:32, "Whosoever therefore shall confess me before men, him will I confess also before my Father which is in heaven," challenging her to claim Him in confession, trusting Him to own her before the Father. In a matter of moments the matter was happily settled.

Mrs. Rice inquired if she were sure about the salvation and the lady responded, "Yes, I am. Jesus said He would not cast me out and I believe what He said." Later she wrote to confirm on paper what she had stated orally.

The John R. Rice family is a soul-winning family. As natural as eating, sleeping or breathing, witnessing and winning are part of their lives. It would be as logical to expect a lifeguard's family to be unable to swim or a professor's family to be illiterate as to suppose anything different. The man who signed his name with the reference of Psalm 126:6 and Luke 11:13 taught his family well the truth, ". . .he that winneth souls is wise" (Prov. 11:30).

*Chapter 16*

# Hymenaeus, Alexander. . .and Peter

*Holding faith, and a good conscience; which some having put away concerning faith have made shipwreck: Of whom is Hymenaeus and Alexander; whom I have delivered unto Satan, that they may learn not to blaspheme.*—I Timothy 1:19,20.

*But when Peter was come to Antioch, I withstood him to the face, because he was to be blamed. For before that certain came from James, he did eat with the Gentiles: BUT WHEN THEY WERE COME, HE WITHDREW AND SEPARATED HIMSELF, FEARING THEM WHICH WERE OF THE CIRCUMCISION. And the other Jews dissembled likewise with him; insomuch that Barnabas also was carried away with their dissimulation.*—Galatians 2:11-13.

DR. RICE'S life, as we have already seen, was anything but free of controversy. Much of that controversy was deliberate. One well-known evangelist stated that he was neither a fundamentalist nor a liberal but a constructionist. Dr. Rice was not only a constructionist, he was a destructionist, too! It is impossible to love flowers without hating weeds; one cannot be for God without being against the Devil; an individual cannot build up for God without tearing down for Satan, and Dr. Rice always sought to fulfill the plain Bible command, "that ye should earnestly contend for the faith which was once delivered unto the saints" (Jude 3).

He was without apology a sworn enemy of evil. The *locale* of that wrong did not make it right in his eyes, and his wrath was not tempered by circumstance or personage. He was as violently opposed to infidels within the church as those without—*actually much more so!*

The Scriptures listed at the head of this chapter show how the Apostle Paul opposed evil men in the church and delivered them unto Satan because of their blasphemy. They also show how he opposed good men, withstanding Peter to his face when he was wrong on the issue of circumcision. It seems that Peter had been eating with Gentiles before some of the brethren came from James, but when they came "he withdrew and separated himself, fearing them which were of the circumcision." Other Jews had followed Peter's example and even Barnabas was "carried away with their dissimulation." Paul said that when he saw "they walked not uprightly according to the truth of the gospel" (vs. 14), he publicly challenged Peter on the issue.

Dr. Rice's ministry has included the unpleasant and tasteless task of controversy: rebuking the Hymenaeuses and Alexanders for their blasphemy, and sometimes publicly rebuking the Peters for going astray in doctrine or practice, leading others astray with them. A few illustrations of these matters of controversy will be given in this chapter.

Remember that he was born in a Bible-believing, Christian home. Saved at an early age, his father was a part-time preacher; and he attended sound Bible churches throughout all of his youth. He received his education at Christian colleges which professed to honor completely God and the Bible. Therefore he had no great awareness of the higher criticism we call modernism until he went to the University of Chicago. In an issue of *The Sword of the Lord* dated January 10, 1936, in an article about modernism in the Southern Baptist Convention, he told how his eyes were opened to this evil. That particular part of the article was subtitled, "When I Saw the Deadliness of Modernism." He wrote:

> It was in the spring of 1921. I was a junior college teacher doing graduate work in the University of Chicago. William Jennings Bryan was brought to the University by the YMCA. When students overran the Kent Theater (the chemistry lecture hall) the meeting was moved to Hyde Park Baptist Church building, where Bryan spoke on "The Bible and Its Enemies." I was an earnest Christian but not very well grounded in the Word of God, and the address was a revelation to me. I had

been taught the evolutionary hypothesis in high school. It had been taken for granted, at least in the two Baptist schools I attended, and in some classes had been actually taught in Baylor University. I had nominally accepted the teaching without realizing that it directly contradicted the Bible. Now I saw I must give up one or the other, and my soul was deeply stirred. I determined to see the thing through and come to a definite stand.

The Chicago University faculty demanded that the YMCA arrange for a meeting in which their representative should answer Mr. Bryan. On a Sunday afternoon, Professor Coulter of the Botany Department spoke in Mandel Hall (then the university chapel) on evolution. He tried to give evidence that would prove the Genesis account of the creation in the Bible was not reliable. To my surprise, he could give nothing more than the suppositions which I had learned in high school, guesses on the basis of fossils, of the comparative anatomy of man and beast, "vestigial remains," etc. That was not conclusive proof for one who really had found Christ and His peace, even though I did not know much about the Bible.

After the lecture, I went on the stage to speak to the professor. He was very cordial, offering to answer my questions. I said, "Will you tell me this, then—do you believe that Jesus Christ is the very Son of God?" Immediately his attitude changed, and he said, "I see it would do no good to talk with you. I do not want to argue."

That settled it for me, and in my heart I resolved that one who could not tell me that about Jesus my Saviour need not tell me anything about His Word! Today I still keep that resolve.

As I went outside, I found an argument in progress on the steps between two freshman boys, each of them seventeen years old. One was the son of a modernist preacher, now on the university faculty, I believe, then the pastor of Hyde Park Church. The other was the son of an American missionary teaching in Robert College at Constantinople, Turkey. The missionary's son first hotly contended for the Bible—the modernist's son that the Bible was a very good Book but not the Word of God and not accurate.

"But I always thought my father believed it all. I wish I could see my father," said the boy who had been sent back to America by his missionary father. "I have always supposed all the Bible was the Word of God with no mistakes."

"But didn't you hear Professor Coulter prove that evolution

is true and the Bible wrong?" said his companion. "Get those old-fashioned ideas out of your head. That is what you came to the university for."

I interrupted, told them my name, found their names and ages, and urged the lad to stay with the faith of his missionary father and mother. But he brushed the tears out of his eyes and started down the steps saying, "Well, I guess a fellow has to get his eyes opened sometime!" And I saw him walk away without his faith, arm in arm with the friend who had been taught by his infidel teacher-father not to believe the Bible but to believe the guesses of men who call themselves scientists.

It was a time of crisis in my life. Standing there on the steps of Mandel Hall that spring afternoon with dusk coming on, I felt burning in me a holy fire. I lifted my hand solemnly to God and said: "If God gives me grace and I have opportunity to smite this awful unbelief that wrecks the faith of all it can, *then smite it I will, so help me God!*" That vow I have tried to keep; and keep it I will by His grace and help.

Soon God laid His hand upon me, and in the Pacific Garden Mission I promised God to preach the Gospel. I left my university classes without finishing the quarter's work and came back to Texas to enter the seminary and begin preaching. I little knew then that the keeping of my vow would lose me some of the dearest friends I ever knew and brand me as an outcast, a fanatic, a "non-cooperating Baptist," a "disturber," a "Bolshevik." But I never regretted it. If there is anything at all to the Christian religion, there is enough to die for. Thank God, He has repaid a hundredfold in this life, and there is still the world to come!

Dear friend, that boy might have been your boy! He nursed at the breast of a believing missionary mother. He was taught to pray by a reverent missionary father. Since then I have seen the same thing again and again. And every time, I renew my vow to God to smite modernism, to have no part with it, not to support it with a copper cent, not to have fellowship anywhere it is allowed. When I saw it was entrenched in Baptist conventions, and embraced or defended by Baptist leaders, then I got out.

Who is on the Lord's side? Then come out from among unbelievers and bear the reproach of Christ outside the camp!

This explains in part why he fought so bitterly against the modernism and socialism of the National Council of Christian Churches, the World Council of Christian Churches, infidelity in denominational colleges and seminaries, the Revised Standard Version, the *Interpreter's Bible,* the Bishop Oxnams, Harry Emerson Fosdicks, Nels Ferres, and the rest of the unbelieving ministerial crowd.

But Dr. Rice not only took a strong stand against modernistic error, he repeatedly fought error when it cropped up in conservative circles. The second chapter of Galatians deals at length with how Paul openly rebuked Peter for his error relative to circumcision, as we previously noted. The editor of *The Sword of the Lord* often did the same of necessity, *never of choice.* His manner was always kindly, the issue was always the principle involved and never the personality; usually he endeavored for weeks or months to straighten out the matter privately and took it to the people only when all other means completely failed.

A notable example, and one for which he was misunderstood by multitudes, pertained to Dr. Lewis Sperry Chafer's book, *True Evangelism.* Dr. Chafer, now in Heaven, was a good man, an earnest believer, a recognized scholar. At the time of his death he was the beloved president of the Dallas Theological Seminary, a fine, fundamental, scholarly school located in Dallas, Texas.

However, Dr. Chafer's book, *True Evangelism,* consisted of an open attack on modern evangelism and proven evangelistic methods. It definitely, outspokenly opposed mass evangelism, called revival "abnormal," criticized the usual preaching of evangelists, discouraged public invitations for sinners to trust Christ openly, and threw cold water on almost every form of personal soul winning—not only in revival campaigns, but other places as well. It was an open attack on the evangelism of D. L. Moody, R. A. Torrey, J. Wilbur Chapman, Gipsy Smith, Charles G. Finney, Bob Jones, Paul Rader, and almost every other greatly-used evangelist in American history. Dr. Chafer himself, in a letter to Moody Bible Institute, named Dr. Torrey and Dr. Chapman as two of the evangelists whom, among others, he opposed. The book had done incalculable harm in many a young minister's life, and Dr. Rice felt it should either be rewritten or taken off the market completely.

He spent a full year and a half trying to get something done about it before writing the first word of public protest in *The Sword of the Lord*. Moody Press was publishing the book at the time; and on December 14, 1944, Dr. Rice wrote a kindly detailed letter to Don Norman, then the manager of Moody Press, stating his objections to the book and inquiring about what could be done. His gracious approach to the unfortunate situation can be seen by quoting one of the letter's opening paragraphs:

> I have had a growing conviction I ought to write you in some detail about the book long published by Moody Press, *True Evangelism*, by Dr. Lewis Sperry Chafer. I have no quarrel with Dr. Chafer or with Moody, as I am sure you know. Dr. Chafer is a good and great man. His clear grasp of the Bible plan of salvation by grace is wonderful and he has been greatly used in that teaching. I regard him as a thorough Bible scholar, a devoted and greatly-used child of God and a lovable Christian gentleman. Some of his books have been widely used, and I can well understand how Moody Press would want to promote the ministry of this good man.

Later, at the first great Sword of the Lord Conference on Evangelism at Winona Lake, on the occasion of a special dinner limited to members of the International Association of Evangelists, the matter was discussed and a resolution relative to *True Evangelism* adopted for presentation to Moody Press. The two evangelists who, at that time, had preached to more people and seen more conversions than any living American, made and seconded the motion to appeal for the book's discontinuance. Over forty evangelists signed the resolution which we are printing here to show the importance of the issue:

> A RESOLUTION TO BROTHER DON NORMAN, DIRECTOR OF MOODY PRESS, AND TO THE ADMINISTRATION OF MOODY BIBLE INSTITUTE
>
> Beloved Brethren:
>
> Greetings in Jesus' name!
> We, a group of forty-seven evangelists (later it appeared that only 41 signed as evangelists) gathered at Winona at the Sword of the Lord Conference on Evangelism, at a banquet given for members of the International Association of Evangelists, respectfully present this petition and memorial to Moody Press and Moody Bible Institute.

I. We thank God for the blessed work done by Moody Bible Institute and Moody Press, for your loyalty to the Word of God and your earnest effort in training Christian workers who believe the Bible and preach the Gospel around the world to the salvation of multitudes of souls. We especially thank God for the contribution of Moody Institute and Moody Press toward the work of evangelism.

II. We express our gratitude to God also for the much good work done by Dr. Lewis Sperry Chafer, devoted servant of God, and we pray the blessing of God upon Dallas Theological Seminary of which he is the honored and greatly loved president.

III. However, we feel that the book, *True Evangelism,* is not true to the Scriptures in certain great essentials, is particularly harmful in discouraging the kind of evangelism believed in and practiced by D. L. Moody, R. A. Torrey, J. Wilbur Chapman, Billy Sunday, and William Biederwolf, as well as that being done by the most earnest and faithful and successful evangelists now living. We believe that the book is particularly unscriptural and hurtful to evangelism in the following matters:

1. It classes full-time evangelists as "false forces in evangelism"; plainly says that there is no place in New Testament Christianity for evangelists like those of today; that a scriptural evangelist should preach only in pioneer missionary areas where there are no churches.

2. It teaches that no evangelist should preach against sin, either in seeking to revive the saints, or in seeking to bring conviction and repentance to sinners.

3. It teaches that the public invitation to accept Christ, such invitations as were given by D. L. Moody himself, by R. A. Torrey and by the best evangelists in all ages, for all people to come openly to confess Christ as Saviour, is a "false force in evangelism." The author makes no exception. To ask people to come forward to take the preacher's hand, to ask people to come at once to the inquiry room, there to be dealt with scripturally, or to ask people to kneel at an altar—these methods are condemned wholesale as unscriptural, as implying false doctrine, as being contrary to the doctrine of salvation by grace. The book says that such public invitations to accept Christ and confess Christ as Saviour implies salvation by works.

4. The book teaches that it is wrong to do personal work except when lost people request it. Such personal soul winning as

was taught and practiced by D. L. Moody, taught by Dr. R. A. Torrey, taught in the Correspondence Course on soul winning in Moody Institute, and we understand, taught in Institute classes; and the kind of personal soul winning which is taught and practiced by the leading evangelists today, is unscriptural and harmful.

5. The book takes up the accusations of the ungodly against evangelists, accusations which in the main are untrue and desperately hurtful, and gives them credence and authority by repeating them. The book intimates that all successful evangelists are interested primarily in money and therefore in numbers to be counted in order to get big offerings. The book repeats the slander that the converts of great revival campaigns are not genuine and do not last. In fact, the book is so critical of evangelism and evangelists, as all of us know it, that not one good word is said for any evangelist, living or dead. Not one word of commendation is given to D. L. Moody, to R. A. Torrey, or to any other evangelist who ever lived. Every word is critical.

6. The book, *True Evangelism,* emphasizes soul winning by prayer. All of us believe in prayer for soul winning, prayer for revivals. But we believe that when prayer is mentioned as the only true force in soul winning and evangelism, evangelistic preaching, the public invitation to confess Christ, personal soul winning, etc., are plainly denounced as false forces in evangelism, that makes the book, in our opinion, untrue to the Bible, desperately hurtful and inimical to true evangelism and to soul winning.

IV. We believe the book thoroughly misrepresents Moody Bible Institute. When this book is advertised in the first pages of the catalog of Moody Press, when this book is heralded as thoroughly scriptural and with the full endorsement of Moody Bible Institute and Moody Press, that puts Moody Bible Institute in the position of attacking the work of D. L. Moody and Dr. R. A. Torrey, the two great founders and builders of Moody Institute and the loved ideals of all true evangelists in America. We believe that the book, if continued, will do irreparable harm to Moody Institute and Moody Press. We believe it will alienate evangelists and their converts and evangelistic pastors. We believe it will have a tendency to line up Moody Institute in the part against true evangelists and their work. That, we feel, would be an unspeakable tragedy which neither the Institute nor any of its friends desire.

V. Therefore, after again expressing our true friendship for

Moody Bible Institute and Moody Press, we respectfully but earnestly petition that the book, *True Evangelism,* by Dr. Chafer, be dropped from publication at once and no more advertised or sold by Moody Press. And this we ask humbly and in the name of our Lord and Saviour Jesus Christ and in the name of souls for whom He died and whom we evangelists most earnestly strive to win.

This resolution prepared on motion by Dr. Bob Jones, President, Founder Bob Jones College, seconded by Dr. Hyman Appelman.

Signed: Hyman J. Appelman, Bob Jones, Sr., E. E. Shelhamer, Jesse M. Hendley, Robert J. Wells, G. Covell Kennum, Edmont Hains, Donald B. Winters, George T. Stephens, Charles F. Weigle, Raymond T. Clover, J. Stratton Shufelt, S. H. Turbeville, George Bennard, Clifford Lewis, Marvin Lewis, Preston Garrett, W. Bryan Green, Tom Presnell, Robert L. Sumner, C. Arnall Jones, Peter B. Weaver, Clarence E. Sharer, Emerson Pent, James H. Nicholls, Wallace E. Jones, G. E. Fisher, L. W. Arnold, Joseph Brookshire, Russell Plummer, John S. Bell, W. C. Pierce, Rolfe Barnard, C. A. Cooper, A. K. Harper, Wm. S. H. Piper, R. Paul Miller, Elmer D. Piper, Joe Henry Hankins, J. Gardiner Clark, John R. Rice.

Dr. Rice and the above-mentioned evangelists were not alone in their objection to this bad book. Dr. P. W. Philpott, former pastor of the Moody Church in Chicago and the Church of the Open Door in Los Angeles, a greatly used evangelist in his own right, objected to the book nearly twenty-five years before Dr. Rice did. Dr. Henry Stough of Wheaton, a classmate of Dr. Chafer's, raised a fight against the book when it was first published and even Dr. Chafer admitted Stough's criticism "was very caustic, claiming that Dr. Chafer was a hindrance to evangelism."

Over twenty-five years before Dr. Rice publicly objected to the book it had been banned at the Philadelphia School of the Bible. Dr. John Brown, famous evangelist and founder of John Brown Schools, and Dr. W. B. Riley, pastor for nearly half a century of Minneapolis' First Baptist Church, both openly opposed the book and Chafer's teaching about evangelism. On at least one occasion, Dr. Riley walked out of a meeting where Dr. Chafer was speaking as a public protest to his bad teaching. Evangelist R.

Paul Miller protested about *True Evangelism* publicly at least twenty years before Dr. Rice did.

Dr. H. A. Ironside, while not wanting to openly disagree with the book, admitted to Dr. Rice privately the book was "a dud." Dr. Will Houghton, president of Moody Bible Institute at the time of the controversy, confessed to Dr. Rice that he himself did not agree with its teaching.

Read again the list of men who signed the resolution protesting the book to Moody Press. Some are little known, but some are the greatest evangelists of the twentieth century. One is the author of the famous hymn, *The Old Rugged Cross*. Another wrote that beautiful song, *No One Ever Cared for Me Like Jesus*.

Every effort was made to get the author to rewrite the book. However, Dr. Chafer wrote Dr. Rice rejecting completely such a proposition and emphasized that if he did rewrite it, "it would be more severe and more drastic in its statements." He even refused to have a conference to discuss the matter. On February 9, 1946, Dr. Rice wrote a long letter to Dr. Houghton pleading for something to be done. To show his fair, kindly attitude, let me quote the following paragraphs from the letter:

> I have worked earnestly, constructively and kindly at the matter of getting this book eliminated for fourteen months. I have spent my own time and money. I have been careful not to cause a breath of suspicion or criticism concerning Moody Bible Institute. I have appealed again and again to the Institute and other evangelists have appealed with me in the kindest and most reasonable language that we knew how to use.
>
> I find that Evangelist Paul Miller made an earnest plea twenty years ago for the book to be discontinued, and it was disregarded. I find that two of the leading Christian editors in America are outspoken in their disagreement with the book; and one great president of a great college and one great president of a great Bible institute have expressed to me their amazement that Moody should continue to publish that which cuts the ground out from under all that D. L. Moody stood for. The evangelists are restive. They feel that they have been betrayed by groups of men they trusted and to whom they had been loyal.
>
> I offered to meet with any group of people that the Moody Press would suggest to discuss this book. I suggested that I

would be glad for Dr. H. A. Ironside, Dr. Hyman Appelman, Dr. Bob Jones and any of the Moody Extension Staff evangelists and faculty members to be present to give their opinions. But nothing came of my suggestion. I gladly acceded to the suggestion that my full review be sent Dr. Chafer and he be asked if he could rewrite the book to make it acceptable to evangelists and other soul winners. Nothing came of it.

I cannot find a single prominent fundamental Christian leader in America outside of Dr. Chafer himself who believes in the doctrines and principles laid down in his book. Not one man rises to defend it. And yet the book is sold by Moody Institute, is widely advertised as "a masterful development of the whole divine program in seeking and saving the lost."

Now I feel that unless you and Moody Institute can be prevailed upon to stop the promotion and sale and distribution of this misleading and hurtful book of false doctrine and attack on evangelists and evangelism, I will have no recourse but to take the matter to the public and warn people everywhere about this book, and, as far as I am able to do so, stop its circulation among and support by Bible believers.

It is my feeling that it would be much better for the book to be stopped privately, taken off sale and the stock destroyed, so that no one could further blame Moody in the matter. Thus, the harm of the book in the future would be largely eliminated. But if it cannot be stopped privately, then I believe the leading Christians in America can be led to repudiate it; and its influence upon people, particularly young ministers, can be counteracted.

I believe that Moody has everything to gain by following what surely must be the convictions of yourself and other Christian leaders there in repudiating and stopping the circulation of this book and I hope you can see your way clear to do this.

Eventually, when every other effort apparently had failed to have Dr. Chafer rewrite the book or Moody Press to discontinue, Dr. Rice wrote and offered to "buy outright the remaining stock of books and the plates if there be any, at your estimation of what the books and plates cost Moody Press. Then you can give your written assurance that the book will not be reprinted by Moody Press, and the earnest request of American evangelists that the book be taken off the market will be fulfilled."

Moody Press replied that "the book was recently reprinted

because of the greatly increased demand for it in recent months" and that they now had "about six thousand copies in stock." They stated that their decision to reprint it had been based on "a matter of good business" and that "economic consideration" would be the only basis on which they would consider its discontinuance. At this writing, however, Moody no longer publishes the book. Another publisher handles all the Chafer publications.

Throughout the entire controversy with Moody Press, Dr. Rice did not become uncharitable nor did he try to hurt the influence of Moody in any way. As a matter of fact, the exact opposite was true. By way of example, in one of his articles protesting *True Evangelism,* he said:

> I sent three workers from my office to Moody Bible Institute. Two of them are still with me. I sent my daughter to Moody. I encouraged my two brothers to attend Moody Institute where both graduated. My advertising manager is a Moody graduate. I have brought a foreign boy nearly ten thousand miles to study in Moody and am helping him meet his regular bills. I am for Moody Institute. But for Moody Institute to publish this book attacking evangelism and evangelists is wrong.
>
> Let us earnestly pray that leaders at Moody Bible Institute will see their mistake and withdraw this book, which has done so much harm, from publication.

On one occasion the Moody Bible Institute sent a paid ad for publication in *The Sword of the Lord,* "the ninth in a series of informative ads dealing with the policy and program of Moody Bible Institute." Titled, "Moody Bible Institute and Evangelism," it was an excellent statement of their evangelistic position. However, one sentence, under the section "Evangelism Is Promoted by Means of Moody Press Literature," advertised the book *True Evangelism* and could not be accepted for publication in *The Sword.* So, turning down the hundreds of dollars the ad would have brought, Dr. Rice refused it, then published the entire article, less the one objectionable sentence, absolutely free of any charge to the Institute!

Right in the midst of the controversy he brought a young black man, John S. E. Thompson, from British Guiana in South America to Moody Bible Institute to train for the Christian ministry, paying his passage and guaranteeing his expenses.

When Dr. Rice finally received word from Moody Press that the book had been reprinted, he wrote them one final protest and said in closing his plea:

> I take my stand with D. L. Moody and R. A. Torrey, founders of Moody Institute. How long can Moody afford to attack those of us who have the same message and the same methods as the men who founded Moody institute?
>
> This has been a matter of long concern, much labor, and of literally days and days of prayer, on my part. With love for my brethren, with malice toward no one, but simply putting soul winning first, I rest my case with God and with Bible-believing people.

There is one other illustration we must give apart from which a biography of the man would not be complete. This controversy dealt with the position Dr. Rice took relative to the Billy Graham crusades. When biblical convictions finally compelled him to repudiate Graham's position, he took his stand knowing full well the high price he would have to pay in criticism, being misunderstood, losing support from sundry sources, and suffering in many other ways. But he felt it was a *Bible* stand, and John R. Rice's decisions were always based upon what he was convinced was the side of the Bible and the Lord Jesus Christ.

First, let me emphasize the truth that he never one time launched an attack against Billy Graham. The issue was entirely one of biblical principle, not mere human personality.

On one occasion I was in a revival at Klamath Falls, Oregon, and a visiting preacher commented to me after the service, "Well, I see Dr. Rice is attacking Billy Graham now." I immediately explained that such was not the case and went to the trouble later of sending him a copy of *The Sword of the Lord* which dealt with the issue, showing the kindly language of the articles dealing with Graham's compromise. The brother did not bother to reply, but I trust his fuzzy thinking relative to the issue was cleared.

Unfortunately, others have misunderstood in the same way

and many wrote to *The Sword of the Lord* to complain about the "attack" on Billy Graham.

Long-time readers of *The Sword* know that for years Dr. Rice was one of Graham's most outspoken defenders and one who rejoiced greatly in the wonderful campaigns he conducted. I think it would not be at all wrong to say their friendship was very warm, if not close.

Dr. Rice asked Graham to serve on the Cooperating Board of *The Sword of the Lord.* In like manner, Dr. Graham begged Rice to serve on the Board of Trustees when he became president of Northwestern Schools; and Dr. Rice agreed, going regularly to all board meetings at his own expense. Dr. Rice flew to Scotland for a week at the All-Scotland Crusade, visited for three days in the Toronto meeting, and always published extended reviews and news releases about Graham's campaigns wherever they were held. He repeatedly told the popular evangelist,"I am not your enemy; I am not even your critic."

Time and again Dr. Rice proved his friendship and love for Dr. Graham. His unsurpassed delight with the results of Graham's campaigns was obvious to every reader of *The Sword of the Lord.* How asinine and childish is the argument of some that Rice's eventual criticism was the fruit of personal frustration and petty jealousy. No one who knows the man could believe that charge for a single moment.

As a matter of fact, he defended Graham so thoroughly against his critics that he lost many friends among the separationists. When Billy spoke unwisely about fundamentalists, Dr. Rice asked his readers to overlook it. When he endorsed the Revised Standard Version of the Bible during his Pittsburgh crusade, Dr. Rice excused him on the grounds of his youth and the advisors about him. He wrote private letters defending him and excusing him when folks wrote objecting to the fact that national magazines had published pictures of Graham's daughters in shorts.

When the *Christian Herald* published an attack on Graham by Tom Rees (from which the *United Evangelical Action,* the NAE's official voice, quoted favorably, and even the *Moody*

*Monthly* quoted approvingly without naming the evangelist), Dr. Rice defended him with a front-page, five-column-headline article entitled, "Billy Graham and Revival Critics." When the editor of *His,* official voice for the Inter-Varsity Christian Fellowship, published an outrageous article slandering Graham's campaigns—without calling him by name—Rice again went to bat in his defense with an article, "Those Bad, Bad Evangelists."

In every way he proved himself a friend of Billy Graham and the Graham crusades. Page after page in *The Sword of the Lord* (worth in excess of $1,000 per page at regular advertising rates even in those days) was used to defend Graham and report his campaigns. He personally prayed daily—and did until his death—for Graham and his meetings. Surely no one could intelligently say Dr. Rice did not prove his friendship a hundred different ways.

When Billy's unequal yoke with modernism became so pronounced that he could no longer condone the popular revivalist's position, in one of his first printed articles of protest—*after repeated* private *attempts to get Billy to change his position*—he described his love and prayerful interest in the evangelist with these two opening paragraphs:

> "God bless Billy Graham in the services at _____. Bless his workers: Cliff Barrows, Bev Shea, Grady Wilson, Jerry Beavan, Paul Maddox." That part of my prayer, I suppose, my children have memorized. I have prayed it so often in family worship, when I have named some fifty or sixty evangelists before the Lord and pleaded for His blessing upon them. Sometimes I have prayed also for Brother Willis Haymaker, for Lorne Sanny and Betty Lowry, etc., but nearly always for those named. Then I got to feeling that my family would think it was too much of a routine matter, so I would sometimes ask God to bless all evangelists, and then alone in secret I would go over them one by one with Him, naming them before the Lord. But for many years, when some evangelist would come to Wheaton or to a Sword Conference, he would be met by one of my workers or one of my family who would say, "I have heard Dr. Rice pray for you so often."
>
> And they could say it also about Billy Graham. How my heart has followed him through the years—his first campaigns in England, then to Los Angeles, to Portland, to Atlanta, to

Columbia, to Dallas, to Scotland, to London, to Toronto, to New Orleans, to Chattanooga, to Louisville. I mention the heart burden of prayer which God laid upon me for Billy Graham because I think it is typical of the burden that many earnest Christians have had for the famous evangelist. Is it not then a matter of proper and deep concern to all of us, as to whether or not he follows God's plan about soul winning and revival?

No, Dr. Rice did not attack Billy Graham. He simply stood for the same principles for which he fought throughout the fifty-nine years of his ministry and which he placed at the heading of *The Sword of the Lord* for forty-six years: "An Independent Christian Weekly, Standing for the Verbal Inspiration of the Bible, the Deity of Christ, His Blood Atonement, Salvation by Faith, New Testament Soul Winning and the Premillennial Return of Christ. Opposes Modernism, Worldliness and Formalism." Let it be clearly understood that Dr. Rice did not change; Billy Graham was the one who changed.

Repeatedly Dr. Graham insisted he would not allow modernists on his executive committees. On one occasion he said to Dr. Rice, with evident distress over what had occurred, "A thing happened in the Atlanta meeting that I am determined will never happen again!" It seemed that before his arrival in Atlanta someone had placed modernists in positions of responsibility and he, in turn, got on his knees to promise God it would never happen again.

On another occasion, when Dr. Rice was visiting the All-Scotland Crusade at Glasgow in 1955, he and Dr. Graham discussed the same issue together in his room at the North British Hotel after one of the evening services. Again Dr. Graham solemnly asserted he had promised God never to have anyone take a place of authority or responsibility in his meetings who was not right on the great fundamentals of the historic Christian faith.

On one occasion Dr. Graham wrote:

It is this sin of apostasy that lies behind the oft-repeated words of the book of Judges: "And the children of Israel did that which was evil in the sight of the Lord." Sin, suffering,

repentance, deliverance—these four words form the constant
refrain of the book of Judges. I have just returned from Europe.
I felt the tension that is in all Europe at this very moment. I
saw what compromise with modernism, naturalism, material-
ism, humanism, and evolution has done to a once proud pop-
ulace. Many times it was my prayer, "Oh, God, help us in
America to fall upon our knees before God, to cease our compromising, to turn back to Thee once again" (*Pilot*, June-July,
1948).

In the same magazine, writing to apologize for an advertising
department slip-up which allowed a book by Harry Emerson
Fosdick to be featured, Dr. Graham declared:

> *The Pilot* represents the orthodox, conservative, fundamen-
> tal theological position. We do not condone nor have fellowship
> with any form of modernism. Dr. Fosdick's position is well
> known as that of an extreme modernist. We do not commend
> his writings to our reading public.

In one of his books he went on record as believing:

> . . .a preacher who is true to the Word of God must not only
> preach the Word (II Tim. 4:2) but must expose false teaching (I
> Tim. 1:3). A minister who is true to his calling must warn peo-
> ple against the danger of heresy and false doctrine. Many times
> he is tempted to soft-pedal because people may misunder-
> stand, and he may make enemies. That is why Paul said, "I am
> praying for you day and night, Timothy." Your pastor needs
> prayer that God will give him courage to stand true. Timothy
> was called upon to "reprove." That was a hard thing for a
> young man to do! Paul told him to "rebuke." That, too, is
> hard! (*Calling Youth to Christ*, p. 33).

How suddenly or how gradually Graham changed from this
firm Bible position, it is not safe to say. However, his open repu-
diation of the separatist stand was made during the National Association of Evangelical's annual convention at Buffalo, New
York, on April 3, 1957. In the manuscript containing the text of
his speech—which Dr. Graham furnished *Christianity Today*
and the emphasis is his own—he said: "First, as to its sponsorship (referring to his then future crusade in New York's Madison
Square Garden), I would like to make myself quite clear. I intend
to go anywhere, sponsored by anybody, to preach the Gospel of

Christ, if there are no strings attached to my message. I am sponsored by civic clubs, universities, ministerial associations and councils of churches all over the world. *I intend to continue.*" Immediately Dr. Rice's endorsement of Billy Graham and his campaigns came to a conclusion. Let it ever be remembered that it was Billy's position which changed, *not Dr. Rice's!*

The grievances of Dr. Rice and other fundamentalists against Billy Graham can probably be summed up in three major points: (1) his inclusive policy whereby he associates and unites in an unequal yoke with modernists and modernism; (2) his statements publicly slurring Bible believers and fundamentalists who have fought in defense of the faith down through the years; and, (3) the modifying of some of his beliefs. These are not "somewhat minor differences," as Dr. Graham stated in his newspaper column that he was "being criticized by some for doing." They are vital, important, pertinently essential matters.

Concerning the inclusive policy, Dr. Rice summed up his position in an article for *The Sword of the Lord,* saying:

> . . .we think it was unscriptural to have a New York Crusade sponsored by the Protestant Council and to have notorious modernists on the general committee and one or more on the executive committee.
>
> We think it was a yoke with unbelievers forbidden in II Corinthians 6:14-18. We think it was bidding Godspeed to and being partaker of the evil deeds of those who do not abide in the doctrine of Christ, forbidden in II John 7-11. We believe it was having fellowship with the unfruitful works of darkness, instead of reproving them as we are commanded in Ephesians 5:11.
>
> We believe that a greater campaign with more honor to God and eventually with more souls saved and more Christians blessed would have been had, had Billy Graham been willing to trust the Lord and go under the auspices of Bible believers and born-again Christians.

Dr. Graham was originally invited to go to New York sponsored solely by evangelical, fundamental churches and organizations. He refused to accept their invitation, insisting instead that the modernist Protestant Council must be included and their support gained before he would go.

In the official Billy Graham *New York Crusade News* the list of sponsors for "The General Crusade Committee" was listed. George Champion was chairman and among the others on the committee were: Dr. Jesse M. Bader, for more than twenty years a strong National Council-Federal Council leader and official; William Randolph Hearst, Jr., the newspaper publisher; Henry R. Luce, editor of *Life* magazine with its frequent articles in support of evolution, its ridicule of the old-time religion, and its prolific whiskey advertisements (Dr. Rice counted 15½ pages of whiskey, vodka and gin ads in *one* issue during the crusade); Dr. John A. Mackay, president of Princeton Seminary, a noted neo-orthodox center; modernist Bishop D. Ward Nichols, "who was among the American delegation which paid tribute to the Communist clergy in Moscow and was entertained by Georgi Carpoi, the atheist major-general of the secret police running the churches in Russia"; Captain Edward Rickenbacker, president of Eastern Airlines; Dr. Ralph W. Sockman, famous Methodist radio speaker noted principally for his modernism; and Dr. Henry P. Van Dusen, outstanding modernist and president of the notoriously infidelistic Union Theological Seminary, branded by the New York legislative committee appointed to investigate seditious activities in that state, the Lusk Committee, "a hot-bed of red radicalism" and a school which cheered the president of the Communist party when he spoke there some time back. Van Dusen later entered into a suicide pact with his wife; she died immediately, he died two weeks later.

When this list was given in the *New York Crusade News,* it said: "These are the people of New York. . .representing a cross-section of this vast city. . .whose advice, counsel and good will are so important in carrying on this tremendous Crusade for Christ." Note that they were the advisors and counsellors and that their advice and counsel was described by the Graham office as "so important" in the success of the crusade.

Daytime meetings of the crusade were held in the Seventh-Day Adventist Center. Notorious liberals were presented to the public night after night and called upon to lead in prayer. Such men as Norman Vincent Peale of the Marble Collegiate Church,

Bishop McConnell of the National Council of Churches, and Dr. Robert H. McCracken, pastor of Riverside Church where Harry Emerson Fosdick (the same man condemned by the Billy Graham of 1948) was pastor emeritus, were among those thus honored.

*The Sword of the Lord* published an article, most kindly and charitable in spirit and tone, by Dr. Tom Malone of Pontiac, Michigan, expressing sorrow over Dr. Graham's compromise and association with modernists. Dr. Graham wrote Dr. Malone, commenting about the modernists helping him in the New York Crusade: "They differ with us on the inspiration of the Bible and on the theories of the atonement."

But the Bible has only one "theory" about the atonement. Anyone who disagrees with that one "theory" is an infidel, not a saved man. It is impossible to be saved and have a different atonement theory than the one in the Bible which teaches that Christ's death was in our place and stead, paying the price in full for our sins and iniquities. When Dr. Graham has a man on his committee who has a different theory of the atonement, that man is an infidel, a child of Satan, without contradiction a lost person.

A very strong evidence of Graham's change in principle and policy concerned Dr. John Sutherland Bonnell, pastor of the Fifth Avenue Presbyterian Church in New York City. Dr. Bonnell was a known liberal, the author of an article in *Look* magazine which stated it was not necessary for Presbyterian ministers to believe in the virgin birth. On one occasion he was featured as the main speaker at the regular Friday evening service of a Jewish synagogue in Miami. Dr. Graham took the issue of *Look* containing Bonnell's article out of his pocket while talking to Dr. Rice in Glasgow, saying heatedly how it offended him and how he objected to it. It had been reported in the public press that Bonnell had gone to Scotland at Graham's invitation, but Billy vigorously denied the report to Dr. Rice. He assured him that though Bonnell had been present in the meeting, he had not recognized him nor invited him to pray. He did admit, however, "One night after I had left the meeting and gone to the inquiry

room, I think that Cliff asked Dr. Bonnell to close in prayer."
But in the New York Crusade, Dr. Bonnell was not only
recognized, he was a committeeman and one of the leading forces
in promoting and organizing the campaign.

At the close of the New York Crusade, the New York City
Council of Churches announced, through its executive director,
Dr. Donald Potter, it had gained 1,300 churches as a direct result
of the campaign. A total of $67,618 of the campaign surplus was
donated to this modernistic council by the Crusade committee.
Riverside Church, where notorious modernist Harry Emerson
Fosdick was a member and pastor emeritus, received 135 decision cards; and the Marble Collegiate Church, pastored by
master psychologist Norman Vincent Peale, received 373 cards,
the largest amount of any church.

Another example of Graham's new inclusivism related to the
Roman Catholic Church. Early in his ministry, he strongly condemned the false doctrines and teachings of Romanism. In his
message, "The World's Crisis Hour," he said he was
"frightened" over three things he had seen in Europe. The first
was Communism, the second was the rapid growth of Moham-
medanism ("the flash of the sword of Islam," he called it), and
this was the third:

> I saw Roman Catholicism. In Spain I saw men on the street
> corners with machine guns, with pistols at their sides. There is
> no religious freedom in Spain today. Any Protestant who tries
> to have a meeting in Spain is in peril of being stoned, beaten,
> arrested, even killed. This is under orders of the Roman
> Catholic Church!
> We are facing a crisis!

While the situation is different in Spain today, it nowhere near
justifies Dr. Graham's embracing of Roman Catholicism. Instead
of being "frightened," as he once was, now he promotes it,
glorifies it, and honors it. He praises its pope and other leaders,
accepts honorary degrees from its schools, has its clerical
dignitaries on his crusade committees and platforms, encourages
its representatives to work in his counseling rooms dressed in
their religious "habit," conducts crusades on its campuses, has

joined in partaking of its mass, and sends his converts to its churches.

That Dr. Graham changed should be obvious to even the most spiritually blind, deaf and dumb! His crusades became so all-inclusive it was difficult to imagine anyone he would not accept.

The second main objection in the Billy Graham controversy related to his public statements slurring earnest, sincere defenders of the Word of God. Repeatedly he refused to refer to himself as a fundamentalist and was quoted in *Christian Life* magazine to the effect: "During Billy Graham's 1955 Scotland crusade a BBC interviewer asked him to define the *fundamentalist* label he had been plastered with. Billy objected, 'I don't call myself a *fundamentalist.*' He said there was an aura of bigotry and narrowness associated with the term—which he certainly hoped was not true of himself."

In his now famous speech at the Buffalo NAE convention, he declared: "The NAE stands at the crossroads—it must steer a course between the extreme fundamentalist that God has by-passed and too much of a position of tolerance." In the same message he said, "I am sure that many of the extreme fundamentalists today would never support Mr. Moody."

In the magazine edited by his father-in-law and to which he donated $10,000 to launch, Graham said: "The old terms, fundamentalism and liberalism, are now passe." In the same magazine he declared, "The one badge of Christian discipleship is not orthodoxy, but love." On another occasion he stated, "I am not a fundamentalist. I am not a modernist. I am a conservative-liberal." Still again he said, "I am not a fundamentalist. I am not a modernist. I am a constructionist."

In addition to his uncomplimentary references to those who paid such a high price in defense of the Faith, he used his influence in trying to harm good, fundamental Christian works, a notable example of which was Bob Jones University. He permitted his biographer, Stanley High (who expressed his appreciation "to Ruth and Billy Graham for their wholehearted approval of the cooperation in this undertaking"), to put Bob Jones and the university which bears his name in a very ridiculous light.

Not only so, but when the school refused to permit a rally at its Rodeheaver Auditorium in behalf of the New York Crusade, an all-out attack was made on the school by those connected with Graham.

The battle was led by Dr. Nelson Bell, the missionary-physician-editor father-in-law of Dr. Graham. He had copies printed of a letter attacking the university by a disgruntled student who had been expelled for repeated and flagrant violation of the rules. He sent it, along with a vitriolic letter of his own containing unreasonable and unfounded charges against Dr. Jones, to nearly every student in the university, the faculty, the staff, the trustees and the cooperating board. The letters were sent to several Presbyterian ministers, other Christian schools, and various Christian leaders.

Primarily the charges were that Dr. Jones did not allow his students to pray for Billy Graham, that he was jealous, a Pharisee, embittered, etc.—all of which were untrue. Two former board members of the university wrote letters of their own, and they, too, were duplicated by Dr. Bell and sent out wholesale. Certainly some, possibly all, the funds for this attack on Bob Jones University came from the Billy Graham organization, part of it from the New York Crusade—the sacrificial money of saints who thought they were investing in a soul-winning business.

Remember that Billy Graham has repeatedly expressed himself as opposing controversy. He even refused to appear in Washington before the Interstate and Foreign Commerce Committee on behalf of legislation to outlaw liquor advertising, calling it "too controversial." But fundamentalists have become increasingly alarmed over his willingness to enter into controversy against them, slander and belittle them, yet be so polite and nice to all the enemies of the Faith.

As Dr. Rice expressed it in *The Sword of the Lord:*

> Dr. Graham seems not to be as sensitive about Bible believers as he is about Catholics, Jehovah's Witnesses, Christian Scientists, and modern infidels. The only ones that he does not mind offending are Bible believers. He accuses the fundamentalists of being "extremists." He said that they

> would not even have approved of D. L. Moody, which is such a
> mistake. I am impressed that he is not acquainted with the
> great mass of literature on D. L. Moody and on the facts which
> R. A. Torrey brought to light so well when Moody's modernist
> son later said that his father was a friend of modernism and
> would have been a modernist had he lived. . . .
>
> He did not primarily warn the National Association of
> Evangelicals that they must beware about yoking up with un-
> believers. He did not warn them that they must beware about
> the false cults that are damning the millions, including
> Catholics and others. No, no. The ones he warned them about
> were Bible believers. They are at the crossroads and they must
> beware not to be taken in by these fundamentalists!

The third cause for Dr. Rice's grief about Graham related to
the modifying of some of his beliefs. In the Stanley High
biography, *Billy Graham: the Personal Story of the Man, His
Message, and His Mission,* High said: "He is not, however, a
word-by-word literalist. In fact, some extreme fundamentalists
are not at all happy at the evidence they see of his departure
from what, by their rigid prescriptions, is the orthodox treatment
of the Scriptures." High said again, "Unlike the extreme fundamentalists, some of whom seem more concerned for their views
about the Bible than about the Bible and who make it a book of
controversy and division, to Billy Graham it is an indispensable
instrument of faith."

Billy Graham's literalism was mentioned again by High when
he said, "So far as his Scriptural literalism is concerned, that
light—as is indicated in a later chapter—has undergone some
modifying." Still again he commented, "There has been, too, a
considerable change which extreme fundamentalists may regard
as dangerous deviationism in the specifics of Billy Graham's
literalism." To illustrate his point, High revealed that Graham
formerly believed in a literal fire in Hell; now he does not.

The evidence that his changing theology seems to be affecting
his public message has been much more pronounced and apparent when Graham has faced exclusively liberal audiences
than it has before his large crusade crowds, comprised chiefly of
fundamentalists.

By way of example, in October of 1957, Dr. Graham addressed

approximately seven hundred students, faculty members and friends of the Colgate-Rochester Divinity School at a regular morning chapel service in the seminary auditorium. He was accompanied by his associate, Grady Wilson, and Dr. Donald Potter of the Protestant Council of New York City. Colgate-Rochester is a notoriously liberal school. As a matter of fact, in the same issue of the school paper which reported Graham's presence it "point[ed] with pride" that Dr. Edwin T. Dahlberg, newly elected president of the National Council of the Churches of Christ, was "both an alumnus and trustee of Colgate-Rochester Divinity School."

The Graham address was reported by William Hamilton in the *Colgate-Rochester Divinity School Bulletin.* Dr. Nels Ferre, noted liberal whose writings have brought reproach on the person and work of Christ repeatedly, conducted a two-day, all-school retreat on the campus two days later and the same article commented on his ministry as well. The following two paragraphs from the Hamilton article illustrate what I mean (the emphases are mine):

> Very few of the school community came to Dr. Graham's address with antagonism. There is very little professional anti-Graham spirit around. Some perhaps came expecting to be bored; but most came gratefully and openly. No one left bored, *and no one left particularly changed.* But we were all grateful for his presence; and, whatever we found in his words, we saw something in the man—or perhaps through the man—that made a real impact on us. In many ways, his talk was a straight-forward and conventional description of the qualities the ministry needs. He spoke directly to the students and allowed the rest of us to overhear. He made two points that stayed with us: the central need for a personal experience of Jesus Christ *(or, he added, what Niebuhr would call an encounter with the living God.* A nice touch, and an impressive example of his extraordinary sensitiveness to an audience), and the utter necessity of personal discipline and prayer.

> These two central points became important retroactively, rather than at the time we heard them. For when the retreat followed close upon, two days later, *we heard and experienced the same two-fold truth from Dr. Ferre.*

Note the following truth from the above revelation: (1) Graham's address did not "particularly change" anyone who heard it; (2) Graham watered down the Saviour's insistence upon the new birth by interpreting it for his hearers as being "what Niebuhr would call an encounter with the living God." No one in his right mind would believe for a moment that what the neo-orthodox Niebuhr meant by "an encounter with the living God" and what Jesus Christ defined as being "born again" are one and the same; and, (3) when students and faculty had heard both Graham and Ferre, they could not tell the difference between their messages, concluding both were talking about the same thing. As a matter of fact, the *Divinity School Bulletin* went on to say: ". . .what they said, or what they meant, at least, was the same thing."

Something is surely radically wrong when an audience of seven hundred cannot tell the difference between a Billy Graham message and a Nels Ferre message—and leave thinking both were about "the same single thing"! That Billy Graham compromised his "methods," no one could deny; that he was gradually compromising his "message" brought grave alarm to hearts of Bible believers everywhere.

Another change had to do with his terminology concerning the results in his crusades. Once they were referred to as "conversions," but that was modified to "decisions." Later they were simply described as "committals to Christ," a popular description used by modernists and meaning almost anything. In the New York campaign he referred to them as "inquirers" and said in print about those who were dealt with after the invitation, "We do not call them converts. We call them inquirers." So it is only fair to say that out of the sixty-odd thousand "inquirers" who reportedly made "committals to Christ" in his New York Crusade, considerably less than half were first-time decisions for Jesus Christ.

One other modification of his beliefs which Dr. Rice and other fundamentalists found very distressing and repulsive related to his position on worldliness. He was for a long time very friendly to the movie industry, but then he began yoking up with them positively.

All of us were distressed when we learned that the film, *The Mighty Fortress,* featuring highlights of his London Crusade, was being shown in commercial theaters. One Chicago theater featured it as an extra attraction the night they presented the movie, *Tonight's the Night,* which was advertised: "Men and women acting like men and women—slightly outrageous!" The advertisement featured a picture of Billy Graham and a picture of a nearly naked woman. The *Chicago Daily News* frankly stated it: "Moviemen here hope the film will help them lure Northern churchgoers away from their TV sets and into the movie houses."

Still later Dr. Graham publicly endorsed Cecil B. De Mille's extravaganza, *The Ten Commandments;* and his testimonial was published in movie ads everywhere, saying, "I was deeply impressed and commend it most highly." On one occasion he called it the "most accurate Biblical picture ever filmed." Actually, the picture was far from the biblical account and was loaded with suggestive sex. *Time* magazine remarked that ". . . what he [De Mille] has really done is to throw sex and sand into the moviegoers' eyes for almost twice as long as anybody else has ever dared to. He throws it very clearly indeed." *Time* also commented that ". . .it is sometimes hard to determine where the fine line between bad taste and sacrilege is to be drawn" in the movie. Young people everywhere began asking their fundamental pastors what the score was with reference to the movies. They reasoned that if a man like Billy Graham approved of them, why couldn't they?

In his newspaper column, *My Answer,* he came out flatly in support of movies—with the exception of *some* bad ones—and condemned by inference all who would oppose the movies simply because there were some objectionable ones. He said in response to the question, "Are movies of the Lord or of the devil?":

> Why not ask, are books of the Lord or of the devil? There are good books and bad books, good movies and bad ones. Unfortunately, many movies play up sin or violence in attractive

ways; and when they do, they are evil for they wield a tremendous influence on people. There have been some wonderful movies, historical stories, and other wholesome pictures which have lifted people up and been a real inspiration. However, such great pictures are in the minority. . . .

Whether in the movies or in books or on radio or television, where sin is made to seem good and attractive, it is wrong; and those who fill their minds with such things find that God is crowded out.

I know that some people feel all movies are evil. If they feel that way, they should not violate their consciences by attending. By the same standard though, we would never read a book because so many of them are evil. Christian discrimination, arrived at by prayer and with a clear leading of God's Holy Spirit in the heart, is the best solution to this problem.

Bible believers were shocked to pick up their newspapers and see a national news service picture of Dr. Graham doing a burlesque, vaudeville-type dance routine with Hollywood actor John Davidson and television personality Mike Douglas. Underneath the picture was the explanation: *"Didn't know that the Rev. Billy Graham tap-danced, did you? Neither did we. Here is Billy with Mike Douglas and that nice young John Davidson, and they're doing a little number during the Las Vegas taping of an upcoming Douglas show."* We were horrified at the thought of Dr. Graham doing a dance routine on national television. It was reminiscent of when, in 1960, during a tour of the former East African country, Tanganyika, he found himself at a communal dance with bare-breasted women and drunken men, and "in a reckless flush of affability, even allowed himself to be momentarily tugged into a few shuffling steps with the dancers." What seems to have been almost an accidental thing in 1960 had become a deliberate, nonchalant act less than two decades later.

It was during this five-day crusade in the Las Vegas Convention Center—when his dance segment on the Douglas Show was filmed—that Dr. Graham told a news conference he was not in the city "to criticize Las Vegas and its sometimes overpublicized lifestyle." But if a preacher is not going to crack down on gambling, booze, nudity and prostitution, hasn't all the *punch* been removed from his *preach*?

Perhaps his most shocking and regrettable endorsement of worldliness related to liquor. Shortly after Jimmy Carter's inauguration as President, Dr. Graham came to the Georgian's public defense over criticism of the latter's consumption of hard liquor. He said, "I do not believe that the Bible teaches teetotalism. I can't. . .Jesus drank wine. Jesus turned water into wine at a wedding feast. That wasn't grape juice, as some of them try to claim." He had previously, in his *My Answer* column, endorsed social drinking. In fact, he admits to some consumption of his own, namely, "medicinal sipping of a hot dram of spirits for an ague once in a while, and in fact, 'after my many trips to Europe,' even began to take a polite glass of wine now and then." He added, "My father would turn over in his grave, I suppose. And that would get me in a lot of trouble from some of the people. But no, I am not a teetotaler."

As you can see, this controversy did not come over minor issues, and the Graham position marked a serious cleavage from the position taken by other greatly used evangelists of the past. It was the Graham office's continual defense that he merely followed in the steps of his predecessors, but it simply is not true that Moody, Torrey, Billy Sunday, J. Wilbur Chapman, and other great evangelists of the past compromised with modernism, slurred fundamentalists, or modified their convictions in doctrinal and practical matters, as has Dr. Graham.

It can rightly be said that *The Sword of the Lord* did not turn from Billy Graham, but Billy Graham turned from *The Sword of the Lord* and the position it had maintained from its inception. Even today, if Dr. Graham would return to his former position of Bible separation, the pages of *The Sword of the Lord* would again be opened to promote and publicize his campaigns.

Sometimes the defenders of the Graham position quote Luke 9:49,50, "Master, we saw one casting out devils in thy name; and we forbad him, because he followeth not with us. And Jesus said unto him, Forbid him not: for he that is not against us is for us." This was hardly applicable, however, for as Dr. Rice wrote:

> . . .nobody objects to Billy Graham's casting out devils. What we object to is his having the devils on the platform, hav-

ing them lead in prayer, turning the new converts over to them, etc. None of us good Christians would object if Billy Graham fought every kind of sin and called for genuine repentance and got drunkards and harlots and convicts saved. So to use that Scripture as if those of us who are standing for the Bible are jealous and want Billy Graham to quit simply because he doesn't follow us, is not only a misrepresentation of the meaning of Scripture, but it deliberately misrepresents entirely the issue which we have plainly made.

The issue is not that Billy Graham casts out devils, but that he runs with them and tries to please them and boost them. Jesus would have approved Peter and John if they had been against the people who wanted others to stay possessed with devils and to call brothers, etc. So are we.

Did the controversy accomplish anything? Did it do any good? That answer is both "Yes" and "No." The answer is "Yes" because many Christian people, both clergy and laymen, had their eyes opened to the real issue of compromise and the damage the Graham crusades were doing to the cause of fundamentalism in America and around the world.

Many who first wrote Dr. Rice very vitriolicly, condemning him for his position, later wrote to apologize and confess sadly that he was right. One lady who wrote rebukingly at first, wrote later to apologize, saying God had shown her she was following Billy Graham somewhat as an idol and that she knew it was wrong to condone yoking up with unbelievers just because he did it. Another man from New York wrote using very sharp language; but before the New York Crusade was over he wrote again, saying:

Dear Dr. Rice:

I have read your letter with great interest. Billy Graham has told his audience several times that he is being slandered and although neither your name, nor that of Dr. McIntire, has been mentioned, it was easy to understand whom he meant. . . .

He does preach the Gospel faithfully, but I am beginning to see that indeed he compromises a great deal. That is a pity! But I do rejoice that souls are getting saved. Yes, it is too bad that those who are supposed to be saved are sent back to their modernistic churches.

Last week Dr. McCracken, the minister of the Riverside

Church, who preaches nothing but social gospel, was invited to sit beside Billy and to pray. He never mentioned the name of Christ. Last year he invited many a modernistic professor to lecture in his church and prove that the Bible was not an absolutely reliable book, inspired from the beginning to the end. I was greatly distressed to see that man beside Billy and to hear him pray.

It is hard to understand why Billy does not see this. . . .

Dr. Bob Shuler, for a third of a century pastor of the large Trinity Methodist Church in Los Angeles, commented in his paper, *The Methodist Challenge,* relative to the position taken by Dr. Rice and Dr. Bob Jones, Sr., concerning the New York Crusade:

I have been asked by various individuals as to my opinion of the stand they have taken. My answer is that, based upon all the information I have been able to obtain, these two old giants are right.

They are biblically right.

They are right according to the tenets and historicity of evangelical Christianity.

They are right, if we are to accept the evidence to be found along the trail left by the truly great evangelists of the centuries.

To prove that they are right, one need only turn to the exhortation of St. Paul in the fourteenth verse of the sixth chapter of Second Corinthians:

*"Be ye not unequally yoked together with unbelievers: for what fellowship hath righteousness with unrighteousness? and what communion hath light with darkness?"*

Continuing in the verse that follows:

*"And what concord hath Christ with Belial? or what part hath he that believeth with an infidel?"*

Here is indeed strong and easily understood language. The line of separation is drawn, not by men, but by the Holy Ghost to whom we correctly yield the credit for having given these instructions to Christians of all the centuries. The words that I have quoted from St. Paul were given to the Christian church for all time by the Holy Ghost (II Pet. 1:21). They came from the day when "holy men of God spake as they were moved by the Holy Ghost."

However, the answer as to whether the controversy has done good is also "No." It did not help Billy Graham. His next big campaign was in the spring of 1958 at San Francisco. This was an even bigger sell-out from the cause of biblical Christianity than the New York Crusade. An impressive array of modernist-liberals was assembled to back and promote the campaign.

The meeting was principally sponsored by the Oakland Bay Council of Churches, an exceptionally strong liberal council because of the influence of Berkeley Divinity School in that area. The treasurer was Fred D. Parr, a member of the "Board of Patrons" of the Pacific School of Religion. This school is as widely known in the West for its infidelity as Union Theological Seminary is known in the East. It annually features such speakers as Nels Ferre, Emil Bruner, Harry Emerson Fosdick, Robert H. McCracken, and others. The noted Methodist modernist, Georgia Harkness, is a member of the faculty, as is a Jewish rabbi, Morris Goldstein. Mr. Lowell W. Berry and Mr. Edward L. Soule were two others on the Graham committee associated with this school of infidelity.

Others on the committee included: Mrs. John Fitzgerald, a member of one of the most liberal Christian churches in the West and president of the Northern California Convention of Christian Churches; Dr. Abbott Book, executive director of the Northern California Council of Churches for many years and a strong ecumenicalist; Dr. W. Earle Smith, past president of the Northern Council of Churches and the San Francisco Council of Churches, a man described as sympathetic with the modernist causes and "a more relentless foe of fundamental Baptist churches could hardly be found." Dr. Smith was co-chairman of the crusade.

Another committee member was Mrs. William Lister Rogers, president of the San Francisco Council of Churches. She was the originator and chairman of the infamous "Festival of Faith" at the Cow Palace in 1955, the same site where the Graham crusade was conducted. In that service, Christian, Jew, Moslem, Buddhist, Hindu and Confucianist each prayed to his own god in his own language, invoking world peace. The whole thing was of the rankest blasphemy, yet Mrs. Rogers was appointed to the Graham committee for the San Francisco Crusade.

Dr. G. Archer Weniger, describing the luncheon for 1,150 ministers, assistants and leaders of that area who met to map out the San Francisco crusade, said: "This meeting was a heterogeneous collection of heretics, modernists, liberals, higher critics, pinks, scoffers of the Blood, deniers of the Bible, rejectors of the Deity, plus a number of fundamentalists. In spite of the smoke, no one could be blind to the fact that there were ecclesiastical decoys present." He went on to describe both fundamentalist and modernist leaders who were brought into the Bay area in attempt to bring the two groups together in harmony for the Graham crusade.

Before we close this chapter, perhaps it should be emphasized that the excuse most frequently given for inviting modernists into the Graham campaigns—to win them to Christ—simply does not work, *nor would doing so be justified even if it did!* We are not to do evil that good may come, the Bible teaches. As has already been stated, Dr. Norman Vincent Peale, master psychologist and minister of the Marble Collegiate Church in New York City, received the most decision cards from the New York Crusade. Rumors circulated freely to the effect that he had been converted and his daughter also had given her heart to Christ. Other reports had him preaching the old-time Gospel as a direct result of Graham's influence. The reports became so prolific and so persistent Peale eventually felt compelled to make a statement in print denying the rumors.

As evidence that he was not helped by the Graham crusade, let me quote from an article in the *Southern Presbyterian Journal,* of which Dr. L. Nelson Bell was then an editor and which praised highly the New York Crusade. The article was written by Rev. William Cooper Cumming and entitled, "What Dr. Norman Vincent Peale Left Out." It seems Rev. Cumming had heard Peale speak to some 2,000 people at the Texarkana Junior College and was hastening to point out what the message lacked. He wrote:

> For example, in diagnosing man's trouble there was nothing said about sin, and in prescribing the remedy there was nothing said about salvation in the sense of being reconciled with God. There was nothing about the cross, and nothing

about Christ as Saviour; and there never is in any of the books, writings, or sermons of Norman Vincent Peale as far as we have been able to observe.

Dr. Peale gives credit to Bible reading and to prayer to give calmness, peace and poise, and indeed it does; but it does it by a method that Dr. Peale never mentions, namely, by bringing lost souls to Christ their Saviour, where they find salvation through the atonement of His shed blood and the peace of God which passes all understanding through the presence of the Holy Spirit who indwells the true believer.

If Dr. Peale came to us as a psychologist or a psychiatrist, we would not expect him to say much more than he says; for what he leaves out is the essential of the Gospel, without which no one can be saved. Therefore, we appraise him as Jeremiah appraised certain of his contemporaries by saying, "They have healed also the hurt of the daughter of my people slightly, saying, Peace, peace; when there is no peace" (Jer. 6:14).

Dr. Peale was not helped by the Graham crusade; and we fear the same has been true of other modernists, in spite of prolific professions to the contrary relating to "unnamed" personalities. It is *never* right to do wrong, no matter what noble motive the sinner might have or who might be doing it—*even Billy Graham!*

Actually, the Billy Graham issue was not a major event in the life of Dr. Rice, although it was certainly important. In revising the biography I was impressed with the amount of space I gave it, due to the fact, no doubt, that it was a fresh and vital issue when the first edition was written. I seriously considered editing the account in the revision, reducing the Graham affair to give the book better balance. I eventually decided against it, since the story as written outlines the principles of biblical separation as Dr. Rice saw them and fought for them. The truth is that both men remained friends, exchanged greetings from time to time; and I am aware of at least one sizable contribution Dr. Graham sent to Dr. Rice for his ministry. And Dr. Rice often spoke, privately and in print, of his gratitude for the souls being reached for Christ through the popular evangelist's ministry. The break was entirely a matter of principle on the part of Dr. Rice.

Perhaps it would be well to sum up the Graham matter with a brief statement Dr. Rice wrote in a letter to a critic, outlining his separation position. He told that brother:

Now let me state my position very clearly. As far as I can understand it, it is based on the clear teaching of the Bible. For one thing, the Scripture says, 'I am a companion of all them that fear thee, and of them that keep thy precepts' (Ps. 119:63). I can have fellowship with those who are born-again Christians and who earnestly believe and try to follow the Word of God. That is a Bible standard which I dare not deviate from.

Second, I am to have fellowship with born-again Christians, even those who are weak in the faith, or who are not well taught on some of the principles of action and so might not agree with me, just so that fellowship does not lead to 'doubtful disputations,' as the Scripture teaches in Romans 14:1.

In the third place, I am clearly forbidden to have fellowship with modernists and other unsaved people (II Cor. 6:14-18, II John 7-11).

In the fourth place, I am forbidden to have fellowship with those who call themselves Christians but who live in outrageous sin (I Cor. 5:11).

From these Scriptures it seems clear I am not to have Christian fellowship with anybody who is unsaved, with anyone who is openly against the fundamental truths of the Bible; and I am not to have fellowship with anybody who is living in outrageous sin, as an idolater, fornicator, or drunkard; but I am plainly taught in the Bible to have fellowship with all Christians who are relatively clean in life and who are true on the great fundamentals of the Faith, even though they may be weak in the faith and even though there may be minor differences of opinion.

I think it would be far greater difference of opinion to differ about eternal security than to differ about the method of Dr. Billy Graham. The method is wrong, but so is Arminianism wrong. Dr. Graham has made this matter a matter of doubtful disputation, a matter of debate and division, and so I cannot have fellowship with him. But if he had not made that an issue, and if it were not a matter of debate and divison, I would have fellowship with Dr. Graham even though on some matters I would feel compelled to tell him he was mistaken and wrong.

Perhaps the strongest controversy Dr. Rice had with his fundamentalist-separatist brethren related to the issue of storehouse tithing. He was accused, *falsely* I hasten to add, of opposing, simply to help his own ministries, the popular modern (we can find no one who espoused it before the 20th Century) view that the local church is now the New Testament "storehouse." That this charge was untrue and unjust can easily be proved from the "Statement of Faith" he wrote as a successful pastor (see Appendix B), insisting that "each Christian is free to give as and where the Holy Spirit directs." Yet this one conviction probably resulted in as many canceled subscriptions to *The Sword of the Lord* as anything following the early days of the Billy Graham-ecumenical evangelism issue.

Any number of preachers have asked me, "Why did Dr. Rice keep 'harping' on that one storehouse note? Why didn't he just state his position and then forget it?"

Perhaps he did overemphasize it, but it was a matter of *very deep* concern to him. In short, he feared history was repeating itself. Explaining it privately to me on one occasion, he said he felt that just as emphases on the "Cooperative Program" had helped undermine evangelical orthodoxy within the Southern Baptist Convention, so insistence upon storehouse tithing would eventually do the same to independent Baptists. The Cooperative Progam had conditioned Southern Baptists to put money into "a program," right or wrong; and he felt storehouse tithing was doing the same thing to the independents.

Dr. Rice strongly believed that all programs and causes— including local churches—should *merit* their gifts. In other words, giving should not be automatic—something that *must* be given *at a certain place*—but offered because the giver firmly *believed in* what the church or organization was accomplishing. He spoke often of the Christian's obligation to invest his gifts where they would do the most good and reach the most souls.

We could call your attention to other controversies in which Dr. Rice was engaged during his colorful ministry, but in each one the issue was "Thus saith the Lord," never a personality. He proved himself to be a friend of "all them that love our Lord Jesus Christ in sincerity" (Eph. 6:24). He could say, and did say, with the Psalmist, "I am a companion of all them that fear thee, and of them that keep thy precepts" (Ps. 119:63). Yet about God's enemies he felt he must say with the same Psalmist, "Do not I hate them, O Lord, that hate thee? and am not I grieved with those that rise up against thee? I hate them with perfect hatred: I count them mine enemies" (Ps. 139:21,22).

Dr. Rice continued, as long as God gave him breath, to oppose sharply the Hymenaeuses and the Alexanders, that they might learn not to blaspheme. In like manner, he continued to lovingly, tenderly oppose the Peters to their faces when they were wrong themselves and leading others away through their dissimulation. As was true of the Scottish reformers, he was "jealous for the crown rights of King Jesus!"

The critics cried, "O thou sword of the Lord, how long will it be ere thou be quiet? put up thyself into thy scabbard, rest, and be still" (Jer. 47:6).

Yet the answer remained, "How can it be quiet, seeing the Lord hath given it a charge. . ." (vs. 7).

*Chapter 17*

# Personality Portrait

*But the fruit of the Spirit is love, joy, peace, longsuffering, gentleness, goodness, faith, Meekness, temperance: against such there is no law. And they that are Christ's have crucified the flesh with the affections and lusts. If we live in the Spirit, let us also walk in the Spirit. Let us not be desirous of vain glory, provoking one another, envying one another. Brethren, if a man be overtaken in a fault, ye which are spiritual, restore such an one in the spirit of meekness; considering thyself, lest thou also be tempted. Bear ye one another's burdens, and so fulfil the law of Christ. For if a man think himself to be something, when he is nothing, he deceiveth himself. But let every man prove his own work, and then shall he have rejoicing in himself alone, and not in another. For every man shall bear his own burden.*—Galatians 5:22-6:5.

*A new commandment I give unto you, That ye love one another; as I have loved you, that ye also love one another. By this shall all men know that ye are my disciples, if ye have love one to another.*—John 13:34,35.

*Though I speak with the tongues of men and of angels, and have not charity, I am become as sounding brass, or a tinkling cymbal. And though I have the gift of prophecy, and understand all mysteries, and all knowledge; and though I have all faith, so that I could remove mountains, and have not charity, I am nothing. And though I bestow all my goods to feed the poor, and though I give my body to be burned, and have not charity, it profiteth me nothing.*—I Corinthians 13:1-3.

*For as he thinketh in his heart, so is he. . . .*—Proverbs 23:7.

JOHN R. RICE was a fighter of the first magnitude. Apparently he never heard the trumpet blow a retreat—or if he did, it was woefully and totally ignored. In a previous chapter we called him a destructionist. He was all of that and more. Yet when we came to write this chapter and meditated long about his most outstanding characteristic, the only distinctive we could seriously consider twice was the characteristic of love.

Does this seem strange or paradoxical? If it does, perhaps we have forgotten the meaning of the word "love." "God is love" (I John 4:8,16), but He is also "a consuming fire" (Heb. 12:29). The God who "so loved the world, that he gave his only begotten Son" (John 3:16) is described in Scripture as hating (Zech. 8:17; Prov. 6:16-19) and as being "angry with the wicked every day" (Ps. 7:11). Hatred is not at all inconsistent with love. It is *what* you hate, *why* you hate, and *how* you hate that determines its good or evil. Such was the case in the personality of John Rice, best defined as an apostle of love. Those who thought of him as harsh, cruel, cutting or bitter because of his bold, dogmatic, uncompromising stand in defense of the Faith simply did not know the *real* John R. Rice!

John Rice honestly, sincerely loved people. He sought to make a friend of every stranger. The continuing of "brotherly love" is defined as being "not forgetful to entertain strangers" (Heb. 13:1,2), and his home was always open for meals and lodging to any and all who might be passing that way.

Not a few are the people I have met in various parts of the country who informed me they "spent the night" with Dr. Rice. He knew no respect of persons—the "nobodies" were just as welcome as the "somebodies" in his home. In his revivals he insisted on shaking hands with every new convert no matter how few or how many; and if an usher started the person to the inquiry room first, he would insist, "Bring that person to me!"

One associate told me of seeing him lean over the platform to shake hands for nearly an hour. Whenever a visitor came into the Calvary Baptist Church he founded and pastored in Wheaton— even though it was Sunday morning and the preliminaries were already underway—he would leave the platform and go personally to welcome the stranger.

Arriving at the Sword office, he waved his hand to everyone

and had a friendly greeting for each employee in sight. When he reached his secretary's office, Miss Viola Walden, he might greet her with some prankish phrase like *"Comment allez vous ce matin?"* meaning "How are you this morning?"

When visitors dropped in at the Sword of the Lord, he showed them every courtesy. I never knew of anyone who came by the office desiring to meet him and was told he was too busy.

And there was an obvious note of sincerity in his friendly greeting, "How are you? I am *so glad* to see you!" If the visitor wanted to see the various departments and all the employees were busy, he personally escorted him on the tour, introduced him to the workers, described their duties, and otherwise made the guest feel welcome. No doubt the visitor concluded that Dr. Rice's work was not very pressing, but several hundred letters might have been waiting for his answer, rush copy for *The Sword of the Lord* needed in an hour, or perhaps several radio broadcasts had to be taped before he could leave the office that day.

Many times he had about five or ten minutes before leaving to catch a plane when someone would want to see him. He never turned one down, although, as a result, his secretary might have had to go along with him to the airport to finish the last bit of work necessary before leaving town. If the visitor was a minister, in all probability he left with a free copy of *Prayer—Asking and Receiving,* or *The Power of Pentecost,* or some new book just off the press.

His sister-in-law, Dr. Bill's wife, Cathy, was speaking of this when she wrote:

> But, busy as he was, his door was always open! He always had time for any and all who needed his counsel.
> I became aware of this when I was just a girl of twenty-one and facing marriage. To tell you the truth, I was scared to death and worried. I was engaged to Bill Rice, the brother of Dr. John Rice, and he was pastor of a small struggling church in Gainesville, Texas. His church was giving him a love offering each Sunday for his support. He always said they didn't love him very much because his offering usually averaged around $3.50 a week. We'd agreed, however, when he was getting $7 a week we would get married. If he could live on $3.50, surely the two of us could live on $7. But I heard the song of

doom constantly. My well-meaning good friends, as well as my aunts, uncles, cousins and so forth, constantly told me what a miserable life I was in for. I knew the prospects looked bleak, but I had prayed about whom I should marry, and I felt that Bill Rice was the one.

One day, however, since I was so worried, Bill suggested that I go and talk to his brother John. Perhaps he could give me some comfort.

"Me speak to him? Why he is so busy, he wouldn't have time for me."

Bill assured me this was a foolish statement and that I would indeed find John Rice would have time for me. So I called on the phone and made an appointment. I'll always remember how kind and gracious and helpful he was to me. I knew he was a busy man, but he still had time to hear my fears and to pray with me and give me words of comfort. And he did not make me feel hurried. He calmed my fears and helped me put my trust in the Lord.

And that's the way it has been through these forty-five years I have known Dr. John R. Rice. He always had time for me. And I know there are thousands who could say the very same thing. I thank God for every remembrance of him.

An employee who had been with Dr. Rice since 1935 and lived in his home for about two decades of that time, wrote me:

When I speak of Dr. Rice, I am not speaking from short acquaintance but on the basis of long and close association. I have seen him at home and abroad. I have seen him when he was relaxed and when under such pressure and burden as would seem enough to crush him. I have seen him surrounded by loved ones and among strangers. I have seen him both sick and well. I have seen him when people praised and loved him as well as when he had lost the dearest of friends because of his uncompromising stand for Christ. In all of these circumstances and during all of this time, his life has been miraculously consistent.

I have never once seen him lifted up with pride or show personal resentment toward those who did him harm, misunderstood him, or misrepresented him. Not once have I seen him take unfair advantage of another. And, perhaps most remarkable of all, not once do I ever remember seeing him discouraged.

I have never seen him other than mild *except* when he had to be otherwise in order to do right. Then I have seen him as bold as a lion, strong as steel, unmovable as a mountain of stone in defending Christ and the Bible or when influences were at work trying to beat him down or turn him from a course he was convinced was right.

I have seen him as objective as a judge on a bench when deciding what was right and what was wrong, even though his own children or wife were involved. I have heard him with holy boldness and unmitigated condemnations expose modernists and other deniers of the Bible. Perhaps I have seen him more rigid with himself than anyone else.

Then this close friend and associate summed it up by saying:

Yet I have never known a person with a greater capacity for loving people. How he yearns after people and prays for them! How he longs to help them!

His treatment of correspondence manifested that love for people. No letter was treated lightly. He answered, often in great detail, many, many problems. A most vitriolic letter might come to his desk bristling with critical animosity and bordering on personal hatred, yet he would take time to answer the critic kindly and thoroughly. This manifestation of love paid big dividends, and many times the offending person wrote back to confess his or her wrong.

His secretary, Miss Walden, sent me a letter which she suggested I reproduce here as representative of the above. It came from a Methodist minister in Ohio who wrote to tell how he had been saved from apostasy and compromise through a series of articles I had written for *The Sword* concerning *The Interpreter's Bible,* a modernist commentary published by the official publishing house of his denomination. His first reaction had been one of anger and indignation, followed by a fiery letter to Dr. Rice. The following paragraphs from his second letter are self-explanatory and indicative of the results Dr. Rice's careful correspondence often produced. This minister wrote:

Dear Brother Rice:

When I wrote you a letter some time ago, asking you to cancel my subscription to *The Sword of the Lord,* I thought it would be the last I would hear from you. The Lord apparently planned it otherwise because your answer made me face up to some of the fundamentals of the Faith which I up to now had found easy to ignore. I have subconsciously been aware of the fact that bit by bit, the essential doctrines of the Faith were being diluted in my thinking until I wasn't sure what I believed. Your letter made me face these questions honestly, and I thank you for this.

It was a misdirected sense of loyalty relative to the infallibility of my Methodist brethren that led to my denouncing you for having denounced them.

Being honest hurts sometimes, but the truth is that after having read one of Brother Sumner's articles I found myself in complete agreement with his remarks. It aggravated me so much that a non-denominational publication could make me lose faith in some of our denominational leaders that the best way to relieve myself of this feeling was to shut the door of the source of my enlightenment. So I asked you to please cease sending *The Sword of the Lord* to me. I was wrong. I not only hope that you will continue to send the paper; but if you would, please send all the back issues relating to *The Interpreter's Bible.* I threw the last few copies away, purposefully ignoring what Sumner had to say simply because I contemplated buying that very set. I promise that *The Sword of the Lord* will receive my reading interest in the future.

. . .I realize that you are a very busy man and I can only feel that it must have been directed of the Lord or you would not have taken time to write me such a thorough letter. Your spirit has truly been that of a Christian. If I expected a letter from you, it, in my thinking, would have been a rebuke. I would like an interest in your prayers and hope someday to become better acquainted with you. . . .

As this incident indicates, preachers were a special delight, holding a very tender spot in the heart of this man who had an international reputation of being "a preacher's preacher." He prayed daily for scores of them by name. Many he helped financially, sometimes paying debts for others out of his own pocket so reproach would not be brought on an evangelist or pastor. When I was pastoring in Texas and a church fire destroyed my library of over a thousand volumes, upon learning of the tragedy, he wrote and suggested I select twenty-five dollars' worth of his books as a gift from him, although I was a total stranger at that time. Eternity alone will reveal what he did for preachers, spiritually and materially.

His love for people was not limited to the saints, but found its greatest fulfillment, perhaps, in a genuine compassion for the souls of the lost. Soul winning was not a theory with him; it was a reality. He witnessed to people wherever he went, and it was not at all unusual for him to return to the office and tell how he won a soldier seated next to him on the plane, or of some other soul-winning experience he had that day. The little chorus he wrote and used so many times in his revival campaigns was merely the beat of his own heart:

**Souls are dying!**
**Brother, do you care?**
**Souls undone, away from God,**
**My brother, do you care?**
**Souls are dying!**
**Brother, do you care?**
**Souls (precious souls) are dying!**

Yet his honest, sincere love for people was manifested just as truly in his role of boss as it was of evangelist and editor. People often asked me what it was like to work closely with Dr. Rice. Frankly, if one did not do his work, it was not a pleasant experience. A perfectionist himself, it was most difficult for him to tolerate inefficiency in others. Yet those who conscientiously did their work could not ask for a finer employer. In all the time I worked in the office, first as an editorial assistant, then as associate editor, I cannot recall a single time he raised his voice at me or even rebuked me in any way. Even when I was obviously wrong, he politely and humbly made suggestions to show me my error. Often he would come into my office and ask my counsel about very important matters as if he were the immature, inexperienced one and I the mature, experienced and qualified one.

His intolerance of inefficiency could be explained by the fact that he himself was a very hard worker. He rarely took a vacation, until near the end of his ministry—and even then it was often a "working vacation." He never took a day off to recuperate after a revival meeting. Regardless of how strenuous the schedule had been or how long the journey home, if he arrived back at home on a weekday, he went immediately to his office and took up his duties. He might stretch out on the couch for an hour's nap in the middle of the morning or after lunch, but he was on the job all of the time. Remember, too, he did not receive a single penny in remuneration of any kind for his work as editor or author.

An illustration of his conscientiousness related to a serious fall when his offices were still in Wheaton, Illinois. Going down the back steps in the dark after taping some radio broadcasts late Saturday night, he fell eleven steps and struck his head on the concrete. For about an hour he remained unconscious on the floor. After regaining consciousness, he found his way in the dark up the stairs, out the back door, down the alley between the office and the railroad tracks, around the corner service station to his automobile, then drove by the post office and mailed the tapes, drove across town to his home, parked his car and came into the house. His chief concern did not pertain to how badly he had been hurt—although it was learned later that he had suffered a fractured skull—but about his duties. He repeatedly asked: "Did I lock the door? I wonder if I mailed the tapes?"

One of the secretaries went back to the office and found the door securely locked. Others looked everywhere for the tapes and could not find them. A few days later word was received from station WMUU at Greenville, South Carolina, saying the tapes had been received. At such a time, shocked and hurt from what turned out to be a double fracture and concussion, duty was still uppermost in his mind—and this was typical of his entire life.

Perhaps listing the length of years some of his employees had been associated with him at the time of his death would be an effective illustration of Dr. Rice as an employer. His personal secretary, Miss Viola Walden, had been with him for more than 46 years. Miss Fairy Shappard, advertising manager, had been with him most of the time for 45 years. Others with over two decades of loyal, faithful service include: Charles Vradenburgh, proofreader, 23 years; Al Byers, business manager, 23 years; Hilda Allen, secretary, 22 years; Rose Gibson, mailroom, 28 years; Sarah Pope, secretary, 21 years; Rex Graby, plateroom, 22 years; Mary Koehler, retail, 25 years; and Dottie Reichel, artist, retired the year before Dr. Rice died after 25 years of service.

The last mentioned employee, Miss Dorothy Reichel, had a physical affliction, and her testimonial of how he treated her is not an abnormal portrayal of his personality. She wrote me:

> Dr. Rice has truly taken the place of my father the last few years. The way he believes, teaches and follows the Bible is so nearly like the way my father did that it seems almost as if "Daddy" is still guiding me through Dr. Rice. He seems to love me nearly as much as my father did, too, because he is so thoughtful of me.
>
> When I came to work at *The Sword* I had not been able to work more than three hours a day. Dr. Rice had a special desk and chair fixed for me almost like one my father made, which I use at home. Then he allowed me to rest fifteen minutes every morning, as long as I could take for my lunch hour, and fifteen minutes in the afternoon. I felt that he was praying for me so that I gradually became stronger and in a few months was working eight hours a day, which I have been doing for the last four years.
>
> He also encouraged me to sing again. I had given up my career as a singer because of ill health. He would ask me to sing from the audience at church, and finally I took a few more voice lessons on his advice. Now I sing solos at church and am able to go to Chicago evenings and sing at rescue missions. I sing twice in one service which includes singing a solo for the invitation at which time I would have previously been very, very tired. I sing the same song over and over while many come forward to be saved: twenty-four the first time, twenty the second time and thirty-nine at another time.
>
> I shall never forget my return to the Sword after taking my first vacation. I did not have a "home" to go to for my vacation, so coming back to the Sword was really coming home for me. At the end of Tuesday morning devotions, Dr. Rice had all the workers stand in a circle with me and sing "Blest Be the Tie That Binds." He told me how he wanted me to feel that this was my true home. . . .
>
> Then it was necessary for me to have a major operation. I have no close relatives and no relatives anywhere who believe in the Bible as I do, so I would have been very lonely if I had not had the love and prayers of Dr. and Mrs. Rice and the Sword people. When I was released from the hospital, Dr. and Mrs. Rice took me to their home for a week and nursed me back to health.
>
> He always seems to sense my need. He never hesitates to

rebuke or compliment accordingly. I would truly feel he did not love me if he failed to administer the rebuke.

In anticipation of this chapter, I requested any employees desiring to do so to make some brief comments relative to their own appraisal of Dr. Rice's personality. Parts of some of them I will quote here. One girl, about to be married, wrote:

> Dr. Rice's clear and complete grasp of the Scriptures has been a constant source of inspiration to me. I was recently graduated from a Christian college, yet being able to transcribe his dictation and to actually see how he uses the Scripture to answer questions and help solve personal problems of preachers, Sunday school teachers, wives and sweethearts, has been a greater help to me than book study or classroom discussion.
>
> Dr. Rice is not just a walking commentary on the Word of God. His personal interest in each of us workers is amazing. You see, he takes each of us under his wing and makes our interest his interest. I am to be married—only twenty-six days from now—and whenever I go into his office, or during office devotions or a sermon at the church, Dr. Rice refers to my leaving him for "some tall, lanky fellow." His teasing is fatherly and actually draws me closer to him. That is wonderful. You see he is making what I am vitally interested in right now part of his life, too. . . .
>
> He is my boss and my pastor, but much more he is my friend, and I thank the Lord for his help in my life.

Another wrote:

> Words cannot express what Dr. Rice has meant to me since I came to work at the Sword. It has been through his preaching that I have grown spiritually, and my complete outlook on life has changed. I know there are very few who live as close to the Lord as Dr. Rice does. The way he talks to God about everything and trusts Him to work everything out is one of the greatest blessings I have learned from him.

Another employee testified:

> When I think of Dr. Rice it isn't usually as a boss (although he is a wonderful boss), but as a friend, counsellor, one who understands, and most of all—as a father. (I kinda adopted him when my father died.)
>
> I have spent many evenings in Dr. Rice's home which I will

never forget—sometimes for games, sometimes for picnics, and other times for advice; but always there was love, understanding, and a happy time.

Some of the features of Dr. Rice that have helped me in my Sunday school teaching and my work in the office, as well as my personal life, are: his love for the Lord, his fight for truth, and his prayer life. There are many more ways in which he has been a great blessing to me. He is truly a great boss and a true friend.

Another said simply:

One of the things that has impressed me (the six years I have been with the Sword) is Dr. Rice's unwavering trust in Jesus Christ! When he asks Him to work out a problem, he expects Him to—*and He does!*

One man who had worked for Dr. Rice more than a decade at the time stated that he had

. . .never found any other man so firm in his belief and with the courage to proclaim it and stick to his convictions. After working with the man for ten years one can tell pretty much what kind of a man he is. I will say that Dr. Rice is a man who lives what he preaches.

Another testified:

My own ministry is greatly indebted to his influence. Through his writings I first began to be a soul winner and to develop strong convictions as a Christian. As a student and as a young preacher his ministry has proved to be an invaluable and faithful guide.

A mother of a teen-aged daughter testified:

When my daughter was quite small I found myself alone and with the responsibility of correcting and disciplining her. It is always easy to tell someone else how a child should be disciplined, but when it is one's own—that is a different matter. About that time I bought Dr. Rice's book on *The Home.* There I found the Bible basis for disciplining and correcting children, and it was truly a blessing.

The thing that has impressed me most about Dr. Rice is the fact of his "bigness"—that is the only word I can think of to describe it. By that I mean that his preaching, his thinking, his writing, his love for people and his burden for soul winning reflect his great love and service for His Saviour. His fight is always for Christ and the Bible. There is never any dislike for persons, and only principles are involved in his fight.

I think it was Sam Jones who used to say, "You can tell a man's religion by the way he treats his cat!" If that is true, and I think most will agree it is, at least in part, one would have learned a lot by visiting the Rice home in Wheaton and seeing the affectionate bond between Dr. Rice and his dog, Flicka. One of the high spots of such a visit was to hear Flicka "sing," accompanied by Dr. Rice at the piano! (And the same kindness could be seen in his treatment of the little poodle, "Honey," given to him by his daughters on Father's Day, some months before his death.)

Several years ago, during a Sword subscription campaign, Dr. Rice was describing the bond between master and dog:

> My toy shepherd, Flicka, stands with her feet on the window sill, her nose against the glass watching for me to come home. When she sees me, she runs to the front door, jumps in a chair beside it so that when I come in she can sit upright in the chair and shake hands with me! She jumps in my lap at every opportunity; sits with her chin on my knee while I eat. And if we don't watch carefully, she brings an old bone to gnaw beside my chair in the living room.

> She loves to jump over a chair or broomstick to please me, or through my encircled arms to get my praise. She sleeps on the couch in my study and has her head on some of my clothes when possible. Last summer at a Sword of the Lord summer conference under a rough tabernacle, she sat very quietly beside me on the bench, and when I preached sat near the front. Once when I was illustrating how in football a man got his breath knocked out of him and I doubled up with a groan as in pain, Flicka leaped to my assistance in concern, thinking I was hurt. She returned to her seat abashed by her mistake when she found I was not hurt! Yes, Flicka wants to please me.

Speaking of love, it is doubtful whether any other man in the world enjoyed being with his family any more than did Dr. Rice. What a glorious time he had when his six daughters, six sons-in-law, 28 grandchildren and 8 great-grandchildren all got together! Because he raised his children by Bible standards and not by the world's theories, many strange and fantastic tales have circulated about his unreasonable rules and how frightened the children were of him. You would not believe some of the rumors which were told, they were so ridiculous, and there is no point in mentioning them here. However, the fact of the matter was that the Rices were among the most affectionate families I have ever known. The first words any of the six girls ever learned were, "I love Daddy!" And they did, too! This was one family that worked together, prayed together, worshiped together, and loved just *being* together.

Dr. Rice loved sports—tennis, golf, baseball—all of which he played well. He never argued about any details of the game he played, but he always played to win and was a fierce competitor.

Dr. Rice was very musical and had a deep appreciation for music. He wrote over seventy-five gospel songs, some of which were, "So Little Time," "Oh, Bring Your Loved Ones," "I Love Thee, My Jesus," "Come, Holy Spirit," "Souls Are Dying," "The Price of Revival," "We'll Never Say Good-Bye in Glory," "Jesus Is Coming," "Jesus, Baby Jesus," "Here Am I," and "Open Your Heart's Door." Part of Dr. Rice's effectiveness in preaching was that he might stop in the middle of a sermon and begin to sing a song that illustrated his message; then, when he finished singing, he would pick up where he left off preaching. He had great sensitivity to the needs of the audience and again and again used music to reach the hearts of his hearers.

All of the Rice children are musical. Many hours were spent in singing gospel hymns around the piano at home, in the car as they traveled, and even at the breakfast or dinner table. Incidentally, on one occasion his mother-in-law was visiting in the Rice home and was terribly shocked when, in the middle of dinner, Dr. Rice opened his mouth, put back his head, and began to sing. Mrs. Cooke reprimanded, "Why, John R., we were taught not to sing at the table." He replied, "That is one of the reasons I got married—so I could sing at my table if I wanted to." And so, through the years, he sang—at the table, in the middle of sermons, at the office, on the golf course, or wherever he happened to be at the time he felt his heart moved with praise.

As a matter of fact, one of his regrets was that he could not take piano when he was in college. He loved to sit down at the piano and pick out favorite melodies. He played two notes in the right hand with a good moving bass in the left. One of his favorites was "Whispering Hope," and that was the song he taught Flicka to "sing" while he played.

It might be well here, while speaking of his love for his family, to quote from a letter by Miss Fairy Shappard:

> I remember in Waxahachie—the first revival in which I heard him—I was invited to a home where Brother Rice and his family were also invited. As you know, just about *everybody* in Texas drinks iced tea in the good old summer time. The hostess on this occasion was serving large goblets of temptingly cool tea. Brother Rice and his family tried to refuse it—but the hostess was rather lacking in understanding. To tell the truth, I wondered then—and wondered many times afterward—why his family did not drink tea at that time.
>
> It was not until two weeks ago that I learned the reason why. A short time before the Waxahachie meeting Dr. Rice and his family were being entertained in a home. On that occasion the hostess offered as one of the beverage choices, iced tea. When she asked Dr. Rice what he would have to drink, he said he would take tea. Grace, then a little girl, was sitting beside him. When the hostess gave her a choice, she also took tea.
>
> He did not feel little children should drink tea and was immediately faced with the realization that if he drank it and refused to let her have it. . .well, that just wouldn't do for him. You see, Dr. Rice does not have one standard for himself and another standard for other people, even his children. For two full years he did not drink tea, and many times I have seen other and similar examples of his consistency in practicing himself what he demands of others.

Yet, as great as was his love for preaching, the brethren, the lost, his employees, and his family, his love for the Lord eclipsed love for anyone and everything else. Here was a man who truly loved God with all his heart! He loved the Word of God. Like Jeremiah he could say, "Thy words were found, and I did eat them; and thy word was unto me the joy and rejoicing of mine heart: for I am called by thy name, O Lord God of hosts" (Jer. 15:16). He spent a lifetime feeding on the Word of God, and God gave him a miraculous insight into the Scriptures. Perhaps this was principally because he digested it so thoroughly and it became such an integral part of him.

His obvious delight in the Scripture was manifested in the way he committed to memory long portions of it. By way of example, he memorized Psalms 1, 8, 15, 23, 24, 34, 37, 100, 103, 121, and 126. He committed to memory John 3 and 14, Romans 8 and 12, I Corinthians 13, Philippians 4, Matthew 28, the Beatitudes, plus hundreds of other passages and single verses. Every Easter Sunday morning the family quoted Matthew 28 at the breakfast table and at Christmas time they quoted together the Christmas story from Luke 2. There are over three hundred verses just in the above-mentioned passages, not counting the Beatitudes or the Christmas story.

His love for the Bible and delight in it made his biblical exposition among the foremost in the world. One lady told me that she had been saved seven years when she first heard him, but could not have found John 3:16 in the Bible without asking someone for help. After sitting under Dr. Rice's preaching for twelve weeks in a big, independent campaign, she knew what the Bible taught about all the major Bible doctrines and also on almost every subject relating to the Christian life—the plan of salvation, baptism, the second coming of Christ, the millennial reign of Christ, and many, many others. As still another commented, his ministry certainly proved false the tritely expressed opinion: "An evangelist is incapable of profound Bible preaching."

This love for the Lord and His Word explains the vigorous defense he made down through the years for the purity of the Saviour's Gospel. In the testimony William McLeod wrote for me, he said:

> My work at the Sword of the Lord has brought me into close contact with Dr. Rice during these years. After six years, I can honestly say my admiration for Dr. Rice has steadily grown. First and foremost, because of his unwavering stand in defense of the Faith.
>
> I can recall many, many times when some issue has come up and perhaps if the decision were left to some others of us here at

the Sword of the Lord we would have taken the road of least resistance. But not so with Brother Rice, who would always insist that we could not, must not, will not compromise what we know to be the truth of the Bible to curry favor of anyone despite the cost. In many instances it could mean thousands of dollars or the loss of many friends.

Only Saturday of last week, I talked with Dr. Rice, giving a report of a trip through the South as far as Florida. I well recall Dr. Rice's statement when I was talking, "Brother McLeod, all we want and all we need is God's people who want to do right and live by the pattern of the Bible." My son David was with me in his office at the time; and when we got into the car to drive home, he said, "I sure do admire his stand for the Truth." We sure need more men like Dr. Rice in these days.

One who probably knew Dr. Rice as well as anyone outside of his wife and private secretary, Evangelist Walt Handford, his son-in-law, wrote me:

Anyone who has worked for Dr. Rice very long is bound to be struck with his staunch stand for the Bible. When controversial issues arise, his question is never "Will it make me popular?"; or "Will this course of action cost us business or financial backing?"; but, rather, "Is this what the Bible teaches?" . . . Though many picture Dr. Rice as a lion, he is a most affectionate man with great capacities for love and devotion. It is not because of any vicious tendencies that Dr. Rice speaks out so plainly and boldly against sin.

Dr. Rice's love for the Lord is evidenced also by his personal prayer life. His private secretary, Miss Viola Walden, wrote me:

How fortunate for me that I have, in a measure, been privileged to pray with him over so many problems—great and small. Some would take faith to remove mountains; others so small it seemed to me hardly worth bothering God about.

For example, he had some tropical fish in his office, plus a parakeet. Recently, several of the fish died. One day as we talked about their treatment, to my surprise he said: "Let's pray about the little things," then proceeded to ask God for wisdom as to how to treat them.

How typical this is of his praying. Many times daily I can hear him praying audibly as he goes about his work—for help in answering his enormous mail, for this person's problem, or concerning details of the promotion of *The Sword of the Lord,* for fellow evangelists, and many other matters.

His prayer life was not a formal or mechanical thing; it was part of his intimate relationship with the Lord Jesus Christ. When Joanna was about thirteen or fourteen, her bedroom was next to Dr. and Mrs. Rice's room. Often she would hear her daddy praying in the night. One night she was awakened and thought he was asking for something, but when she went into his room to inquire what he wanted, he said, "I didn't want anything. I was just talking to a Friend of mine." Joy, in a Father's Day tribute to him, related, "Often at night in the room next to mine, I would hear him say, 'Lord Jesus, help me.' He prayed aloud even in his sleep." And Libby, in a letter to him, thanked him: "You taught us that God answers prayer. Then you prayed for things—specific, enumerated, definite things. We saw God give you specific answers to your prayers."

Along this line, Miss Shappard was telling me how she happened to begin working for Dr. Rice. It was during the depression; jobs were very hard to get, and she was the only one of her family working at the time. She wanted to join Dr. Rice's staff and he wanted her to come, but he did not feel it would be right for her to join him in what would have to be sacrificial pay as long as she was the only one in her family working. One Saturday afternoon in June, 1935, she went to Dallas and reminded Dr. Rice that she felt God wanted her in the work. He said, "Well, why don't we pray that you will lose your job and your father will get a job." He stopped and had prayer then and there. She was working in a government office and, as far as she then knew, had a job as long as she wanted it. But Monday morning when she went back to work she was told that her job had been discontinued. The same day her father got work, and the next week she went to Dallas to begin working full-time for Dr. Rice and for *The Sword of the Lord.* And she was still there when he died, forty-five years later!

Another evidence of his love for the Lord was his unselfishness and the strong sacrificial spirit with which he supported the Lord's work. His selflessness was amazing to behold. Perhaps it would have been hard to convince the Internal Revenue Department about how he spent his money, but it was nevertheless so.

On matters pertaining to himself, he was one of the most frugal persons imaginable. Most of his clothes, for example, were gifts from others. Yet he was as liberal pertaining to the Lord's work as he was frugal about his own. The contrast was amazing. He abhorred waste. Mrs. Rice had to find many ways to fix leftovers; none were thrown away at his house. Poor Flicka got only the crumbs from her master's table (plus dog food), not the leftovers. When Dr. Rice returned from a revival, he asked what Mrs. Rice needed for the family, then often gave the rest of his love offering to his "Ministers and Missionary Fund," or sent it to some work of the Lord. Even as a pastor he was not on a regular salary, but was dependent upon designated offerings. Many a Sunday his personal contribution was greater than the money he received from the offerings of the people.

His daughter, Libby, in the letter just referred to, reminisced: "You told us what God expected of His children in sacrificial living. Then you demonstrated it. You gave, joyfully and without complaint, of all your resources—money, emotions, time. Remember the poor bums you'd bring home from a mission service, and how, occasionally, they'd be gone before daylight, with what little money there was in the house? 'No matter,' you'd say, 'I'd rather make a mistake helping someone who isn't sincere, than to not help someone who does mean business for the Lord.' "

Already mentioned is how he brought a boy from British Guiana, John S. E. Thompson, and put him through the Moody Bible Institute. That is, he and some others guaranteed the boy's expenses and helped him considerably. He gave so much money to TEAM that on his desk was a "Life Membership" from that organization, stating, *"This certifies that The Evangelical Alliance Mission hereby confers upon Dr. John R. Rice the rights and privileges of Life Membership in recognition of deep interest in Foreign Missions."* Other mission organizations made similar gestures. For example, Lifegate, Inc., presented him with a plaque replica of the original engraving of the tract "God's Simple Plan of Salvation" in appreciation "for generous support of the Ford Porter Memorial Ministries." And Baptist International Missions, Inc., gave him a plaque "for faithful stewardship of life and ministry for more than fifty years."

Yes, in the heart of John R. Rice beat a fierce and all-consuming passion for Jesus Christ. It could be said of him, as was said by the Jews concerning our Lord's affection for Lazarus, "Behold how he loved him!" Part of this love is expressed in Dr. Rice's hymn, of which he wrote both words and music, "I Love Thee, My Jesus":

> What words can I find to tell Jesus I love Him,
> Because He first loved me:
> Because of my ransom He paid with such suff'ring,
> Upon the cursed tree.
> O come, let us magnify Jesus together,
> For praise becometh Thee;
> And blessings about me I owe to my Saviour,
> Who all things bought for me.
> May never my praises be slow or be silent.
> Nor e'er my love be dumb.
> This sinner is saved and my sins all forgiven,
> The Saviour's work is done!
> O how can I love Thee enough, dear Redeemer,
> How e'er repay my Friend?
> I'll spread the glad sound of my praise and my heart love
> On every joyful wind!
>
> > In the morning, at the noon-time,
> > And when come evening shadows,
> > I love Thee my Jesus,
> > I love Thee my King,
> > In rejoicing and in sorrow,
> > In lightness and burden,
> > I love Thee my Saviour and Lord.

The Boss is out! He will not mind, however, our peeking in at the busy corner of his spacious, beautiful office in Murfreesboro, Tennessee, where we glimpse his loaded desk and empty chair awaiting his return. To the right we see but the first of 12 bookshelves filled with some 6,000 volumes in his personal library, contained in his "L" shaped office, back-to-back, library fashion. To the left we see his piano, presented to Dr. Rice by his workers on his 68th birthday, upon which he picks out the melodies of many of the songs that originate from his heart and mind. Behind that is a portion of the more than 32 feet of window space, a feature which Dr. Rice is proud of since moving South. About a third of his office did not get in the picture.

*Chapter 18*

# A Giant Goes Home

*The beauty of Israel is slain upon thy high places: how are the mighty fallen!*—II Samuel 1:19.

*Know ye not that there is a prince and a great man fallen this day in Israel?*—II Samuel 3:38.

*. . .and died in a good old age, an old man, and full of years; and was gathered to his people.*—Genesis 25:8.

March 8, 1978, started out like any other day. The sun rose in the east, roosters crowed, families gathered around the breakfast table, people went to work, and pastors started finalizing plans about prayer meeting that evening. As was his custom, Dr. Rice rose early, enjoyed a breakfast prepared by his wife, had the normal time of family devotions, then went to the office. About 90 workers gathered in the Sword auditorium, and Dr. Rice led in the daily devotions as usual, apparently without any difficulty. After going upstairs to his office, however, he complained to his secretary that he was short of breath; he was perspiring heavily and seemed to be in considerable distress.

Following consultation with Dr. Al Byers and Dr. Ron English, he was rushed across town to Rutherford Hospital; and Dr. Rice's personal physician, Dr. S. C. Garrison, met him in the emergency room. Dr. Rice felt the problem was merely "lung congestion, tension and pressure," and assured everyone he expected to be dismissed very shortly. But it was not until March 22, after two full weeks in the "coronary care" unit, that Dr. Garrison signed a release permitting him to return home.

*It was Dr. Rice's first heart attack, experienced after more than eighty-two practically trouble-free years of glowing health!* At least it was the first insofar as his medical records gave evidence.

His secretary, Miss Viola Walden, is not so sure, feeling he may have suffered two mild attacks previously. The first time was on May 30, 1974, in Indianapolis. He was speaking at the commencement exercises of the Indiana Baptist College when he had to stop, unable to continue, and was taken by ambulance to Methodist Hospital. Someone notified me about what had happened and I immediately phoned the hospital, only to be informed that no patient by that name had been admitted. Dr. Rice, waiting in the emergency room to be treated, began to feel better and characteristically decided he did not want to hang around. He went out, hailed a cab, rode to the airport, caught a plane, and flew back home. He blamed the problem on an "upset stomach and continuing pressure in the great heat of the service, with a hot robe on."

The second incident happened about a year and a half later, on the Sunday following Thanksgiving. Dr. and Mrs. Rice, along with Miss Walden, had driven to Chattanooga for services with Dr. Charles J. Thompson at the Trinity Baptist Church. He had not been feeling well, but spoke in the morning services without incidence. Since some of the symptoms of the Indianapolis problem were present, the ladies wondered if perhaps they should take him back to Murfreesboro. At first he said no. However, the situation worsened as the afternoon progressed; and eventually he permitted them, most reluctantly, to call Dr. Thompson and be excused from the evening service. Whether or not he actually suffered mild attacks on these two occasions, it cannot be determined with certainty.

Dr. Rice gradually regained his health and strength following the March, 1978, hospitalization and, thanks to careful diet, exercise and loving care, he was able to resume a reasonably normal work load for the next two years.

Then, on Saturday morning, April 5, 1980, he suffered another heart attack and was again taken to Rutherford Hospital, finding himself once more in the coronary care unit. After one week he was transferred to a private room, finally being dismissed on Saturday, April 19, two weeks after the attack. Since I needed to go to Murfreesboro anyway with a book manuscript, I spent about a week of that time helping out at the office, answering letters, speaking in devotions, reviewing books, and otherwise trying to prevent a backlog of his work.

Although he did not remain in the hospital any longer this time than previously, apparently the latest attack was much more severe. He was never able to be in the office after that any more than a few hours at a time, and some weeks he came in only once or twice all week. His secretary went to his home daily with the mail he needed to see, took his dictation, went over Sword copy with him, and otherwise helped him make it through the next seven or eight months.

The last month or so was especially strenuous for him. He had trouble breathing and it was difficult for him to remain awake. Oxygen was kept handy for his use around the clock. Several times he was taken to the hospital emergency room for treatment; and one night, November 17, he was in such distress he concluded his time was very short. Summoning Miss Walden to his home, he dictated sweet letters to Mrs. Rice, Miss Walden and Miss Fairy Shappard, putting in writing how much they had meant to him over the years.

The final attack—in the form of cerebral thrombosis, a stroke caused by a blood clot in the brain—came early December 17, less than a week after his 85th birthday. He had read on and off throughout the night, unable to sleep, and had asked Mrs. Rice for breakfast at an early hour. About 5 a.m., when the meal was ready, she went to his chair and could not arouse him.

She immediately called the Ed Martins, parents of son-in-law Roger Martin, who worked as caretakers on the farm and lived next door, then summoned an ambulance and several of the Sword workers. When the three ambulance attendants could not wake him, he was taken to Rutherford Hospital. He never regained consciousness, as far as anyone could tell, although when loved ones talked or sang to him there would be an occasional moving of his hands or tears in his eyes.

Christmas, always such a high day with the Rice clan, saw this warrior helpless on a hospital bed, but nonetheless comforted by the sweet Holy Spirit. Dr. Rice's Christmas letter to his friends, written a short time before the fatal stroke, was especially precious; and we quote four paragraphs here to show how his heart continued to beat for souls and in love to his Saviour right to the end. He said in that letter:

> This year I was slowed down once again with another heart attack. But I am 85 years of age! And how well and strong I have been through all this time! Up until just a few years ago, I could still beat my sons-in-law in both golf and bowling! Oh, God has blessed me in so many ways. Of course, I yearn to be about my Father's business, but He knows all about it; I am in His hands to use—or not to use—as He now sees fit. I often find comfort in these inspired words: 'Even to your old age. . .even to hoar hairs will I carry you: I have made, and I will bear; even I will carry, and will deliver you" (Isa. 46:4).
>
> I still, from my arm chair, "preach" in great revival campaigns. I still vision hundreds walking the aisles to accept Christ. I still feel hot tears for the lost. I still see God working miracles. Oh, how I long to see great revivals, to hear about revival crowds once again!
>
> Talking about revival in a Christmas message to friends? It would be no Christmas to me without the sense of the breath of God upon me still, weak and frail as I am. I want no Christmas without a burden for lost souls, a message for sinners, a heart to bring in the lost sheep so dear to the Shepherd, the sinning souls for whom Christ died.
>
> I will have the comfort and company of my faithful wife, my sweet girls' arms around my neck, grandchildren to be proud of and to hear tell of their plans for God's service; I will give and receive presents and surprises, and carols will be heard the day long, along with feasting and fellowship with family and workers. All this will be sweet, of course. But may food be tasteless, and music a discord, and Christmas a farce if I forget the dying millions to whom I am debtor, if this fire in my bones does not still flame! Not till I die, or not till Jesus comes, will I ever be eased of this burden, these tears, this toil to save souls.

Early Sunday, December 28, Dr. Rice's condition seemed to worsen. He developed a high fever, infection set in, and his breathing became very heavy and difficult. Shortly after mid-

night, between 1:30 and 2:00 Monday morning, December 29, the
warrior laid down his sword and shield and entered into rest. He
was Home at last!

   He had experienced what he described in his greatly-used *Bible Facts About Heaven,* "A glorious promotion." There he had
also enthused, ". . .how sweet it will be when I can see Him in
person. Then hope will change to glad fruition, faith to sight, and
prayer to praise. Then I can put my finger on the nail prints and
my hand in His side. Then I can hold His feet as did Mary
Magdalene and the other Mary, or lean upon His bosom as John
did. It will be Heaven enough to be with Jesus. We love Him now
having never seen Him. How we must love Him when we see His
face!"

   What an abundant entrance into Heaven this giant for God
must have experienced! While any description would have to be
in the realm of imagination, of course, Dr. Rice's gifted daughter
Grace wrote a beautifully moving poem at the time of his death
which she called, "Someone Special Is Coming Home!" It went
like this:

A shiver of excitement shimmered through the crystal air.
"Someone's coming! Someone special!" angels whispered on the stair.
As an angel told a seraph (angels love to tell good news!)
And the seraph told another in the language seraphs use.

The tidings spread like wildfire, and the balconies began
To be filled with wondering watchers as the word like ripples ran,
"God's special, chosen servant has begun the journey's end!"
"Oh, I know him! I must see him when he's coming down the bend!
I must be up close to see him," says an eager, sweet-faced soul.
"Why, he won me to the Saviour," cried another bright and whole.

"These robes of white I'm wearing are because he preached the Word."
"Down in Dallas. . ." "Back in Wheaton. . ." "Buffalo his witness heard."
And the praise to God kept growing as the word was flashed above.
"Praise the Lord that he was faithful and kept telling of God's love."
"And, oh, you know his prayers—he could reach the ear of God,
Pouring out, prevailing, pleading, till he saw the answering nod."

His coming Home was not as easy as some thought it should be.
(It takes some time just to organize things.)
So he lingered, and that mighty heart, so strong for fighting wrong
Now bent to the task in a valiant effort,
Needed time to run more softly, take a cadence new and low.
The clock ticked on, but quietly, and the great heart struggled slow.

Breathing, long easy, now took on a labored tone.
Loved ones gathered, watched and waited, sensed those others, not alone.
As he groped among the midlands, neither here nor wholly Home;
And in time—no, in eternity, where time has lost its sphere—
There came an order and delight to all the pulsing plans.

The crowd of those who loved him when he led them to the Lord—
Well, that group kept on growing, a cheerful, eager horde.
From countries far, and counties near, from years both fresh and dim
They cried with joy and a snatch of song, "My salvation came through him."
But another group gathered with different stance, more a wistful, longing
    glance,
"My darling son! It's been so long! Now I'll hold you close again!"
"It's my brother John," a glad voice says, "and I've loved him all my life,
Like brother, father, teacher, friend, I learned all I know from John.
Let me be the one, dear Lord, I plead,"
Said a creature tall and strong, still learning to walk in a broad new gait,
"Let me saddle his heavenly steed."

Whatever they do for a favorite son, that's what they're doing up there:
A robe and a ring, some fabulous thing—God's love gift of welcoming cheer.
And the angels, I know, don't have to be told
His name or how to pronounce it. For down through the years,
When the call comes with joy, "Rejoice! A Sheep has come home;
Write the name in the Lamb's Book of Life!"
"Who spread the Word? Whose beautiful feet published the tidings of joy?"
"A boy named John R., a poor college boy,"
"A hard-working Corporal Rice." "A preacher. . ." "A pastor. . ."
    "Revivalist"
"Writer. . ." "An elderly saint—John R. Rice."

A few days passed—on earth, that is—and the loved ones waited still
While he hovered yet in some vestibule, held by the hand of God's will.
They were eager to have him Home at last, and free from the body's clay,
Yet reluctant still to say goodbye, see the spirit slip away.

Finally all was ready. It took but a look
From Father to Son: "Let him come!
All things are ready; his place is prepared."
Nail-scarred hands join in welcoming reach.

A flutter of flags, a fanfare of trumpet, a burst of angelic chorus,
The cloud-curtains part, and in glorious splendor
That shining new creature steps forth.
"He's here! Home at last! See the joy on his face!
No sorrow or sighing or frown."
The Saviour with infinite love and compassion embraces the newest arrival.
All Heaven breaks forth, pealing praises to God;
He's Home, Home at last! Oh, welcome the soul winner Home!

Yes, indeed, someone special *had* come Home!

## THE MEMORIAL SERVICE

Dr. Rice went to be with the Lord early Monday; and two days later the Memorial Service was held on Wednesday, December 31. Even though there was little time to let people know of his death and others simply could not get plane reservations, both auditorium and balcony of the Franklin Road Baptist Church were packed with friends, loved ones, co-workers and dignitaries. The crowd contained a veritable "Who's Who" of Fundamentalism. In fact, one preacher commented that if Satan wanted to take a giant step in destroying the soul-winning element of Fundamentalism, he would only need to blow up the church that afternoon! It would be difficult to say exactly how many states were represented, but they were present from the farthest reaches of America. And the church auditorium was completely encircled with memorial wreaths, sent from both far and near as expressions of love and affection.

Dr. Walt Handford was in charge of the service; and after a few words of welcome, he explained it would be a lengthy service and that the family wanted it to be a triumphant time of rejoicing. To emphasize the latter, the Franklin Road Baptist Church choir, joined by some of the grandchildren and directed by son-in-law Don Sandberg, opened the service with the "Hallelujah Chorus" from Handel's *Messiah,* one of Dr. Rice's favorite selections.

This was followed by remarks from the church's pastor, Dr. Bob Kelley, who spoke of the love Dr. Rice had for him and for the church. He said, "He stood behind it. He loved the local church. I don't believe I ever met him anywhere, anytime, in his office or his home, when he didn't ask, 'Preacher, how is the church going? Brother Kelley, how many souls did we have saved last Sunday?' He was always interested in souls. He never asked me how many we had in Sunday school first; he always asked how many we had saved first." Dr. Kelley also spoke of his concern for "little people," the time he always had for them, and how he loved children and children were drawn to him.

I led in prayer next; and then Dr. Lee Roberson, pastor of the great Highland Park Baptist Church in Chattanooga and chancellor of Tennessee Temple University, spoke, saying his mind had been drawn to I Corinthians 13:13, "And now abideth faith, hope, charity, these three; but the greatest of these is charity." The characteristic about Dr. Rice that he said "kept coming back to me was his love." Dr. Roberson spoke of his love for horses and dogs, his love for music, his love for the Word of God, his love for work, but, most of all, "he loved the Lord supremely. He was at home with the Lord in his prayer life, in his devotional life, in his preaching life; but he is at Home with the Lord now."

Dr. Al Byers told how, after he was saved at the age of eighteen, he became acquainted with Dr. Rice through some of his books and through *The Sword of the Lord.* He spoke of his long association with him and what a tremendous influence he had been upon him and upon his family. Dr. Rice married Al and his wife, Marcella, rejoiced with them in the birth of their four children, wept with them when he buried their 9-day-old daughter, and baptized the other three following their conversions. Dr. Byers spoke especially of how he had bathed his ministry in prayer and walked by faith, closing his remarks: "Dr. Rice was the most consistent man I have ever met."

The internationally-noted song writer and soloist, Dr. Al Smith, who had worked with him in many of the Sword Conferences, sang Dr. Rice's favorite song, "Jesus, I My Cross Have Taken." He used the occasion to point out how much Dr. Rice had meant in his life over the years, serving as a bulwark of inspiration to him.

Rev. Allan MacMullen spoke next, telling what a privilege it had been to be a son-in-law. He noted that while Dr. Rice loved working, he also loved playing, describing him as a good competitor and a great deal of fun. He also spoke of the example Dr. Rice's character had been to him, saying, "Dad stood for right even though often it hurt. He was consistent and always dependable. I was constantly amazed at his fairness in dealing with people. Regardless of the cost, he did what was right by them even when it was inconvenient and not to his advantage. Never did priorities conflict with what was right."

Dr. John Rawlings, pastor of the Landmark Baptist Temple in Cincinnati, one of the largest churches in the nation, spoke of the long relationship he and his wife enjoyed with the Rices, having known them personally over forty years. Dr. Rawlings emphasized Dr. Rice's great faith, his soul-winning zeal, his prayer life, and his courage. Of the latter, he said: "To me, John Rice was a man of steel. He wasn't afraid of man oi beast or Devil. And this has left a lasting impression on me. I like to be around a man who has the courage to fight. I never did like a sissy. And with that bulldog jaw and those piercing eyes, you knew when you were around John Rice you were around a real soldier." Dr. Rawlings also paid tribute to the women in his life: Mrs. Rice, the six daughters, and the secretaries who had been associated with him so long.

Rev. Charles Himes reminisced about his first meeting with Dr. Rice, during the days of his courtship with Mary Lloys, then what it meant to him to be a member of the Rice family. He also spoke of the example Dr. Rice had been, saying, "The thing that characterized his life was that everything he did was in absolute dedication and surrender to the Lord."

Dr. Kelley spoke next of a wee morning hour experience the month before Dr. Rice died, when he felt the end might be near and had called his secretary to dictate some letters: one to his wife, one to Viola Walden, and one to Fairy Shappard. Then he read to the congregation the letter to Mrs. Rice, given earlier in this book. The congregation then sang the song mentioned in the letter, "The Solid Rock."

Dr. Bill Rice, III, spoke next, saying how impressed he had always been with his uncle's consistency and balance. He said: "All of us have our claimed strengths and obvious weaknesses. All of us, I fear, tread on tangents in our lives. It is very seldom that you see a man who is noted for his intellect on the one hand and compassion on the other. It is rare that you see a person noted for being loving and being strong. And while it may be sad to say, it is nonetheless true, that very seldom do you hear of a man who is noted as a defender of the Faith and as a soul winner. Dr. John R. Rice was the most consistent, most balanced Christian I have ever had the privilege of knowing. He was a man who could say right is right, wrong is wrong, good is good, bad is bad, and mean it—and weep at the same time. He was a man whose life was noted by his fierce determination, his solemn conviction, and his obvious compassion. God give us men like that."

Mr. Jack Cornelius spoke of how he had been reached for Christ through the ministry of Dr. Rice and rejoiced that it had been his privilege since May of 1978 to travel with him. He said, "I acted as his valet, his companion, his burden bearer; and if he just felt like picking on somebody, I was there for that, too," adding that the thing impressing him most about Dr. Rice was his prayer life. He pointed out that Dr. Rice was known to others as "evangelist, editor, publisher, author, song writer, soul winner, Christian extraordinary, defender of the Faith, rock-ribbed fundamentalist," but he said, "To me he was friend, counselor, teacher, pal, prayer partner, and an adopted daddy."

Dr. Walt Handford reminisced about Dr. Rice from his days of courtship with his daughter; then, quoting Joshua 1:8, spoke of how impressed he had been that Dr. Rice was a man of the Book. He said, "Down through the years the Book of God was his constant companion. He loved it; he slept with it; he quoted it constantly; he read it avidly, and he loved it."

Dr. Bill Harvey, another gifted soloist and song leader who worked in many conferences with Dr. Rice, said the family had asked him to sing the marvelous song Dr. Rice had written, "So Little Time," noting, "This displays his heart, I believe, as no other song he wrote." He mentioned that he never sang this song as a solo if Dr. Rice were present, since Dr. Rice would always step to the podium and join him on the chorus. Commenting that it would be emotionally difficult for him to sing the song alone, he requested the congregation to join him on the chorus after each verse, just as Dr. Rice had done.

This was followed by Dr. Jerry Falwell, pastor of Thomas Road Baptist Church of Lynchburg and chancellor of Liberty Baptist Schools. He called Dr. Rice's passing "the passing of an era.

There has not been one like him before him, and there will not likely be one like him after him. He was God's man for the hour. I looked on him as the guardian of fundamentalist truth for this generation. More than any other person, he was the most trusted man in Fundamentalism." Dr. Falwell emphasized that while his death was the passing of an era, it was not the passing of a movement. And he closed his remarks by saying: "No one more appropriately fits the fulfillment of the promise, '. . .and their works do follow them,' than John Rice. He left behind a family. He left behind an arsenal of written material that says who he is, what he believes, and with whom he had a personal relationship. He set the standard in the pulpit ministries of thousands of pastors and evangelists. So we pay tribute to one someone has called 'a titular leader of Fundamentalism,' but who has now distributed that to thousands of us. The mantle has fallen, not on one or two or five or ten, but on thousands. We must see to it that everything John Rice stood for never ceases to be the way it is."

Don Sandberg reminisced briefly about how Dr. Rice referred to him as the "pink-haired Swede" in the family, then mentioned as his heritage from him four memorial stones. He listed them as a strong belief in and practice of the Word of God, the practice of "in everything by prayer," his love and appreciation for good music, and his strong sense of family.

Next, Joy read the poem Grace had written at Dr. Rice's death, "Someone Special Is Coming Home," quoted earlier in this chapter, and then the six Rice girls sang, "Finally Home."

Hundreds of letters, telegrams, telephone calls and personal messages were received from friends, pastors, church leaders, civic dignitaries and political VIPs. Dr. Ron English read a few selected comments from Mr. Tommy Martin, insurance executive and bank director known locally as "Mister Murfreesboro"; Mr. Jack Weatherford, chairman and chief executive officer of the Murfreesboro Bank & Trust Company; Mr. Hollis Westbrooks, mayor of Murfreesboro; State Senator John Rucker; United States Senator James Sasser; United States Senator and newly-elected Senate majority leader, Howard Baker; Evangelist

James Robison, Southern Baptist evangelist and television minister; Billy and Ruth Graham; and President-elect Ronald and Nancy Reagan.

Evangelist Pete Rice spoke of how fortunate he was to have known his uncle and learned so much from him. He referred to Dr. Rice's teaching on the Holy Spirit and on prayer, plus his example in the home, as being of special benefit. He closed his remarks by noting "to whom much is given, much is required," reminding those assembled that each was accountable to God.

Dr. Tom Malone, pastor of the Emmanuel Baptist Church in Pontiac and chancellor of Midwestern Baptist College, spoke of the help Dr. Rice had been to him in his early ministry. He also referred to Paul's statement that "we brought nothing into this world, and it is certain we can carry nothing out." saying: "Dr. John R. Rice, I am sure, never had one thought in all of his many years of taking anything out of it. But I think he constantly thought of leaving something in it, and he surely did. He left men by the thousands who respected him, loved him, and looked to him. He left a tremendous family who not only loved him, but followed him enthusiastically. He left thousands who are saved because of him and, I think we could say, millions who are richer because of his ministry. I sat down and wrote a few little words a few days ago, even before Dr. Rice went to be with the Lord. I wrote:

> If men are trees, he was a giant redwood;
> If men are streams, he was a mighty Amazon;
> If men are lights, he was a flaming lamp.
> If men are stars, he was a mighty galaxy;
> If men are flowers, he was a garden of beautiful colors.

"I never knew a man I thought was more in Christ than Dr. John R. Rice. In Christ, his soul found liberty and peace. In Christ, his mighty intellect found expansion. In Christ, his versatile personality found fulfillment. In Christ, his capacity to love found its greatest release. In Christ, his capacity for arduous work and labor found its greatest challenge. He was a powerful preacher, a potent pen, a picture of purity, a princely person, and a friend no one could ever forget."

Rev. Billy Carl Rice said it was while serving in the Air Force in Korea that he received his first copy of *The Sword of the Lord*, then ordered Dr. Rice's book, *A Know-So Salvation.* He gave the latter, after first reading it himself, to a fellow serviceman whom he had led to the Lord. Then he laughingly told of going to Wheaton College after the war, getting a job as janitor at the Sword of the Lord, and eventually marrying the boss' daughter! He, too, spoke of Dr. Rice's impeccable consistency of life. He said, "Dad practiced what he preached. He was the same in private life as he was in public life."

Ray Hart, a former Metropolitan Opera tenor greatly used in revival work and a soloist in numerous Sword conferences, sang "Until Then," dedicating it especially to Mrs. Rice. Then Dr. Jack Hyles, chancellor of Hyles-Anderson College and pastor of the First Baptist Church of Hammond, one of the world's largest, spoke. Although scheduled by the family to be the final speaker, because of the lateness of the hour he asked Dr. Curtis Hutson to exchange places with him. Dr. Hyles was one of Dr. Rice's closest and most intimate friends, and they had been on Sword Conference platforms together all over America. Excerpts from his message are as follows:

> Over 2,200 times I have sat on the same platform and preached with Dr. John R. Rice. Many a time I have shared motel rooms with him. Hundreds of times I have sat across the table and shared a meal with him. These hands have touched him. These eyes have gazed upon him. These ears have heard him speak. I have held his hand, caught his tears, felt his burden, and seen his heart.
>
> Dr. John Rice walked far above most of us, yet he was willing to stoop to walk with us. I never thought he quite ever talked on his own level. He always had to bend beneath his level to meet the rest of us. He was greatness clothed with humility. He was maturity clothed, for our sakes, with a touch of childhood. He was theology bathed in practicality. He was profundity choosing to wear the garment of simplicity that we might understand him.
>
> He was an eagle willing to fly with us sparrows so we could fellowship with him. He was depth appearing to be shallow in order to lead us shallow ones to greater depths.
>
> He was eloquent. His eloquence was ever present but seldom used in order that we might understand him. He was a deep-

sea diver willing to wade with little children. He was royalty who was somewhat timid to be seen on his throne. He was scholarship veiled with propriety.

He could quote Shakespeare and make it appear like a nursery rhyme. He could blend beautifully the graduate school with the grade school. He was a marriage of grace and truth. He was strength betrothed to beauty. He built the structure of zeal upon a foundation of knowledge. In him, mercy and truth kissed each other. He was a rare combination of honor and majesty; love and justice walked arm in arm; compassion and conviction merged, and courage and patience were joined.

Can I forget him crawling in the back seat of a Volkswagen so we younger ones could sit in the front?

Or could I forget his preaching with tears to nine people in Sioux City, Iowa, one morning?

Or always ordering the cheapest thing on the menu? He could sign the check. I never saw John Rice eat a steak unless I paid for it. He wouldn't sign the check. I have seen him get up and leave restaurants because he wouldn't eat anything that cost that much, though he could have signed the check and charged it to the church.

Can we forget his singing "The Windows of Heaven are Open" with Bill Harvey in a restaurant in Houston, Texas? Or giving away his love offering at Tokyo? Or on his knees at 2:00 in Tampa, when I found him praying for America? Or his volunteering to preach first on the program and letting me preach last? Or saying to the stewardess on the plane when she would bring me some hot tea: "Stewardess, put a little arsenic in that, if you would please"? Or, "Good morning, Dr. Hyles. Whose side are you on this morning?"

Speaking directly to the family, Dr. Hyles added:

Thank you, Mrs. Rice, for all the goodbyes, for all the nights alone, for all the holidays without him, for all the empty places at the table, for going seventeen years without kitchen cabinets in Wheaton, for sharing him with me.

Thank you, Grace, Jessie, Mary Lloys, Libby, Joanna and Joy for letting John Rice be daddy to us all. He was everybody's daddy, every preacher's pastor. We all thought of him as our daddy. You will forgive us if we feel like we are part of the grieving family. Thank you for letting the rest of us have him.

He closed his remarks with an original poem, "How to Make Another John R. Rice," written some years before during a Sword Conference at Colorado Springs:

"What will we do when he is gone?"
Why we'll just make another one.
I think you'll find this will suffice
To make another John R. Rice:
From Paul take all the churches' care,
And stir with David Brainerd's prayer;
Put in some Billy Sunday fire,
With some Bob Gray's intense desire.
Of Mueller's faith please add a part,
And Jeremiah's broken heart,
And Larkin minus all his charts;
Throw in a touch of Mark Twain's wit,
With John the Baptist's holy grit;
Add then an R. A. Torrey mind
With all the love that you can find,
Sam Jones' intense attack on sin,
Knute Rockne's strong desire to win;
Add quickly Spurgeon's mighty pen,
The strength of David's mighty men;
Then take Will Roger's honest face,
And add some Falwell charm and grace;
Some Evel Knievel, but not much,
And Dennis the Menace, a little touch.
Then add Jack Dempsey's mighty arm
To some of Ronald Reagan's charm,
The eloquence of R. G. Lee,
Muhammad Ali's poetry,
Some of Drew Pearson's better side,
With faith from gentle Praying Hyde.
Then add a little Roloff zeal
To J. R. Faulkner's kind appeal,
And then so deftly, quietly blend
A Jonathan-type, a true-blue friend
Who stands beside you to the end.
Then place a large and generous part
Of Dr. Weigle's happy heart.
Add to Bill Harvey's winsome gift
A little of Jack Benny's thrift;
Some Winston Churchill leadership,
Don Meredith's light and folksy quip.
Equip him with Goliath's sword,
And turn him loose to preach the Word.
Then add Lee Roberson's kingly air,
His leadership, and godly care;
Adventure from old Lewis and Clark,
The bravery of a Sgt. York.
And let him walk o'er fifty years
With men of passion, power, and tears.
With Jones, and Riley, and Shuler, too,
And Gipsy Smith, to name a few;

With Dr. Bob and Ironside,
And others long known far and wide.
Then let him travel all around
With just a pinch of Charlie Brown.
Then give him, to his strength renew
A wife as sweet as Joseph knew,
Who loves our hero through and through,
A brother like John Wesley had,
And don't forget to make him Dad
Of six fine daughters all who've been
Long married to fine preacher men;
All six of them so well employ
The Spirit's fruit from Grace to Joy.
Then give him workers by his side
Who will be tested, true, and tried;
A Walden, Shappard, and a Byers,
As yielded as a pair of pliers.
Then add a touch of Eisenhower,
With Charles G. Finney's mighty power,
The wisdom of dear old Bob Jones,
The preaching of a Tom Malone.
Then add some Theodore Roosevelt,
The courage that MacArthur felt.
And while you make him don't destroy
That charming touch of a little boy
That millions get to oft enjoy.
And when you've finished, then, of course,
Please put him on his favorite horse;
And let him give a tender tug
To his beloved General Doug.
Then we can look with high esteem
For he's the captain of our team;
And we together will have shown
The greatest man we've ever known.

Dr. Roger Martin was the final son-in-law to speak. He called "the balance, the breadth of his ministry," the most striking part of his influence upon him. Then he listed three areas where this balance and breadth amazed and impressed him: his fellowship with all who feared God, his doctrinal preaching, and his personal life. He summed it up: "Oliver Goldsmith once said in tribute to the King of England, 'He lived all the days of his life.' For Dr. John R. Rice, this was true."

Don Holmes, minister of music at Franklin Road Baptist Church, sang the number by Sarah Doudney and Ira Sankey, "The Christian's Good-Night," the song Sankey sang at the memorial service of another pulpit giant, Charles Hadden Spurgeon. He was followed by Dr. Curtis Hutson, Dr. Rice's successor as president of the Sword of the Lord Foundation and editor of *The Sword of the Lord* magazine.

Dr. Hutson said: "It is no exaggeration to say that no preacher in the twentieth century has affected the lives of so many so profoundly as John R. Rice. . . . Measured by any one of a dozen standards, John R. Rice was one of the greatest men America has ever produced." His message listed some of the outstanding features of Dr. Rice's life and ministry, giving illustrations for each. He pointed out: (1) First and foremost, he was a man with a consuming zeal and undying burden to win souls. (2) He was a man of great courage and conviction. (3) He was a man of profound wisdom. (4) He was a man of wisdom because he was a man of prayer. (5) He was a man of unbelievable accomplishments. (6) He was an example of sacrificial living. (7) He was a man of sympathetic understanding. (8) He was an earnest contender for the Faith. (9) Through it all, he was a humble man.

He summed up his remarks by promising: *"We at the Sword of the Lord are committed to carrying on the great work which he began, promoting soul winning and revival, strengthening and helping local churches, and standing without compromise for the fundamentals of the Faith."*

Mr. Russell Anderson, a Michigan businessman and very dear friend of Dr. Rice, led in the closing prayer. The congregation remained standing to sing one of Dr. Rice's songs, "We'll Never Say Goodbye in Glory," a selection he himself sang often and loved much.

Interment followed at the Bill Rice Ranch; and Dr. Rice's body was laid to rest beside those of his evangelist brothers, Dr. Bill Rice and Evangelist Joe Rice.

The words Ulrich Zwingli (1484-1531) penned in his will could easily be the charge Dr. Rice left to his co-workers and companions in the Lord's army: **"May God send his thunder and hail upon us if we allow the Holy Scriptures to be distorted. Take care that the divine Word is loyally proclaimed amongst you. . . . Listen to the Word of God! That alone will set you right again."**

*Chapter 19*

# His Works Do Follow

*And I heard a voice from heaven saying unto me, Write, Bless-
ed are the dead which die in the Lord from henceforth: Yea,
saith the Spirit, that they may rest from their labours; and
their works do follow them.*—Revelation 14:13.

*And they that be wise shall shine as the brightness of the firma-
ment; and they that turn many to righteousness as the stars for
ever and ever.*—Daniel 12:3.

Why did God so wonderfully bless the life and ministry of John
R. Rice? Perhaps one significant and vital key can be seen from
his philosophy of life. On one occasion, when someone wrote to
ask what that philosophy was, he replied:

> I promised the Lord long ago that I would honestly try to put
> Him first and serve Him with all my heart at any cost. That
> meant to lose any friend I ought to lose; to be poor when I ought
> to be poor; to be misunderstood by friends or foes if that should
> come.
> I set out: first, to know the Bible, love the Bible, take it at
> face value, to follow it at any cost. Second, I determined to put
> soul winning as the one big aim and labor of my life. Third, I
> have made it a practice to continually wait upon God for
> wisdom, power and provision.

That philosophy worked so well that what Henry Wadsworth
Longfellow wrote of Senator Charles Sumner could easily be applied to Dr. John R. Rice:

> **Were a star quenched on high,**
> **For ages would its light,**
> **Still traveling downward from the sky,**

**Shine on our mortal sight.**

**So when a great man dies,**
**For years beyond our ken,**
**The light he leaves behind him lies,**
**Upon the paths of men.**

Since this is being written less than seven months after his death, there has hardly been time to literally show how his works are following him. However, an exciting and fascinating—one could easily use such adjectives as "sweet" or "precious"—incident took place which illustrates what can be expected in the days ahead, if our Lord tarries.

On June 29, exactly six months to the day after Dr. Rice's promotion to Heaven, Rev. T. A. Powell and his family from Suffolk, Virginia, were enjoying their first full day at the Bill Rice Ranch's "Founder's Week." Setting out to see the sights and desiring first to visit the memorial park where the Rice brothers were buried, the Powells made the long walk up the hill to the grave sites. As they approached, they were somewhat surprised to see a man seated at the foot of the monument at Dr. John's grave, but when they got closer they saw he was carving an inscription: the favorite verses of Dr. Rice, Psalm 126:5,6.

After watching for a few moments, Pastor Powell introduced himself, made a comment or two about the inscription, then asked the worker if he had known Dr. Rice. Receiving a negative response, the preacher surmised he might not be a believer, so pressed him about salvation. When the gentleman freely admitted his lost condition, the soul winner took his New Testament and carefully explained God's wonderful plan of salvation. At the conclusion, the two men knelt on the grass in the front of Dr. Rice's grave; and the sinner asked the Lord Jesus Christ to forgive his sin, come into his heart, change his life, and eventually take him to Heaven.

After the prayer and some counseling about assurance, the new convert confessed he had been to church many times, but never before had anyone explained how to be saved in a way he understood. He was excited, happy, thrilled! Pastor Powell said later, "I felt as if I could almost hear Dr. John clapping his hands, for in his death he gave Gene the opportunity to accept the Saviour who made Dr. John R. Rice the man he was." And in fulfillment of the promise being inscribed on the monument, Pastor Powell added, "Then I went forth rejoicing."

It is mankind's common lot to ignore greatness during an individual's lifetime; then, human nature being what it is, after death the public will hasten to "build the tombs of the prophets, and garnish the sepulchers of the righteous" (Matt. 23:29). While we do not think Dr. Rice's *true greatness* has been recognized even yet, there was, indeed, a large measure of acclaim by his peers during his lifetime.

Many honors came his way in addition to those mentioned earlier in this volume. Two prestigious awards were given to him in the very year they were inaugurated. One was "The Bob Jones Memorial Award for the Defense of the Scriptures," bestowed upon *The Sword of the Lord* on May 27, 1970. In making the presentation, Dr. Bob Jones, Jr., then president and now chancellor of the university, called *The Sword* "a publication that stands against the compromise of scriptural principles and ecumenical alliances and one that has promoted scriptural evangelism, Biblical preaching, and the winning of souls to Christ. It has strongly stood for New Testament principles and affairs of the church."

The other was the "D. L. Moody Award for Distinguished Service in the field of Christian Literature," conferred by the Moody Bible Institute and Moody Press. It was presented on July 25, 1974, by Floyd Robinson, Moody Press sales manager, at the Minneapolis Auditorium and Convention Hall during the annual Christian Booksellers Association Convention. The Moody Press news release describing the event explained that "Dr. Rice was presented the first annual D. L. Moody Award because his wide distribution of Christian literature reflects the pioneering spirit of 19th Century evangelist, educator and innovator Dwight Lyman Moody."

It noted that the Sword of the Lord Foundation "distributes millions of pieces of literature on a free or subsidized basis in parts of the world less affluent than the United States." And it concluded: "Founder of Chicago's Moody Bible Institute,

Dwight L. Moody instituted paperback books in a Book of the Month Club in an age in which such concepts were unknown. Such innovations were designed to make Christian literature available to all economic strata of society. Dr. Rice's extensive distribution of Christian literature in the 20th Century has perpetuated the same spirit, distinguishing him as a pacesetter among Christians throughout America."

Dr. Jack Wyrtzen and Harry Bollback, directors of Word of Life, presented him with a plaque on January 23, 1978, recognizing him as "Great Proclaimer and Defender of the Faith."

A number of cities and communities honored Dr. Rice in different ways, although records were not kept of many of them. One certificate found in his effects, dated August 3, 1975, and signed by the mayor and secretary of the city, said: "GREETINGS. Be it hereby known that Dr. John R. Rice has, on this day, been made an HONORARY CITIZEN OF DALLAS, TEXAS, and under this charter shall hold and enjoy a place of high esteem in the minds and hearts of the people of this City." He was given the key to the city of Winder, Georgia, on December 6, 1969. And Indianapolis Mayor Richard G. Lugar (now a United States Senator) proclaimed August 12-18, 1974, as "Sword of the Lord Week," noting, "Dr. John R. Rice, founder and editor, has been providing this Christian publication for forty years to families in the United States and around the world."

On January 15, 1970, Mayor Bryant Liggett of Pensacola, Florida, issued a proclamation describing Dr. Rice as one of God's "most dedicated and effective evangelists." On November 8, 1978, Mayor Ann A. Crichton of Decatur, Georgia, released a proclamation welcoming him to that city, with "our heartfelt prayers that his visit among us will be blessed and rewarded with a great spiritual revival in our area." On March 18, 1969, Mayor Joseph E. Klen of Hammond, Indiana, presented with a certificate appointing him an "honorary citizen of the City of Hammond." And on August 29, 1979, Governor William P. Clements, Jr., commissioned him "Admiral in the Texas Navy with all rights and privileges appertaining thereto and with the duty of assisting in the preservation of the history, boundaries, water resources, and civil defense of the State"!

On September 9, 1972, Dr. Rice and the Sword of the Lord were both given the "Liberty Award" by the Congress of Freedom in recognition of "outstanding service in a meritorious effort to restore individual freedom and states' rights, as originally guaranteed by the Constitution of the United States, so that future generations may once again enjoy the God-given blessings of Liberty." The institution of his early ministry, Wayland Baptist College, where he taught and coached following his graduation from Baylor, on its 60th anniversary, September 9, 1968, presented Dr. Rice with a certificate in "grateful appreciation" for his "faithful service" on the faculty and expressed "gratitude for every contribution to the growth and stability" of the college. And in January, 1978, The Pilgrim presented him with its Preacher of the Month Award.

On May 4, 1970, the Memphis Baptist College gave him a certificate "in recognition of our appreciation" to him, saying, "We acknowledge with gratitude every act of kindness and labor of love which you have expressed toward the ministry and welfare of Memphis Baptist College." On December 6, 1967, the American Ministers Association of Georgia presented him with its "Outstanding Citizen" Award, recognizing "his contribution to the religious, economic, political and social welfare of the nation; his faithful service to his fellow men and the Kingdom of God," along with "many other outstanding services."

At its 1980 meeting in Louisville, the loosely knit but large and prestigious Southwide Baptist Fellowship, at a special service in his honor, lovingly presented him with a plaque which says: "Dr. John R. Rice, whom we commend as a giant of the Faith. We gratefully acknowledge manifold years of service to God, manifesting his love for mankind." The local executive committee at the Texas Sword Conference presented him with a large and beautiful plaque, saying: "In behalf of the cooperating 78 churches, we express our deepest appreciation for bringing the National Conference on Soul Winning and Revival to Dallas and Fort Worth, Texas, August 3-6, 1975." His co-workers at the

Sword of the Lord honored him in so many ways on so many occasions it would take a special chapter to describe them all.

Pastors and local church congregations seemed especially appreciative of Dr. Rice's ministry. Dr. Barry Bagwell and the People's Baptist Temple of Greenville, North Carolina, presented him with a plaque inscribed: "Mr. Fundamentalist, Dr. John R. Rice, For Over Three Quarters Of A Century Standing for Bible Truth." Dr. William W. Pennell and the large Forrest Hills Baptist Church of Decatur, Georgia, on November 12, 1978, made Dr. Rice "A Lifetime Honorary Member of Forrest Hills Baptist Church, With All the Spiritual Privileges That Accompany Church Membership." Dr. Clyde H. Box and the Brook Hollow Baptist Church of De Soto, Texas, on November 19, 1978, presented Dr. Rice a plaque proclaiming him "World's Greatest Fundamentalist."

Dr. Terry Smith and the Longview Baptist Temple in Texas honored him twice, the first time on November 21, 1971, with a plaque calling him "20th Century's Defender of the Faith." Then on April 25, 1976, on its "Thank God For Our Heritage Sunday" during America's Bicentennial Celebration, the church presented him with a scroll saying:

> In appreciation of those faithful men of God who have down through the centuries exhorted the inerrant truths of the Bible and thus provided for our generation a heritage of strong Bible-believing churches, Spirit-filled preachers to stand in the pulpits of our country, and the freedom to continue the proclamation of these same eternal truths—
>
> We the people of the Longview Baptist Temple gratefully acknowledge Dr. John R. Rice, Editor of *The Sword of the Lord*, as a voice standing out in this 20th century to protect and advance that same heritage. He has defended victoriously the fundamentals of the Faith, has given courage and stamina to countless thousands of God's men, and preserved in writing much of his God-given wisdom to be passed on to the next generation.

He was honored also many times by the church where he held membership during the last two decades of his life, the Franklin Road Baptist Church of Murfreesboro. Other churches giving him plaques included the North Houston Baptist Church in Texas; the Temple Baptist Church of St. Paul, Minnesota; the First Baptist Church of Rosemont, Minnesota; the Central Baptist Church of Milwaukee, Wisconsin; and literally a host of other churches.

One of the finest tributes given Dr. Rice was on the occasion of his 75th birthday, at a birthday luncheon held at the Southern Diplomat Restaurant in Murfreesboro. Part of the remarks of the speaker, Dr. Monroe Parker, general director of World Baptist Missions, were framed and now hang on the wall with other memorabilia at the Sword Foundation. The tribute said:

> One of America's most eloquent speakers, Dr. Bob Jones, and one of her most successful pastors, Dr. Jack Hyles, paid tribute to Dr. John R. Rice last night; and Europe's most dynamic preacher, Dr. Ian Paisley, delivered a sermon which was indeed a beautiful tribute to this great leader. It would seem that anything that could be said today would be anticlimactic; but since nothing is so eloquent as sincerity and nothing is so powerful as truth, I shall speak sincerely and truthfully of this wonderful man, this effective evangelist, this powerful writer, this spiritual giant, this beloved friend, Dr. John R. Rice.
>
> He is a man, reared in a place and in a day where and when most men were men. Dr. Rice is as gentle and as tender as a mother, but he is no sissy. He had courage. This bronc-bustin' Texas football player from Decatur Baptist College is a line ripper of the old school. As a man, Dr. Rice is a sinner saved by grace, baptized and filled and endued by the Holy Ghost for the great ministry that today we all so deeply appreciate. God endowed him with a rugged body which he has kept pure and strong and in subjection to the Lord Jesus Christ. Only a man with an unusual physical constitution could be such an indefatigable worker.
>
> God endowed Dr. Rice with a sound and a brilliant mind; and that is a rare combination. He is one of the finest scholars and teachers. His commentaries on some of the books of the Bible reveal brilliance and scholarship of the finest quality. His practical treatment of those subjects reveals soundness and spiritual insight so lacking in most of the commentaries. In all of his writings, whether on the subject of Home, Courtship and Marriage, or the Holy Spirit, or Prayer, or the Bible, or Soul Winning, or Modernism, or Neo-orthodoxy, or New Evangeli-

calism, there is the throb of the evangelistic heart. Then there is the literary gift. He has a poetic soul and a love for the beautiful, but he will not allow gorgeous rhetoric to thwart his purpose in writing. Few men possess such literary acumen.

What is true of Dr. Rice's writing is equally true of his preaching and of his daily walk.

The story is told of St. Francis of Assisi that one day he said to a young monk, "Let us go down to the marketplace and preach." They went down to the marketplace and walked around for a while and returned to the monastery. The young monk in astonishment said, "I thought we were going to preach." St. Francis answered, "We have been preaching." I have never felt that I was so holy that I could just walk around and drool piety, but it is true that what we do sounds out so loudly that people can hardly hear what we are saying. Dr. Rice's life is an eloquent and effective sermon bringing inspiration to thousands and glory to God.

We all know that Mrs. Rice is an helpmeet for her husband, and we are grateful for the beauty of her soul that shines through Dr. Rice's life and for their lovely daughters and their faithful co-laborers.

The influence and power of Dr. Rice's life and ministry are being felt in every fundamental church and school in the land and in thousands of places throughout the world.

Thank you, Dr. Rice, for your faithfulness, and your love for the Lord Jesus Christ, and your commitment to Him.

May God continue to sustain and bless *The Sword of the Lord* and of John R. Rice!

Dr. Rice belonged in any "Who's Who" or "Hall of Fame" for those who stood for the Faith and sought to evangelize the world. Many of his peers recognized this. Dr. Tom Smith and the Phillips Drive Baptist Church of Atlanta presented him with a "Heavenly Hall of Fame" plaque in recognition of "his years of outstanding leadership through the ministries of *The Sword of the Lord.* " The San Francisco Baptist Theological Seminary and the Lucerne Christian Conference Center elected him to their "Fundamentalism's Hall of Fame" and hung his picture with others thus honored at the Conference Center in Lucerne, California. The Forrest Hills Christian School elected him to its Liberty Chapel "Patriot Hall of Fame." And as soon as his death made him eligible, the most prestigious of all the Halls—the

Christian Hall of Fame at Canton, Ohio—hung his portrait and made him the one hundred and first thus honored. Other men featured in the Canton Hall include early church fathers, reformers, missionaries, evangelists and pastors.

After Dr. Rice went to be with the Lord, a steady stream of telegrams, letters, telephone calls and other messages flooded Murfreesboro, both at his home and his office. Several of the civic leaders who knew him personally and appreciatively as a man and as a Christian gentleman sent stirring communications.

Dr. Rice made an impact on people everywhere, so it was no surprise that community leaders where he lived and worked respected him and loved him. Typical, we think, is the statement from Tommy Martin, the man local people affectionately call "Mister Murfreesboro." (An insurance executive who has received many honors—Life Member, Million Dollar Round Table; Hall of Fame; National Quality Award, etc.—Middle Tennessee State University had just announced the establishment of the Tommy Martin Chair of Insurance.) He wrote, in part:

> I have considered it an honor and privilege to know Dr. Rice over these past seventeen years. His dedication as a Christian leader has been evidenced by the many souls that have been led to Christ, by the many ministers that he helped, and by the sympathetic understanding he had with his associates. As a subscriber to *The Sword of the Lord* since 1963, and a collector of many of Dr. Rice's wonderful books, I feel that I am a much taller man and that I have been blessed in so many ways by having known this man of God.
>
> Our hearts were deeply saddened when we learned that Dr. Rice had passed away. But we realize that his examples of loyalty to his friends, devotion to his family, and love for his God will continue to live on through those of us who knew him.
>
> We shall miss Dr. Rice—this man who always held high the Banner of Christ—but Murfreesboro is a better place in which to live and we are better people because he passed this way.

Another personal friend, Jack O. Weatherford, chairman and chief executive officer of the Murfreesboro Bank & Trust Company, said in part: "Continuing thoughts of Dr. John will be meaningful because he was such an exemplary model as a Chris-

tian, a father, a husband, a businessman, and a community
leader. His influence in those areas has been outstanding and
unique to many of us."

Mayor W. H. Westbrooks of Murfreesboro spoke of Dr. Rice as
"one of the outstanding people who has come to our community
during the past few years"; then added, "The organization which
he brought to Murfreesboro has been outstanding in its contribution to our community."

The congressman from his district, the Honorable John Bragg,
acknowledged a loss in his death that could not be refilled, yet
admitted everything was now perfect for Dr. Rice. Then he said:

> More than any man of God, Dr. John typified the true
> evangelist. Not with great fanfare and not with the sounding of
> trumpets, but with a human, sincere, and caring approach, he
> touched men wherever he stood and everywhere he was heard.
> He could walk with kings, but he never forgot the common
> touch.
>
> Before I ever met him, I knew about him from my conversa-
> tions with Dr. Bill Rice. I distinctly remember the first time I
> met Dr. John, and the first time I ever heard him. I don't
> believe any person could forget either experience. I have
> watched him through the years and marveled at his dedication,
> his steadfastness, and his encouragement as he told the world
> The Way.
>
> We shall all miss him, and we are all fortunate that so many
> of the seeds he planted fell on good ground and his work will
> bear fruit in all the years to come.

The junior United States Senator from Tennessee, Jim Sasser,
called him "a dedicated and talented Bible scholar and writer
whose insights will be sorely missed." And he added: "His was a
full and fruitful life and one which should set an example for all
citizens."

United States Senator Howard Baker, the senior senator from
Tennessee and now the Senate majority leader, wired Mrs. Rice:
"It was with deep sorrow that I learned of the passing of your
husband. Dr. Rice has been the titular head of the fundamentalists in this country and one of the most powerful pens through
his 45 years with *The Sword of the Lord* and the numerous books

he has written. My heartfelt condolences are with you and your six daughters during this time."

Tennessee Governor Lamar Alexander's message to Mrs. Rice spoke of her husband's service to God during his lifetime, how it had benefited so many and would be remembered so long. Then he added, "Honey and I will keep you in our thoughts and prayers."

President-Elect Ronald Reagan wired Mrs. Rice: "Nancy and I were saddened to learn of the death of your husband, John. His life and his great faith were an inspiration to millions through the years. In this hour may the peace of God comfort you and your family. With warmest personal regards."

On the national and international scale, hundreds of evangelical leaders sent messages. Dr. Fred M. Barlow, evangelist, author and Sunday school expert, testified: "My memories of Dr. Rice go back to 1948 when he invited me to a Sword of the Lord Conference on Evangelism in Chicago. Those were hallowed and holy days in my life. I made holy vows regarding my service for the Saviour and evangelism. Suffice it to say, there are multitudes of men like myself preaching today whose lives and labors were blessedly touched by the person and pen of Dr. Rice."

Dr. Hugh F. Pyle, another evangelist and author, declared: "In the early days of my preaching ministry, Dr. John R. Rice, along with *The Sword of the Lord,* sparked my life with soul-winning power. He has encouraged and helped my writing ministry as no other. Through the years his faithfulness to the Bible and the Saviour has been a challenge and an inspiration. My association with this great friend of preachers has been sweet, indeed. The world needed him. We all loved and will miss him. But now we look forward to renewed fellowship where the gates swing outward never."

The man they call "The Walking Bible," Dr. Jack Van Impe, an internationally known evangelist and radio speaker who also conducts a nationwide television ministry, sent this message:

In 1950, while attending the Detroit Bible College, I picked up my first issue of *The Sword of the Lord*. I have never missed reading one issue from that day until the present hour. It has been a source of blessing and inspiration to me throughout all of these years.

Dr. John R. Rice became one of the men to whom I looked for spiritual guidance over these years as I read *The Sword*. What a thrilling day it was when, as a young man, I became acquainted with him. I learned to love him. I learned to appreciate him, not only as a brother in Christ, but as a great leader. Many were the times I called him for advice as to the direction I should take in my ministry.

Because of the call of God and the inspiration provided by Dr. Rice and *The Sword of the Lord*, I decided to enter citywide evangelism in 1969. At that point I had conducted 800 local church crusades. After receiving the call of God through the Holy Spirit and Dr. Rice's pleadings, I conducted 250 mass citywide endeavors, preaching to some 10 million people; a total of 500,000 decisions were recorded. And when, at the Judgment Seat of Christ, rewards are distributed, Dr. Rice will be the one God honors for having encouraged the heart of a young preacher to take this stand.

Another well-known television minister and evangelist conducting gigantic crusades, James Robison, sent this word: "Even in the face of grief over the parting of Dr. John R. Rice, I can see the glory of the light of the Lord through this great holy man of God. Perhaps no man in this century has influenced more preachers to be true to God's Word, to win souls, to stand firm, and to refuse to compromise. John R. Rice has been an immeasurable influence on my life and ministry. The effect of his efforts lives on throughout all eternity through the glory of our great God. My prayers are with you."

Dr. E. J. Daniels, another famous preacher of both television and united crusades, testified:

Every time I think of Dr. John R. Rice, I think of God's declaration that there were "giants in those days." Dr. Rice was a giant measured by any standard. He was a giant mentally, spiritually, morally, doctrinally and in his influence around the world. Few men have shaped history as has he. This giant has not fallen, but lives on, even in this world, through his books, Sword publications, and the thousands of preachers he has influenced for better.

He has been my dear friend for nearly fifty years. Heaven is now more precious to me because he is there.

Rev. Ron Adrian, pastor of the First Baptist Church at New Castle, Delaware, said: "Speaking in behalf of my entire family of seven independent, fundamental Baptist pastors, Dr. John R. Rice has had a more profound influence on our ministry for fundamentalism, soul winning, and church building than any other man in America today. We love him and respect him and hold him in high esteem."

The pastor of the large Temple Baptist Church in Detroit and president of Baptist Bible College East, Dr. A. V. Henderson, said in part:

> As a young preacher I'd been delighted with his stand for fundamentalism and his unmovable stand against modernism. He made an impression on me that the uppermost thing in his mind was the salvation of the lost. Through *The Sword of the Lord* he not only inspired me in the efforts of evangelism, but made it possible for me to sit at the feet of the great preachers of another generation. In the Sword Conferences of which I have been a part, there was always a spirit of concern and cooperation. I have counted John R. Rice one of my special friends.

Dr. Harold Henniger, pastor of the huge Canton Baptist Temple where the Christian Hall of Fame is housed, said:

> Dr. John R. Rice has been one of the great soul winners of this century, not only personally, but he promoted and encouraged revival and soul winning and evangelism among thousands of preachers and churches through *The Sword of the Lord* and Sword conferences. His numerous books had an enormous impact upon the spiritual life of fundamental Christianity. He stood as few men have stood for what he considered biblical convictions, even when it meant standing alone. His family is the example of family life based on the Bible. We will miss this choice servant of God and cherished friend. Our loss is truly Heaven's gain.

An evangelist of the old school and long a personal friend, Dr.

Hyman J. Appelman, sent a wonderful testimonial; and we give just a part:

> Dr. Rice was a man who comes, perhaps, once in a genera-
> tion. The Holy Spirit had endowed him with many talents. As
> a gifted author of most helpful books; as a noted, effective
> pulpiteer—matter of fact, I can say a giant of the pulpit; as a
> pastor; as an evangelist; as a protagonist and leader of noble
> causes—many, many times sacrificing himself. Above all, as a
> Titan in the realm of soul winning. Tens of thousands, aye,
> hundreds of thousands have been saved, reclaimed, added to
> the churches under his impassioned appeals. Truly, hundreds
> of others will join me in my own fervent, unreserved testimony
> that I am the better man because John R. Rice came into my
> life.
>
> Beyond any of these things, great as they were and are, John
> Rice was a Christian through and through—a gentle, compas-
> sionate, Spirit-filled Christian, sacrificially going out of his
> way in many ways to help us lesser people. May I say from the
> depths of my soul, thank you, Lord, for giving us John R. Rice
> for so many years. God, please, the prayer of my soul, bless his
> wife and wonderful children and grandchildren; and may they
> carry on the superlative tradition of this giant of giants in
> Christ's name. Amen.

Dr. John Powell, pastor of the Reimer Road Baptist Church in Wadsworth, Ohio, said:

> Dr. John R. Rice was my hero and friend. The paper which
> he edited, *The Sword of the Lord,* has been a tremendous bless-
> ing to me. I was privileged to have Dr. Rice in my pulpit
> regularly for the last nine years. We have men now serving on
> our deacon board who were saved and influenced under his
> preaching ministry. Our people loved Dr. Rice. In fact, we ded-
> icated our last new building in his honor and a large picture of
> him is hanging in our foyer.
>
> His books have been such a help to me through the years of
> my ministry. But most of all, his life has been an example for
> me to follow. He lived what he preached and wrote. He was one
> of the most unselfish and loving men I have had the privilege of
> knowing. I believe he was more like Jesus than any man I have
> ever known.

A long, glowing tribute came from Dr. Dino Pedrone, pastor of the Open Door Church at Chambersburg, Pennsylvania, too lengthy to reproduce here. He told of the blessing Dr. Rice had been throughout his ministry and of his first visit to the Open Door Church. Then he said:

> Since then God has allowed me to build a Sunday school which averages over 1,600 in a small community. We have had numerous big days, including setting many state Sunday school records, one of which was over 11,000 in Sunday school two years ago. At my request, Dr. Rice returned to our pulpit on a yearly basis. It was through his encouragement that I have written several books.
>
> To many he will be remembered as "The 20th Century's Mightiest Pen," the editor of the world's foremost revival weekly, evangelist and a revivalist; but to this preacher he was the difference between a mediocre ministry and a ministry that has influenced thousands of people. Personally, I loved him as a father, looked to him as a leader, and thank God for his example. This is the way that this preacher shall always remember him.

The pastor of the Lavon Drive Baptist Church at Garland, Texas, Dr. Gary Coleman, said Dr. Rice was truly his hero, then added:

> Since the first time I heard Dr. Rice speak in a Sword of the Lord conference at the old Galilean Baptist Church back in the early 1960s, I have looked up to him and depended on him for leadership. I will never forget, as a young preacher, how I wrote him for advice with regard to some principles to live by. I received a long reply from Dr. Rice, giving me some excellent advice about principles that should govern a pastor's life. It had a profound impact on my life as a preacher of the Gospel.
>
> All his books are in my library and have been a great blessing. Especially his books on the home and prayer had an influence on my life as a young preacher. . . .
>
> The Bible says, 'The memory of the just is blessed,' and I can truly say that Dr. Rice's memory is one of the most precious memories that I have in my ministry and life.

Another lengthy but truly wonderful testimony came from Dr. Bill Pennell, pastor of the Forrest Hills Baptist Church in Decatur, Georgia. After several paragraphs of tribute to Dr. Rice, he said:

Many years ago now I went to a Sword of the Lord conference as an officer of my denomination to criticize Dr. John R. Rice and Dr. Jack Hyles for their extreme positions and hyper-aggressive evangelism. I was a fruitless, powerless and lifeless preacher of a small, struggling church which had great potential located in a small Southern city. I had heard of this fire-breathing monster, this denominational vampire, this money-grabbing church leech, this fanatical fundamentalist agitator; but I found he was none of those when I heard him preach.

The Holy Spirit gripped my heart and set my life on a course of soul winning and church building that included the definite power of the Holy Spirit. I can, and others can, mark the turn-about in my soul winning and church building, the beginning of depth and growth in my church and my life, from that very important date and to the powerful ministry of Dr. John R. Rice.

Later Dr. Rice became a close, personal friend and a sought-after advisor. I found him always warm, interested and knowledgeable about any subject one chose to discuss with him. His advice was based on Scripture, not emotions; on right, and not personalities. . . .

Dr. Rice was a true friend of our Lord, of poor lost sinners, of needy preachers, of Christians worldwide, and my dear friend who has now marched away to his place beside Jesus, our best Friend.

Dr. Tom Wallace, pastor of Beth Haven Baptist Church in Louisville, told of the tremendous influence Dr. Rice had been in his life and ministry. Then he said:

He has been my teacher, counselor and friend. He has been like a father to me. This evangelist extraordinary, powerful preacher, enlightened editor, successful soul winner, blessed broadcaster, writer of sweet songs, author of bountiful books, pamphlets, and tracts, pleasing poet and faithful friend has surely been a man sent from God. As the Lord tarries, Dr. Rice will continue to preach on to multitudes for years and years to come through his books, pamphlets, tracts and printed material. As Dr. Rice joins the crowd in heavenly grandstands to watch the revival and soul-winning activities of those of us left to do the work, we can be sure he is shouting "Hallelujah!" and "Glory to God!" every time a soul comes to Christ. Dr. Rice is gone, but not his influence. "He being dead yet speaketh" (Heb. 11:4).

Dr. Adrian Rogers, pastor of the tremendous Bellevue Baptist Church in Memphis—one of the nation's 10 largest—and past president of the Southern Baptist Convention, paid him a glowing tribute in a personal letter just a few weeks before Dr. Rice went to be with the Lord. He wrote:

> You have been a blessing to my heart and a strength to my life for almost 30 years. I believe that some of the basic convictions I have were first born in my heart from reading *The Sword of the Lord* as a nineteen-year-old college student.
>
> Your books and your life and your convictions have been a strength and a testimony to me. You have stood like the Rock of Gibraltar, yet with a love and a compassion and a tenderness that I have seen in few men.
>
> . . .I am grateful to be counted as one of your friends.

Mr. John Beiler, businessman from Elkton, Maryland, and a Sword of the Lord board member, said: "When I think of Dr. Rice, I also think a lot of a man who looked to God for his needs. It proves that God is for real because God answered his requests and did meet his needs as he relied on the Lord. Dr. Rice has greatly influenced my life in these areas—how to live the Christian life the way we should!"

Another businessman, Sam Moore, president of Thomas Nelson, Inc., in Nashville, declared:

> As an evangelist, Dr. Rice was a giant of a giant. Although physically he stood tall, he called himself one of the little people, the people to whom he proclaimed the message of salvation. His great compassion for the lost showed no favorites.
>
> It truly has been both an honor and blessing to have known Dr. Rice for the past decade. His sincerity and convictions have been a tremendous force in the Christian world. His dedication to reaching the lost has been an inspiration to those whose lives were touched, and his living concern for the new Christians nurtured through growing faith.
>
> Dr. Rice was a true scholar who devoted his energies toward helping lay people understand the message of the Gospel. The clarity of his writing penetrated hearts and minds of many nationalities. It has been my privilege to share his final work, the Rice Reference Bible. His notes and references, over which he prayerfully labored, culminate a lifetime goal of spreading God's love throughout the world to all people.

Dr. N. A. Woychuk, in the Scripture Memory Fellowship *Digest* he edits, reported Dr. Rice's death:

> Dr. Rice was a courageous and yet gracious defender of the faith. His ministry was characterized by a warm compassion for people. Soul winning was the theme of his life, and this was so effectively demonstrated in his preaching throughout America, in his writing of many substantial books, and in the production of the strong weekly paper, *The Sword of the Lord.* Dr. Rice had a tremendous influence on many pastors and Christian leaders throughout the world. His books on prayer and Heaven have been much appreciated as awards in SMF, and we thank God for the kindly consideration shown us by this dear man of God and his good staff.

Dr. Bruce D. Cummons, pastor of the Massillon Baptist Temple and president of Massillon Baptist College, reported Dr. Rice's death in his church paper under the heading "My Friend Has Gone Home!" He told of his long association with Dr. Rice, then said: "The preaching, teaching, and publishing ministry of this man who walked so closely with the Lord has touched and influenced the lives of thousands of preachers, and tens of thousands of laymen. His books, sermons, and ministry of *The Sword of the Lord* has greatly influenced my life and ministry."

When news of Dr. Rice's death reached Australia, Sidney W. Hunter, editor of the *Biblical Fundamentalist,* said in his lead editorial:

> Some twenty years ago a friend gave me a copy of *The Sword of the Lord* edited by Dr. John R. Rice. I immediately subscribed. Through its pages God began giving me a very real heart's concern to win the lost to Christ. It also made me aware of the modernism and theological compromise which was taking place in many church groups and seminaries. God used it to encourage me to win souls, stand true to the fundamentals of the Christian faith, and have a sincere desire for my life to count for the cause of Christ.
>
> God used Dr. Rice, *The Sword of the Lord* magazine, and many of Dr. Rice's books to be a real blessing and encouragement to me in my Christian life. *Prayer—Asking and Receiving* helped me tremendously in my prayer life. I enjoyed his heartwarming, down-to-earth, practical, evangelistic applica-

tion of the Word of God to the everyday issues of life. I thank
God for the influence his work has had on my life.

In the Trinity Baptist Church paper of Jacksonville, *The Baptist Beacon,* Dr. Bob Gray described the funeral service, saying:
"The new church auditorium, which seats approximately 1,700
people, was completely filled and people were standing around
the walls in the downstairs part of the auditorium. Those
preachers participating in the funeral service, which lasted for
three hours, made up a list that could easily have been called the
'Who's Who in Fundamentalism' in America!"

He went on to tell of the personal influence of Dr. Rice in his
ministry, then said: "The exemplary family life of Dr. and Mrs.
John R. Rice has provided a role model for every fundamental
preacher in the country! How can you even begin to measure the
life and ministry of this great preacher? Suffice it to say that 'I
am a debtor,' and gratefully so. A place in the ranks of fundamentalism will be vacant that no one else can fill."

In an issue of *The Branding Iron* dedicated to his memory, his
nephew Evangelist Bill Rice, III, referred to his character, saying:

> It is not simply that he was a great man in public whose
> mourners would include thousands of Bible believers across
> this nation, great fundamentalist preachers, and the President
> of the United States. He was a godly man at home with his
> children and his dear wife. He loved the Lord (and it was
> evident) during breakfast on Monday morning just as certainly
> as he loved the Lord (and it was evident) as he preached to a
> great crowd on Sunday morning.
>
> No man is worthy of bouquets or our remembering simply
> because he has an effect on multitudes. This world is filled with
> "prominent people" whose public life is quite different from
> their private life. Men who quote the Bible on Sunday but cannot live it on Tuesday! Men who are kind in public, but crude
> in private. Men who speak of affection and say "I love you" to a
> television audience of millions, while divorcing their wives and
> leaving their children. Fame and greatness are two entirely
> separate matters!
>
> The honest truth is, there are men in the public eye whom we
> perceive to be great, who are quite often shallow and hollow in
> person. Find a man who appears good or even godly before

thousands on a Sunday or a Monday, and you have found a person of fame. But when you find a man who is consistent in his home, you have a godly man.

Then he went on to illustrate how Dr. Rice was exactly that kind of a man in his home.

Our conclusion is that John R. Rice was one of the truly great men of God, not only in our generation and our century, but of all time. Rebecca Byers, the daughter of the Sword general manager, penned a poetic tribute to him which we will use to conclude this biography. She wrote it around the time of his death when she was only seventeen, a junior in high school. Expressing the emotions of her heart, she declared:

> **There was greatness here amongst us**
> **Such as some will never know—**
> **A man of God, a prince of prayer,**
> **A fervent fighter of the foe.**
> **A man of great compassion**
> **With love for all he knew,**
> **Yet not afraid to stand**
> **No matter with how few.**
> **He left a shining example,**
> **Let us follow in his way**
> **Praying, trusting, working, caring**
> **As we live from day to day.**

## APPENDIX A

## "WHAT MUST I DO TO BE SAVED?"

### By Evangelist John R. Rice

What must I do to be saved? Here in the simplest, shortest form is put the question to which every man must learn the answer, or spend eternity lost, away from God, suffering the torments of the damned! Thank God, this question is asked and answered in the Word of God so simply that every soul can understand it. There are other questions in God's Word which affect the soul's welfare, and many places in the Bible is the plan of salvation made plain, but only one place is this question given word for word, and there, too, we find the answer. Paul and Silas were in jail in the city of Philippi, and at midnight they sang and prayed until God broke down all the doors and broke the stocks which held their feet, with a mighty earthquake. The poor jailer, frightened and convicted of his sins, came to these two preachers and asked this question. Read it in Acts 16:29-31.

> Then he called for a light, and sprang in, and came trembling, and fell down before Paul and Silas, And brought them out, and said, Sirs, what must I do to be saved? And they said, Believe on the Lord Jesus Christ, and thou shalt be saved, and thy house.

"What must I do to be saved?" "Believe on the Lord Jesus Christ, and thou shalt be saved!" There is God's plan of salvation, the only plan He has for every man, woman and child who was ever born into the whole world.

## WHAT MUST I DO?

Sinner, there is something you *must* do if you would be saved. There was hope for this jailer because he saw himself a lost sinner and came trembling to inquire, "What *must* I do?" Reader, you are a sinner. The Word of God from beginning to end emphasizes that fact. In Isaiah 53:6 we learn:

> *ALL we like sheep have gone astray; we have turned EVERY ONE to his own way; and the Lord hath laid on him the iniquity of us ALL.*

We have all gone astray! The Lord is not content for sinners to be left believing themselves good. In Romans, the third chapter, how positive, how certain is the Word of God that every man, woman and child is a sinner!

> *What then? ARE WE BETTER THAN THEY? No, in no wise: for we have before proved both Jews and Gentiles, that they are ALL under sin; As it is written, There is NONE righteous, NO, NOT ONE: There is NONE that understandeth, there is NONE that seeketh after God. They are ALL gone out of the way, they are together become unprofitable; there is NONE that doeth good, NO, NOT ONE!*—Rom. 3:9-12.

In verses 22 and 23 it is stated again that "there is no difference: For all have sinned, and come short of the glory of God." That is the reason that Jesus said to Nicodemus in the third chapter of John, "Marvel not that I said unto thee, YE MUST BE BORN AGAIN." And a little later in the same chapter, verse 18, He said that the man who has not believed in Jesus is already condemned.

Certainly these Scriptures must make it clear to every man who believes the Word of God that he is a sinner; and until he has believed in Christ and has been saved, he is a lost sinner and needs saving. The heart is wrong, and only God can make that right. Then if you want to be saved, you must admit in your own heart, *"I am a sinner. I am lost and need to be saved."* No one ever was saved without coming for salvation as a sinner.

## CHRIST DIED TO SAVE SINNERS, NOT GOOD MEN

Oh, I beg you, see it today! You are a poor, lost sinner, a Hell-bound sinner! Your heart is black. You have hardened your heart; you have resisted the call of God; you have rejected Christ. However good you are in man's sight, you are a terrible sinner; and unless you turn to Christ, you must spend eternity in Hell. A SINNER! That is what you are. Admit it in your own heart; confess it to God. You are a sinner, and you need saving worse than you need anything else in the world.

If you have settled in your heart that matter, then you are ready to learn God's answer to your question, "What must I do to be saved?"

## BELIEVE ON THE LORD JESUS CHRIST

Here is God's simple way to be saved. You are a sinner; your heart is wrong; you cannot save yourself; you are already condemned. The thing you are to do then, to be saved, is simply to trust the Lord Jesus with that matter. When you do trust Him, then you have God's promise "thou shalt be saved."

I do not mean that you are simply to believe that there is a God or that there is a Saviour. Devils believe that and tremble (James 2:19). You can believe that a certain physician is a good doctor without calling him to be your doctor when you are sick. You can believe that a certain man is a good lawyer without taking him as your lawyer to defend your case. You are not just to believe the truth about Jesus, you are to believe on Him, that is, depend upon Him, risk Him, trust Him; and when you do, you are saved.

## NOT SAVED BY GOOD WORKS

Of course, you do not deserve salvation. There is nothing you can do that will make you worthy of it. You cannot be saved by keeping the Ten Commandments, for the Scripture clearly shows that you have not kept them. Romans 3:20 says:

> *Therefore by the deeds of the law there shall no flesh be justified in his sight: for by the law is the knowledge of sin.*

The same thing is told in Galatians 3:11 which says:

> *But that no man is justified by the law in the sight of God, it is evident: for, The just shall live by faith.*

Many, many Scriptures repeat again and again that there is no salvation through human goodness.

> *Not by works of righteousness which we have done, but according to his mercy he saved us, by the washing of regeneration, and renewing of the Holy Ghost.*—Titus 3:5.

> *FOR BY GRACE ARE YE SAVED THROUGH FAITH; AND THAT NOT OF YOURSELVES: IT IS THE GIFT OF GOD: NOT OF WORKS, LEST ANY MAN SHOULD BOAST.*—Eph. 2:8,9.

We had as well admit, then, that no man deserves saving and no man can save himself. Salvation must be free or the sinner could never get it. In fact, it takes blood to pay for sin, for the Scripture says:

## "WITHOUT SHEDDING OF BLOOD IS NO REMISSION"—HEBREWS 9:22

> *For when we were yet without strength, in due time Christ died for the ungodly.*—Rom. 5:6.

> *All we like sheep have gone astray; we have turned every one to his own way; and the Lord hath laid on him the iniquity of us all.*—Isa. 53:6.

Peter tells us that all of us are bought by the blood of Christ:

> *Forasmuch as ye know that ye were not redeemed with corruptible things, as silver and gold, from your vain conversation received by tradition from your fathers; But with the precious blood of Christ, as of a lamb without blemish and without spot.*—I Peter 1:18,19.

Every lamb, bullock, heifer, goat, turtle dove and pigeon offered in the Old Testament times on the altar pictured this: that man, a guilty sinner, must have some innocent one to shed his blood to pay for one man's sins. Jesus died for our sins; and, thank God, salvation is bought for every man in the world, if he will have it, as the free gift of God.

> *For the wages of sin is death; but the GIFT of God is eternal life through Jesus Christ our Lord.*—Rom. 6:23.

Dear sinner, remember that church membership will not save you. If you have been baptized, that cannot save you. Baptism does not save, does not keep anybody saved; it is only an act of duty for those who have already found Christ as their Saviour. A moral life or lodge membership or good citizenship, these must all fail to bring salvation, for it is "not by works of righteousness which we have done, but according to his mercy he saved us" (Titus 3:5). Don't depend, then, on what you do, but on what Jesus did and promises to do for you.

## WHAT ABOUT REPENTANCE?

Does not the Bible say that we must repent? Yes, the Bible plainly says that "God. . .commandeth all men every where to repent" (Acts 17:30), and again, "Except ye repent, ye shall all likewise perish" (Luke 13:3,5). This was the preaching of John the Baptist, of Jesus, of Peter and of Paul, that men should repent. And certainly repentance is God's plan of salvation. The trouble here, however, is that men misunderstand what repentance means; and there has grown up an idea that repentance means a period of weeping and mourning over sin, or sorrow for sins. This idea comes from the Douay Version of the Bible which instead of "repent" says "do penance." So the place of inquiry in revival meetings, where people should be taught the plan of salvation from the Bible,  became "the mourner's bench"; and thousands of people have been taught that God would not hear their prayer nor forgive their sins until they went through a process of sorrow and mourning over their sins!

Do not misunderstand me. God is anxious for you to have a penitent, broken heart over your sins. You have gone away from God. You have trampled under foot the blood of Jesus Christ, wasted years of your life which you can never live over again. You have served your father the Devil. There is plenty for you to weep over, and I am not surprised if you feel deep shame and sorrow in your heart that you have so mistreated the God who made you and the Saviour who died for you. I am not surprised if you cannot keep back the tears! But what I want you to know is that tears or no tears, however much sorrow you may have in your heart, or not have, those things do not save you.

You ought to be sorry for your sins and ashamed of them. "Godly sorrow worketh repentance" (II Corinthians 7:10)—the right kind of sorrow leads to immediate repentance, but mourning is not itself repentance.

> Could my tears forever flow,
> Could my zeal no respite know,
> These for sin could not atone;
> Thou must save, and Thou alone.

To repent literally means to have a change of mind or spirit toward God and toward sin. It means to turn from your sins, earnestly, with all your heart, and trust in Jesus Christ to save you. You can see, then, how the man who believes in Christ repents and the man who repents believes in Christ. The jailer repented when he turned from sin to believe in the Lord Jesus Christ.

## INSTANT SALVATION!

The jailer did not go through a period of mourning. He was told to believe on the Lord Jesus Christ; he did just that and was saved, and his whole family was saved the same way, immediately, the same hour of the night. Everywhere you look through the New Testament you find that people were saved all at once without any process, without any period of mourning. Zacchaeus, up a tree, trusted Jesus and made haste and came down, and received Him joyfully (Luke 19:6-9). Jesus said, "This day is salvation come to this house." When Peter told Cornelius and his assembled household that they could be saved by believing, immediately "while Peter yet spake these words," the Scripture says the Holy Spirit came on them and they were happily saved (Acts 10:44-48). The thief on the cross, wicked sinner that he was, who a few minutes before had been railing at Jesus, was saved immediately when he inquired of Jesus (Luke 23:42,43). In the first chapter of John, verses 35 to 49, we see where Andrew, Simon Peter, Philip and Nathanael were all converted, one by one, immediately by faith in Christ. There is no record of any person in Bible times who was ever told to wait or mourn or weep over his sins before trusting Jesus and being saved! One who believes in Christ has repented. Repentance and faith are the same thing put in different words, and neither requires a long period of time nor a process of mourning and sorrow.

Salvation is instantaneous. All that keeps you today from being saved is the wickedness of your heart that holds on to sin and will not run to Jesus to trust in Him for salvation. I beg you, turn in shame and sorrow from your sins this minute, and trust in Christ and be saved!

## CAN ONE BE SAVED WITHOUT PRAYER?

In the Bible there are many cases of sinners who prayed like the thief on the cross or the publican in the Temple. In fact, Romans 10:13 says:

> For whosoever shall call upon the name of the Lord shall be saved.

Many people believe that a sinner cannot be saved without a period of prayer, without consciously calling on God. However, the Bible does not say that a sinner must pray in order to be saved. In fact, immediately following the verse in Romans 10:13 is an explanation which shows that calling on God is an evidence of faith in the heart and that it is really faith which settles the matter. Read it again.

> For whosoever shall call upon the name of the Lord shall be saved. How then shall they call on him in whom they have not believed?—Rom. 10:13,14.

The Lord encourages the sinner to pray; and the Lord hears and answers the sinner's prayer, if that sinner trusts in Jesus Christ for salvation when he prays. He heard the prayer of the thief on the cross, of the publican in the Temple, of blind Bartimaeus. But the Scripture says, "How then shall they call on him in whom they have not believed?" Certainly everyone who is to be saved must believe. Prayer is evidence of faith. No matter how long one prays, if he does not trust in Christ, he can never be saved. If he trusts in Christ without conscious prayer, then he is saved already. There is just one plan of salvation and just one step a sinner must take to secure it. That step is to believe on the Lord Jesus Christ!

Some way we preachers have left the impression on this poor world of sinners that God is hardhearted and that it takes many tears and loud cries and long periods of sorrow before He will hear and save the sinner. We have left the impression that God does not care whether sinners are saved or not, and that sinners must some way touch the heart of God and get Him ready to forgive. What a slander on a good and holy God who "so loved the world, that he gave his only begotten Son, that WHOSO-EVER BELIEVETH in him should not perish, but have everlasting life." Man's sins are already paid for; God's wrath is already turned away from any sinner who wants to be saved. Both the Father and the Son are a million times more anxious to save every sinner than the sinner can be to get saved! Thank God, I do not have to beg God to forgive my sins. He will do it the minute I am willing to trust it with Him.

## HOW TO GET THE CHANGE OF HEART

This simple way of being saved by faith seems so easy,and it is. Some sinner may say, "But I thought one must have a change of heart." So you must, dear sinner, but that is God's part. Jesus was talking to Nicodemus when He said, "Ye must be born again," and in the same chapter He tells Nicodemus how to get the new birth.

> For God so loved the world, that he gave his only begotten Son, that whosoever believeth in him should not perish, but have everlasting life.—John 3:16.

The change in your heart, sinner, is God's part; and you may be sure He will attend to that. Your part is to simply believe in Him. Whatever else is necessary in your eternal salvation, the Lord attends to when you trust in Him or believe in Him.

## HOW SHOULD I FEEL?

Some people have an idea that the change of heart is a matter of feeling. Some do not want to claim Christ as Saviour until they have the mysterious feeling that they want. Do not let the Devil deceive you here. I believe in heartfelt religion, and thank God for the joy which He gives to me day by day. But the Bible nowhere tells how one must feel before he is saved, nor does it anywhere say how you feel after you are saved. In fact, people do not feel the same. Feeling varies with the person saved. Some cry when they are saved, some laugh, and a few shout aloud the praises of God. One is no more saved than the other. What you want, dear sinner, is salvation; and you should be satisfied to feel any way that will please the Lord, just so He forgives your sins.

Be sure you notice another fact, too, and that is that you cannot feel right until you get right. Rejoicing does not come before you trust the Lord. One does not feel the result of medicine before he takes it. The children of Israel, in the wilderness, bitten by fiery serpents and at the point of death, were not healed and did not feel healed until they looked to the brass serpent on the pole (Numbers 21:6-9). People are not saved by feeling; they are saved by trusting in Christ. The prodigal son, away from home in the hogpen, decided to arise and go to his father; but he did not feel good. He was without shoes, clothed in rags, without the ring of sonship, without any evidence of his father's forgiveness, perishing with hunger! Yet he arose and came to his father not by feeling, but by faith in his father. Thank God, his father received him like God receives every sinner who will come. And when the prodigal boy has sat down at his Father's table, with shoes of the Gospel of peace, clothed in the garments of the righteousness of Christ, with the ring of sonship on his finger, eating the fattened calf at the right hand of the Father, happy in His love, then he has plenty of feeling. Feeling comes after salvation. Leave the feeling with the Lord and come to the Saviour by faith today.

After you are saved, you will get peace and joy out of following the Lord in baptism, reading His Word, winning souls and otherwise pleasing Him. You need to go to the Lord again and again day by day for the joy of a Christian life. But thank God that salvation is settled once and for all when you simply depend upon Christ as your Saviour.

## WHAT ABOUT PUBLIC CONFESSION?

Every person who is saved ought to publicly confess Christ. Matthew 10:32 and Romans 10:9 plainly teach that God will claim as His child any of us who will claim Christ as our Saviour, but we simply confess with the mouth what we have already trusted in our hearts. Romans 10:10 concerning that very matter says:

> For with the heart man believeth unto righteousness; and with the mouth confession is made unto salvation.

To claim Christ as your Saviour simply proves that you trust Him in the heart. Likewise with all other promises in the Bible about how to be saved. "Him that cometh to me I will in no wise cast out," says John 6:37, and salvation is promised in John 1:12 to as many as receive Jesus. But you could not come to Christ without trusting Him, and John 1:12 shows that receiving Jesus is the same as believing on His name.

Dear sinner, do not make this a difficult matter. There is one simple step between you and Jesus. When you trust Him, everything else is settled, and you have repented; you have come to Christ; you have received Him; you have done everything necessary to be saved. Take the answer in Acts 16:31 at face value: "BELIEVE ON THE LORD JESUS CHRIST, AND THOU SHALT BE SAVED." All through the Bible in dozens of Scriptures, salvation is promised to those that believe. Read carefully the following Scriptures and see that again and again, many, many times, God has promised all any poor sinner would ever need when he believes on the Lord Jesus Christ.

> But as many as received him, to them gave he power to become the sons of God, even to them that BELIEVE on his name.—John 1:12.
>
> And as Moses lifted up the serpent in the wilderness, even so must the Son of man be lifted up: That whosoever BELIEVETH in him should not perish, but have eternal life. For God so loved the world, that he gave his only begotten Son, that whosoever BELIEVETH in him should not perish, but have everlasting life.—John 3:14-16.
>
> He that BELIEVETH on him is not condemned: but he that BELIEVETH not is condemned already, because he hath not BELIEVED in the name of the only begotten Son of God.—John 3:18.
>
> He that BELIEVETH on the Son hath everlasting life: and he that BELIEVETH not the Son shall not see life; but the wrath of God abideth on him.—John 3:36.

*Verily, verily, I say unto you, He that heareth my word, and
BELIEVETH on him that sent me, hath everlasting life, and
shall not come into condemnation; but is passed from death
unto life.*—John 5:24.

*And this is the will of him that sent me, that every one which
seeth the Son, and BELIEVETH on him, may have everlasting
life: and I will raise him up at the last day.*—John 6:40.

*Verily, verily, I say unto you, He that BELIEVETH on me
hath everlasting life.*—John 6:47.

*To him give all the prophets witness, that through his name
whosoever BELIEVETH in him shall receive remission of
sins.*—Acts 10:43.

*And by him all that BELIEVE are justified from all things,
from which ye could not be justified by the law of Moses.*—Acts
13:39.

Read again the Scripture we started with:

*What must I do to be saved? . . .BELIEVE on the Lord Jesus
Christ, and thou shalt be saved.*—Acts 16:30,31.

## TRUST JESUS, THE GREAT PHYSICIAN

If you were sick and about to die, and there was some good doctor whom you could trust, would you not risk him to take your case, give you the necessary treatment, and with God's help get you well? Then just like that, trust in Christ, depend on Him for your salvation, and turn it over to Him today. With the same kind of faith that will call in a doctor and risk him for your body, you can call in the Lord Jesus Christ and risk Him to forgive your sins and save your poor lost soul! He said, "They that are whole need not a physician, but they that are sick" (Luke 5:31). He is the Great Physician and will heal your soul instantly if you will trust Him. As you would trust a doctor, submit to his treatment, depend on him for results, so trust Jesus today about your soul. To be sure, human doctors fail many times; their results at best are gradual, and so no doctor is a perfect picture of Jesus. The doctor can work no miracles, but Jesus can; and the change that is needed in that poor, wicked heart He will make immediately, instantly, without any further effort on your part, when you trust Him!

## JESUS IS OUR LAWYER

If you had committed a crime and were thrown in jail, probably the first thing you would do would be to send for some lawyer in whom you had confidence and trust him with the entire matter of your defense. In God's sight you are a criminal, condemned already with the wrath of God upon you day by day. But God has provided Somebody to take the part of us poor sinners, criminals before the bar of God's justice, and Jesus is that Lawyer, for the Scripture says:

> If any man sin, we have an advocate [or lawyer] with the Father, Jesus Christ the righteous: And he is the propitiation for our sins: and not for our's only, but also for the sins of the whole world.—I John 2:1,2.

Jesus will not only be your Lawyer to defend your case; He has already paid the penalty and you may safely trust Him to have you immediately pardoned and justified! Why not simply risk Jesus as you would risk a good lawyer? Jesus is better than any lawyer, of course, and you do not have to pay Him a fee, and He never fails.

## A WEDDING

A young man and young woman stand together, side by side, before the preacher. The preacher says, "You will join right hands." Then to the young man he says, "Do you take this young woman to be your lawfully wedded wife, to love her and cherish her until death do you part?" He answers, "I do." To the young woman the preacher says: "Do you take this man to be your lawfully wedded husband until death do you part?" She answers, "I do." Then the preacher says: "I pronounce you man and wife," and they are married in the sight of God and man. What a simple picture of salvation! Jesus is the Bridegroom and we who trust Him are to be His bride. Already Jesus has loved you and has long urged you to accept His love. Jesus invites you to believe in Him right now and be saved and so become a part of His bride. Will you not right now, with the same simple faith of that young woman who takes a husband, accept Jesus as your Saviour and say to Him, "I do"?

## MAKE IT SURE—CLAIM HIM TODAY!

The way is plain and you can be saved this moment if you will.

Surely it has become plain, dear lost sinner, that it is your own fault if you are lost! Do you hate Jesus Christ? Will you hold on to your sin and go to Hell for your stubbornness? Nothing in the world could show your wickedness like postponing this matter. You can be saved right now, this minute. I beg you, do it now. Turn your whole heart from sin to trust in Christ. Choose for Heaven against Hell; choose for Christ against Satan. Do not let Satan deceive you any longer. If you delay, it may result in a hardened heart, a wasted life and a tortured soul in Hell! And if you are not saved, when God has made the way so plain and paid the price for your sins, then you have no one to blame but yourself. Will you trust Jesus Christ today and be saved?

> *Boast not thyself of to morrow; for thou knowest not what a day may bring forth.*—Prov. 27:1.

> *Behold, now is the accepted time; behold, now is the day of salvation.*—II Cor. 6:2.

> *To day if ye will hear his voice, Harden not your hearts.*—Heb. 3:7,8.

God has given you this heartbeat, this breath, this moment in order to trust Christ, but there is no promise of another. I beg you do it right now, and then claim Him as your Saviour.

If you realize that you are a sinner, if you believe that Christ died for you, if you will honestly trust Christ as YOUR Saviour, depending on Him to forgive all your sins, will you not sign the following statement and send it to me, so that I may rejoice with you? Then you have the assurance that Jesus will confess you before His Father, as you confess Him before men, for He said:

> *Whosoever therefore shall confess me before men, him will I confess also before my Father which is in heaven.*—Matt. 10:32.

You are saved when you trust Christ, but much of the assurance and joy you get when you claim Christ and He claims you and sends the Holy Spirit to make you happy. If you are willing to claim Him, then just say so today in the following statement.

_____ , 19____

Realizing that I am a sinner and believing that Christ died for my sins, I here and now trust Him to be my personal Saviour, depending on Him to forgive all my sins, change my heart, and give me everlasting life as he promised to do. I am glad to confess Him as my Saviour and gladly mail this to let you know.

SIGNED_____

ADDRESS_____

Get others to decide if possible, and send in their names, too. Either clip out this statement and mail it or write on postcard or letter.

One who trusts Christ should then publicly claim Christ before men. It is God's plan that after trusting Him you should be baptized and join in with His people. I hope you will join a church and let yourself be known publicly from this time forth as a child of God.

## APPENDIX B

# STATEMENT OF FAITH *

Fundamentalist Baptist Church of Oak Cliff, Dallas,
Texas, Adopted July 31, 1932, at Its Organization

WE BELIEVE:

I. That the Bible is the inspired, reliable Word of God, verbally inspired, reliable in science, history and every other matter it discusses, as God gave it in the original manuscripts; that it should be our sole guide in faith and practice.

II. That Jesus is very God, one with the Father and the Holy Spirit; that He was conceived by the Holy Ghost, born of a virgin; lived without sin, died on the cross for our transgressions, arose from the dead bodily and ascended into Heaven.

III. That man was created in the image of God, not by evolution, but by direct act of God; that since Adam's sin all are sinners and can only become children of God by being born again.

IV. That salvation is a gift of God, is received only by faith in Christ, and is not of works.

V. That the sinner is immediately saved and receives everlasting life when he believes in the Lord Jesus Christ; that he then shall not come into condemnation as a lost sinner any more, and shall never perish.

---

* I do not think this statement, which appears to have been hastily written to meet a deadline, is typical of Dr. Rice's work and writing. However, since it shows his theological position at this phase of his ministry—in a pastorate—I felt it valuable to include here. Note especially the teaching of the "pastor" relative to "storehouse tithing"—a position many of his critics have charged to his "evangelist" status! Incidentally, Dr. Bob Kelley, his pastor during the last years of his life, spoke glowingly of his support of the local church, saying that in one two- or three-month period, when they were having pressures in a building program, Dr. Rice gave the church "gifts totaling $16,000 without batting an eye."

VI. That the saved shall live eternally with Christ and that those who die without trusting Him as Saviour will enter into everlasting punishment in Hell.

VII. That the Holy Spirit convicts sinners and dwells in the Christian to guide, comfort, make fruitful and powerful; that each Christian should be filled or baptized with the Holy Ghost; that the evidence of this baptism is not sinless perfection or speaking in tongues, but the soul-winning power as promised in Acts 1:8 and the fruit of Galatians 5:22,23.

VIII. That a New Testament church is a local body of baptized believers independent of every other earthly body, following the Bible alone and being led by the Holy Ghost in conducting its affairs; its officers being pastors and deacons (or servants) elected by the church.

IX. That Bible baptism is the burial of the believer in water, symbolizing the burial and resurrection of Christ and the believer's death to sin and resurrection to a new life; that all saved people should be baptized.

X. That Christians should constantly watch for the return of Christ in the air to meet His bride, the saved; that then the Christian dead will be raised bodily and living Christians will be changed and caught up together to meet Christ; that after a great tribulation on the earth, Christ will return to the earth with all the saints and angels, will destroy the Antichrist and will reign on the earth from David's throne at Jerusalem; that after a thousand years' reign on earth, the unsaved dead will be raised up bodily, will be judged according to their works and be cast into the lake of fire; that the earth will be purged by fire and made new; that then God the Father and the heavenly Jerusalem shall descend to the earth and Christ shall turn the kingdom over to His Father.

XI. That the work of the church is soul winning, baptizing converts, and teaching the Bible; that it should reach every creature possible; that a church has no obligation to maintain secular schools and hospitals, nor to follow in its work any plans submitted from outside the local church, nor to cooperate in any work except as the church decides.

XII. The denominational bishops, secretaries, conventions, boards, conferences and presbyteries, not being authorized by the Bible, have no authority, legal or moral, over any New Testament church, its officers or members.

XIII. That the support of a soul-winning and Bible teaching ministry should be supplied through the tithes and free will offerings of God's people; that each Christian is free to give as and where the Holy Spirit directs.

XIV. That Christians should be careful to maintain good works, to grow in grace and knowledge of the Bible and faith, should especially pray for and help weak Christians, should win souls, should withdraw from them that persist in walking disorderly, and live in separation from sinful amusements and work by the Spirit's help.

This statement of faith was designed to state in simple, explicit language the fundamental doctrines of the Bible upon which Christians ought to be agreed in order to prevent hurtful divisions. Many other great Bible teachings upon which Christians do not materially differ are not here stated, since it is thought best to make the statement as brief and simple as possible. . . .

The church has no other written articles, no constitution nor by-laws, nor church covenant. We go by no church manual. We claim the Bible as our only rule of faith and practice and this statement is not meant to supplant the Bible, but merely to state what we believe the Bible teaches on the principal great doctrines.

## APPENDIX C

# BOOKS AND PAMPHLETS WRITTEN BY DR. RICE AND THEIR CIRCULATION THROUGH DECEMBER 29, 1980 (the time of his death)

*Title*

| | |
|---|---|
| Abortion | 127,650 |
| Adultery and Sex Perversion | 24,552 |
| All About Christian Giving | 20,120 |
| All Have Sinned | 146,349 |
| All Satan's Apples Have Worms | 65,431 |
| Always Rejoicing! | 7,390 |
| Amazing Power of the Gospel in Print | 10,197 |
| American Heritage | 23,992 |
| Amusements for Christians | 53,690 |
| "And God Remembered. . ." | 55,119 |
| Angel's Christmas Message | 65,908 |
| Apples of Gold (compiled) | 59,218 |
| Are You Going to Heaven? | 21,027 |
| Attack on the Bible | 33,985 |
| Backslider, The | 232,763 |
| Banquet Invitation, R.S.V.P., The | 22,277 |
| Beautiful for Thee (compiled) | 16,997 |
| "Behold, he Cometh!" (Commentary on Revelation) | 16,913 |
| Best of Billy Sunday (compiled) | 25,186 |

| | |
|---|---|
| John R. Rice Bible Stories | 19,658 |
| King of the Jews (Commentary on Matthew) | 34,674 |
| Know-So Salvation, A | 17,264 |
| Last Judgment of Unsaved Dead, The | 194,963 |
| Lodges Examined by the Bible | 164,233 |
| Lot | 33,196 |
| Missing God's Last Train for Heaven | 42,753 |
| Neglect—the Shortest Way to Hell | 140,606 |
| Negro and White | 49,239 |
| Never Alone—Never Forsaken | 97,699 |
| New Solos & Duets | 9,431 |
| "No One Cared for My Soul" | 5,217 |
| Open your Mouth | 35,230 |
| Our God-Breathed Book—the Bible | 19,663 |
| Our Loving Friend, The Holy Spirit | 25,199 |
| Our Perfect Book, the Bible | 52,251 |
| Personal Soul Winning: How to Do It | 70,817 |
| Poems That Preach (compiled) | 102,621 |
| Power of Pentecost, The | 47,172 |
| Prayer—Asking and Receiving | 362,413 |
| Preaching That Built a Great Church | 5,052 |
| Predestined for Hell? No! | 26,498 |
| Prize-Winning Evangelistic Sermons (compiled) | 10,155 |
| Rebellious Wives and Slacker Husbands | 173,020 |
| Religious—But Lost | 271,925 |
| Resurrection of Jesus Christ, The | 28,889 |
| Revival Appeals | 25,104 |
| Revival Specials No. 1 (compiled) | 35,528 |
| Revival Specials No. 2 (compiled) | 30,570 |
| Ruin of a Christian, The | 43,671 |
| Saved for Certain | 117,254 |
| Scarlet Sin, The | 25,793 |
| Second Coming of Christ in Daniel, The | 120,614 |
| Seeking a City (Novel) | 6,451 |

Sermon From a Catholic Bible                                147,099
742 Heart-Warming Poems (compiled)                           31,076
Seven Secrets of a Happy, Prosperous Christian Life          78,913
Sin of Formalism, The                                        41,889
Six Fine Gospel Songs on Soul Winning                         1,253
Some Great Bible Characters                                  16,737
Son of God, The (Commentary on John)                         14,849
Son of Man, The (Commentary on Luke)                         21,043
Songs of John R. Rice                                         7,537
Soul-Saving Sermons for Sinners                               6,375
Soul-Stirring Songs and Hymns (compiled)                    250,456
Soul-Winner's Fire, The                                     141,287
Soul Winning                                                 78,692
Southern Baptist Convention Approves
  Liberal Commentary                                         10,205
Southern Baptist Leaders Now Committed Liberals              89,653
Southern Baptists and Wolves in Sheep's Clothing              6,118
Southern Baptists, Wake Up! (compiled)                       16,577
Speaking With Tongues                                        58,118
Spectators at the Cross                                      42,778
Steps for New Converts                                       81,783
Storehouse Tithing—Does the Bible Teach It?                  33,339
Success-Prone Christians                                      6,811
Sunday or Sabbath—Which Should Christians
  Observe?                                                  200,226
Sweet Family Ties in Heaven and Hell                          2,904
Sword Book of Treasures, The (compiled)                      15,213
Sword Scrapbook, The (No. 1)                                 26,750
Sword Scrapbook No. 2 (compiled)                             17,423
Sword Special Songs (compiled)                               33,148
Tears, Blessed Tears                                         10,454
Tears in Heaven                                              47,807
Ten Messages That Changed Ten Thousand Lives                  6,997
These Bible Christians Fell Through Compromise               56,554

| | |
|---|---:|
| Tobacco: Is Its Use a Sin? | 226,085 |
| Trailed by a Wild Beast | 159,408 |
| Twelve Tremendous Themes | 33,527 |
| Unequal Yoke, The | 160,536 |
| Verbal Inspiration of the Bible | 124,990 |
| War in Vietnam | 35,935 |
| Was Pope John Paul I a Born-Again Christian? | 4,791 |
| Watching Jesus Die | 9,730 |
| Watergate Mess, The | 10,300 |
| We Can Have Revival Now! | 15,750 |
| What Is Wrong With the Movies? | 32,914 |
| What It Costs to Be a Good Christian | 19,148 |
| What Must I Do to Be Saved? (English) | 32,921,765 |
| What Was Back of Kennedy's Murder? | 82,709 |
| What Will Happen When Jesus Comes? | 77,905 |
| What's Wrong With the Dance? | 31,192 |
| When a Christian Sins | 101,826 |
| When Skeletons Come Out of Their Closets! | 31,877 |
| Whosoever and Whatsoever When You Pray | 9,857 |
| Why Our Churches Do Not Win Souls | 18,538 |
| Why Pray? | 36,226 |
| Why Preach Against Sin? | 31,926 |
| Winning Your Loved Ones | 39,499 |
| "Woman Thou Gavest Me, The" | 27,671 |
| Wonderful Jesus | 27,631 |
| World-Wide War and the Bible | 20,000 |
| You Must Be Born Again | 31,561 |

Total (English):  44,812,720

# FOREIGN TRANSLATIONS AND FOREIGN EDITIONS

## "What Must I Do to Be Saved?"

| | |
|---|---|
| Angami (India) | Not Reported |
| Arabic | 40,000 |
| Armenian (Lebanon) | 5,000 |
| Australian | Not Reported |
| Bangala (Africa) | 25,000 |
| Chinese (Formosa) | 295,000 |
| Chinese (Mandarin) | 110,000 |
| Dutch (Holland) | 132,500 |
| Finnish (Finland) | 100,000 |
| French | 200,000 |
| German | 510,000 |
| Gujarati (South India) | 50,000 |
| Hausa (Africa) | 15,000 |
| Hindi (India) | 350,000 |
| Ilocano (Philippines) | 6,000 |
| Ilongo (Philippines) | 10,000 |
| Italian | 305,000 |
| Japanese | 8,489,000 |
| Javanese (Indonesia) | 13,000 |
| Kamba (East Africa) | 15,000 |
| Kanarese (South India) | 25,000 |
| Korean | 1,100,000 |
| Malayalam (India) | 110,000 |

| | |
|---|---|
| Marathi (India) | 250,000 |
| Portuguese | 800,000 |
| Samoan | 10,000 |
| Singapore | 50,000 |
| Sinhelese (Ceylon) | 35,000 |
| Spanish (American Edition) | 1,808,745 |
| Spanish (Spain) | 90,000 |
| Swedish | 200,000 |
| Syriac (Lebanon) | Not Reported |
| Tagalog (Philippines) | 150,000 |
| Tamil (India) | 95,000 |
| Telugu (India) | 100,000 |
| Ukrainian | 32,000 |
| Urdu (Bangladesh) | 1,000,000 |
| Urdu (Pakistan) | 50,000 |
| Zulu (South Africa) | Not Reported |

Total (Foreign "What's"): 16,576,245

Grand Total, English and Foreign: 61,388,965

We have made no effort—because of the insurmountable problems in attempting it—to total foreign translations of Dr. Rice's other books and booklets. *Prayer—Asking and Receiving,* for example, has been published in Dutch, German, Japanese, Spanish, Korean, Ukrainian and Danish, yet we have no idea how many copies were printed.